# Management for Professionals

More information about this series at http://www.springer.com/series/10101

Richard Thomas Watson

# Capital, Systems, and Objects

The Foundation and Future
of Organizations

 Springer

Richard Thomas Watson
Department of Management Information Systems
University of Georgia
Athens, GA, USA

ISSN 2192-8096             ISSN 2192-810X   (electronic)
Management for Professionals
ISBN 978-981-15-9417-5     ISBN 978-981-15-9418-2   (eBook)
https://doi.org/10.1007/978-981-15-9418-2

This Springer imprint is published by the registered company Springer Nature Singapore Pte Ltd.
The registered company address is: 152 Beach Road, #21-01/04 Gateway East, Singapore 189721,
Singapore

*To*

*Alice, Ned, & Sophie*

# Preface

I have always enjoyed puzzles, particularly those with fuzzy rules that encourage creative and tangential thinking. For much of my life, I have pursued the solution of one puzzle: I've been trying to identify and fit together the pieces of a jigsaw that would give me a general understanding of how humans, organizations, and societies work. This is a wicked jigsaw because there are no edge pieces to frame the puzzle and the pieces rarely fit together cleanly. Even so, there are moments of elation when I see a connection between two pieces and can mash them together within my mind. Sometimes I see how a series of pieces connect to create a landscape that is a significant leap forward for me in solving my idiosyncratic jigsaw. This book is about four of these landscape moments. First, I realized that the object-oriented thinking of computer science could be applied to the design of organizations. Then, over a period of about a decade, I gradually conceived the notion that an organization is a capital creation system. In mid-2017, over a period of a few months, I identified five systems that I will argue are the building blocks of all social systems. Finally, in the fall of 2017, I connected the capital creation and fundamental systems chunks to understand how systems create capital.

In this book, I describe each of the pieces, how they connect, and why understanding their intertwining is important for those who shape the present and future of organizations. Rather than write a series of articles, I abide by Lane's[1] recognition that "a book is still the best way to layout a vision of how facts might relate to each other across the whole fabric of science." My vision is a composition of concepts such as social capital and systems of inquiry, and I use facts and cases to bring these concepts to life in practical settings. Most importantly, I show how the core concepts of capital creation and systems connect to create organizations and societies, and I provide an explanation of the operation and purpose of human institutions that spans millennia. Finally, I show how digital connectivity gives us an object-oriented canvas for organizational design.

This book is heavily footnoted, maybe obsessively so, because I wanted to provide you with the sources of many of the jigsaw pieces so you can, if you wish, reassemble them for your personal world view. In developing my mosaic of capital,

---

[1]Lane, N. (2015). *The Vital Question: Energy, Evolution, and the Origins of Complex Life.* WW Norton & Company.

systems, and objects, I have been sensitized to seek facts and opinions that fit my evolving understanding. This can be myopic, so feel free to challenge my view, and more importantly, fashion an appropriate vision for your needs and circumstances.

This book is a celebration of the ingenuity of humans to build a system that has raised the standard of living of billions. While many of the examples are about economic capital creation, this is not the only focus. Rather, I assert that the quality of life for each person is a synthesis of six types of capital, and we should strive to create national and organizational environments in which humans can achieve a self-determined blend.

A broad discussion of capital creation must consider a major threat to the system—global climate change—as it is disrupting natural capital production, the foundation of life and the kick-starter of the human capital creation system. If you have an issue with acknowledging the need to redesign the capital creation system to operate on a renewable energy platform, then you might disagree with portions of this book. I ask, however, that you recognize that the capital creation system continually adapts to environmental and technological disruptions, and that understanding how it operates is critical to dealing with all perturbations.

Many organizations are currently addressing two important transformational issues: ecological sustainability and digitization. Sustainability is a goal, an end, and digitization is a process, a means to achieve a goal. This book introduces a flexible model that can be applied to current and future organizational challenges, including sustainability and digitization, because the fundamentals are constant. Capital creation and conversion are what societies have done for thousands of years by applying five basic systems. Leaders will continue to design their organizations' future by creating and refining systems for capital conversion.

In one sentence, this book argues that *organizations and societies are the result of five fundamental systems that are used to create and maintain six types of capital.* Infinitely, many ways in which these elements can interact and be fashioned have created and sustained the broad and diverse canvas of civilization. Today, object-oriented thinking is used to reshape and populate that canvas.

This book paints a generally rosy view of capital creation systems, but keep in mind Mahatma Gandhi's comment:[2]

> *Capital as such is not evil; it is the wrong use of capital that is evil. Capital in some form or other is always needed.*

Please join me in putting together the pieces, so that I might contribute to your personal jigsaw of life. May the pieces be with you.

Athens, GA, USA                                                         Richard Thomas Watson
2020

---

[2]Freeman, I. A. (2014). *Seeds of Revolution: A Collection of Axioms, Passages, and Proverbs (Vol. 2).* iUniverse. p. 437.

# Acknowledgments

I appreciate the outstanding work of Tie Nakata in converting the graphics into a consistent and visually interesting form. She also took the original text and converted it to InDesign for professional publication.

I thank the following for reviewing the early drafts and giving me helpful feedback: Lynda Applegate, David Bray, Kevin Desouza, Eduardo Morgado, Leyland Pitt, Stefan Seidel, and Madeline Weiss.

Clare Watson, as usual, for listening attentively to my many progress reports. She also proofread the book and slides.

Thanks to Rachel Paul for her careful copyediting.

Blame me for all errors and omissions, and more importantly, let me know when you spot one <rwatson@terry.uga.edu>.

# The Value Proposition

Organizations face a continuing barrage of new ideas and technologies. In recent years, you have likely heard multiple references to digitization, blockchain, sharing economy, and a host of other managerial and technological innovations. These are means and not goals. It is too easy to become enchanted with a means that seems to solve multiple problems, but the long-term concern must be the enduring goals that a means can help achieve.

**Capital creation** is the enduring goal for all organizations. All are concerned with creating a mix of one or more types of capital: economic, human, natural, organizational, social, and symbolic. All need to focus on raising their capital productivity, $C'$ (C prime), to a level greater than their industry competitors.

There are **five fundamental systems** for creating capital: systems of engagement, framing, inquiry, production, and record. An organization, a capital creation system, has to continually modify, effectively manage, and efficiently integrate each of its multiple variations of these systems to enhance its $C'$.

Breakthrough leaps in $C'$ in recent years can be understood in terms of **object-oriented organizational** design. Uber, for example, is based on the premise that drivers and riders are objects that can receive and respond to digital messages through their smart devices. In a connected world, nearly every person and the asset is an object that can be networked electronically in innovative ways to create new organizations with higher levels of $C'$.

In recent decades, the capital mix of organizations has changed. For the S&P 500, 32% of firms invest more in intangible than physical (economic capital) assets, and 61% of their market value is intangibles such as research and development (human and organizational capital), customers linked by network effects (social capital), brands (symbolic capital), and data (organizational capital). Additionally, there is no discernible link between CEO authorized investments and results.[3] Executives need a new frame for thinking about capital investments.

---

[3]https://www.economist.com/leaders/2020/02/06/what-it-takes-to-be-a-ceo-in-the-2020s

Leaders who want to change the game, need to know three things:

- What's the game?
- How do you play the game?
- What's the modern form of the game?

This book gives you a set of integrated frameworks—capital, systems, and objects—that transcend managerial or technology hype by focusing on the long-term fundamentals that sustain organizational success. Read this book if you want to be an effective capital creator—the world's number one game.

# How to Read This Book

This book is designed to serve two purposes: first, to present you with three conceptual foundations for designing and operating organizations (capital, systems, and objects; Part I); and second, to provide a reference source for implementing these ideas in your organization (Parts II and III).

Part I of the book, Chaps. 1 Through 7, sets forth the conceptual foundations. The chapters mix concepts and practical examples to give you a new way of thinking about the setting in which you likely work many days each year.

Part II provides details and associated examples of every one of the thirty-six forms of capital conversion. It also illustrates how the five foundational systems support capital conversion in a variety of ways.

Finally, Part III is about measuring capital and systems, based on the premise that without measurement, you are in the dark and the future is even darker.

I recommend that you read Part I, over the next few days to gain a broad understanding of the book's key ideas. In particular, learn about the general notion of a capital creation system. Then put the book aside so that your thinking about capital, systems, and objects can mature by using these new lenses for observing and understanding the world. With this new way of comprehending the world, you will see the ideas in action frequently, and this will deepen your understanding and build your collection of cases.

When you are ready to start applying the book's ideas, pick the chapters in Part II, that are most relevant and use the vignettes within them to stimulate your thinking. For example, if you are particularly concerned about human capital productivity, then consult Chap. 9. Alternatively, if you decide to assess your current standing, then read the final two chapters and start building new measurement systems for capital and systems to guide future efforts to raise $C'$.

Of course, if you find the book too engrossing to put aside, which I hope you will, feel free to read all the chapters without pause.

# Contents

# About the Author

**Richard Thomas Watson** is a Regents Professor and the J. Rex Fuqua Distinguished Chair for Internet Strategy in the Terry College of Business at the University of Georgia. In 2011, he received the Association for Information Systems' LEO award for exceptional lifetime achievement in Information Systems. The University of Liechtenstein has established with government support a Consortium for Digital Capital Creation based on the ideas in this book.

# Part I
# Capital Creation Systems

Part I introduces the notion that humans have established over many centuries a capital creation system that is built upon, and operates in parallel with, the several-billion-years-old natural capital creation system. The earth has become a capital creation system, with natural capital one of the six forms of capital. The others are economic, human, organizational, social, and symbolic.

Chapter 1 introduces the concept of the earth as a capital creation system. The key determinants of the state of human systems—capital productivity, $C'$, and energy efficiency, $E'$—are defined, as are the six common types of capital that a capital creation system converts from one form to another. It also introduces the five fundamental systems for creating capital.

The concept that all organizations are capital conversion and creation systems, the central theme of this book, is introduced in Chap. 2. A linkage is also made to the role of government as a creator of capital to advance its societal $C'$.

An introduction to each type of capital and some key historical events in its growth are presented in Chap. 3. The role of incremental and radical change with respect to $C'$ is also considered.

In Chap. 4, the five fundamental systems of capital creation—systems of engagement, production, record, inquiry, and framing—are defined. Their historical emergence is reviewed, and their virtuous interaction is described.

Chapter 5 discusses recent development in $E'$, because we are in the midst of an energy revolution that has important implications for capital creation and $C'$.

Object-oriented enterprise design is introduced in Chap. 6 as a means of understanding how the network age facilitates the rapid creation of organizations that are built by networking the existing capital creation systems in novel combinations.

Finally, some speculations and conjectures on the future of the capital creation systems are presented in Chap. 7.

# A Capital Idea

Since life emerged, the earth has become a capital creation system. Capital creation has changed the face of the globe from a collection of rocks, gases, and water to an ensemble of forests, plains, cities, and other forms of capital. Formally, scholars define *capital* as a durable and transforming factor of production generated by a prior investment,[1] but we take an extended view. Capital is also an investment created by an animal or plant to increase its survival and reproductive prospects. Animals, for example, generate body fat from the food they eat to enable them to survive periods when food is unattainable. Some animals go beyond storing capital as fat. Some ants and bees, for example, create nests—a capital investment that enables them to store the food they harvest and provide a protective environment for their young.

Humans, the world's preeminent capital creation species, initially accumulated some capital, such as skins and baskets, but once they started to settle and farm, they created substantial capital, such as arable plots and buildings. Since the dawn of agriculture, we have built a civilization based on investing in capital and capital creation capabilities to develop the sociotechnical environment in which we currently live. It was a long journey to our current capital creation system.

The earth coalesced from galactic dust about 4.5 billion years ago. While our original endowment of atoms and molecules has been added to by the occasional meteor or comet crashing on earth, our inanimate inheritance was essentially established when the earth was formed. Some 4 billion years ago, bacteria emerged, and this was the only form of life for about 2 billion years. Complex organisms, plants, animals, fungi, and so forth appeared about 1.5–2 billion years ago.

---

[1] Dean, A., & Kretschmer, M. (2007). Can ideas be capital? Factors of production in the postindustrial economy: A review and critique. *The Academy of Management Review, 32*(2), 573–594.

R. T. Watson, *Capital, Systems, and Objects*, Management for Professionals, https://doi.org/10.1007/978-981-15-9418-2_1

The ability to create capital, in the form of energy, is the foundation of life. Fundamentally, all living cells are powered by a flow of protons (positively charged hydrogen atoms). You can think of these protons as similar to the electrons of electricity. Cells burn food to create energy, which is used to pump protons across a membrane to create an energy store, capital, on the other side of the membrane (a battery). An energy store is a bridge between feasts. The flow of protons in the reverse direction enables the stored energy to be used. The proton gradient is universal among all earthly life.[2] It is the way cells harvest and store energy, and it is why energy is central to evolution and the development of a capital creation system.

Energy is needed for life, and life and energy have been intertwined since the beginning of cellular forms. Stored energy was the first capital created on earth; the rest was inherited. My premise is that without capital creation, life is a very precarious existence because cells would literally live by hand and mouth with no reserves to handle environmental vicissitudes. Furthermore, those life forms that extend their capital creation capabilities enhance their prospects of survival and reproduction.

There are two forms of natural capital creation. Some organisms, such as plants, process a stream of photons using photosynthesis to create energy stores, such as sugars. Other living cells generate energy from food (plants and animals) and oxygen, and they store it in a variety of forms, such as fat for humans. These two processes are responsible for creating the world's renewable capital.

## 1.1 Converting Sunshine to Capital

The earth's capital creation system is based on **photosynthesis**, by which plants convert sunshine, water, and $CO_2$ to sugars[3] and oxygen. Sugars are a form of capital because they are an energy stored for future use. **Respiration** is the process by which a plant uses stored sugars to fuel its metabolism, and in the process, $CO_2$ and water are released. A plant typically generates more sugars than it needs, and this store is available for others to consume. Herbivores gain the energy they need to drive their metabolism by eating plants and storing energy in the form of fat and protein. Herbivores are in turn a source of energy for carnivores, who also store energy in the form of fat and protein. Furthermore, carnivores might eat others of their ilk (Fig. 1.1). All species are in the business of creating capital as some form of energy. They convert energy from one form (e.g., sugar) to another (e.g., fat). Each stage of the conversion process has energy losses. A steak, for instance, contains about 10% of the nutritional energy of the plants eaten by a steer to grow the meat.

---

[2]Lane, N. (2015). *The Vital Question: Energy, Evolution, and the Origins of Complex Life.* WW Norton & Company.
[3]Compounds of carbon, hydrogen, and oxygen. Sucrose is $C_{12}H_{22}O_{11}$.

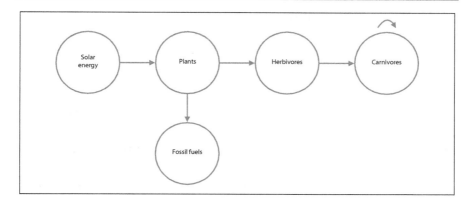

**Fig. 1.1** The energy capture process

Fossil fuels were formed over hundreds of millions of years from the energy stored in dead plants and organisms. Plant remains not consumed by bacteria settled on the seafloor or in oxygen-deprived water, where they were transformed by heat and pressure into liquid and gaseous compounds of carbon and hydrogen.

These energy sources, formed over millions of years, provided the energy for the industrial revolution and enable our current standard of living. However, when they are burned at a large scale, such as is the case today, they release $CO_2$ at a rate that significantly increases its level in the atmosphere and creates a greenhouse effect. Prior to the Industrial Revolution, atmospheric carbon was around 280 ppm, and in 2015, it exceeded on an annual basis 400 ppm for the first time.

Sunshine has created and supported the earth's flora and fauna, its natural capital, for millions of years. It is also responsible for creating another natural capital, fossil fuels. The former is renewable, with a cycle time measured in months or years, whereas the creation of fossil fuels takes millions of years. Humans have demonstrated that they could exhaust the world's fossil fuels in a few centuries, which is having long-term harmful effects on the environment. Clearly, we need to find alternative renewable and ecologically sustainable energy sources to maintain our standard of living and capital creation system.

## 1.2   The Earth as a System

There are several systems perspectives regarding the earth, including Humboldt's single living organism theory, Lovelock's Gaia concept, and more recently, the massive chemical battery concept. The capital creation view, another systems perspective, is focused on human life on the globe.

## 1.2.1   The Living Organism

*Humboldt's Unifying Vision*

Alexander vonHumboldt, a nineteenth century polymath, was likely the first to envision the earth as a single large living organism.[4] He saw multiple levels of connectedness and understood the need to examine the parts while keeping in mind the whole. His general systems perspective recognized that in an organic system, the whole is shaped by its many parts, an idea that later was refined and is now generally known as a *complex adaptive system.*[5]

Humboldt explored the world with the intention of learning how "all forces of nature are interlaced and interwoven—how organic and inorganic nature interacted." Thus, when exploring Lake Valencia in Venezuela, he realized that human deforestation of the region around the lake had caused local climate change. However, he recognized that humans were not the only destructive force. He noted that plants compete for light and nourishment, and that life is an ongoing battle between species. His views ran counter to the prevailing notion that nature was harmonious and that each species had a divinely determined role that preserved an ordained equilibrium.

Humboldt's thinking is reflected in Darwin's theory of evolution. Indeed, Darwin took with him on HMS *Beagle* Humboldt's seven-volume record of his Latin American expedition because it had inspired him to volunteer as the ship's naturalist for a global voyage that commenced in 1831. Humboldt's systems thinking and his observations on the relentless struggle for life are echoed in Darwin's research. Humboldt provided Darwin with a lens for viewing the world that likely sensitized him to imagine the process of evolution.

*Gaia*

In 1979, biologist James Lovelock presented the Gaia[6] hypothesis, which argues, as Humboldt did, that the earth is a macroorganism.[7] He extended Humboldt's thinking to add a purposive perspective by asserting that this mass organism maintains the necessary ecological conditions to sustain life on earth. He assigns Gaia a motivation, whereas Humboldt and Darwin see ongoing competition that can be destructive and purposeless, and need not result in sustained harmony. Lovelock sees humans as the cause of our present ecological problems, which would seem to be at odds with the notion of the earth as a macroorganism, as humans are a product of evolution on earth. Humans might well now be the dominant and most influential species, but they are an integral part of Gaia. Maintaining his purposive perspective,

---

[4]This section draws upon Wulf, A. (2015). *The Invention of Nature: Alexander Von Humboldt's New World*. Knopf Publishing Group.
[5]Holland, J. H. (1995). *Hidden Order: How Adaptation Builds Complexity*. Basic Books.
[6]Gaia was a Greek goddess who personified the earth.
[7]Lovelock, J. E. (1979). *Gaia: A New Look at Earth*. Oxford University Press.

Lovelock asserts that the earth has not evolved solely for the benefit of humans and that our actions threaten its existence.[8]

Viewing the earth as a complex adaptive system of organisms embraces both Humboldt's and Lovelock's principles. There are many interacting organisms competing for the resources necessary to live and reproduce, but to suggest the earth is a single macroorganism providing a unity of purpose is hard to accept. Such a model does not embrace cataclysmic events such as the asteroid that ended the reign of the dinosaurs and destroyed three-quarters of the earth's species.[9] We should view the earth as a collection of interacting organisms continually adjusting to a wide range of environmental changes. Despite major extinction events, life has continued to exist for about two billion years.

## 1.2.2   The Battery

The earth can also be viewed as giant chemical battery.[10] Hundreds of millions of years of solar-powered photosynthesis have slowly created billions of tons of biomass, such as forests and fossil fuel reserves. The battery has been trickle charged by solar energy over hundreds of millions of years. Over the recent millennia, starting with agriculture, humans have exploitatively discharged this battery, with the rate accelerating considerably with industrialization and population growth.

While the cycle time for regenerating fossil fuels is very long, biomass is being continually created by the steady flow of solar energy and photosynthesis converting photons to biomass. However, in the last two thousand years, it is estimated that humans have reduced the earth's biomass from $\sim 1,000$ to $\sim 550$ billion tons, because of deforestation, changes in land use, pollution, and desertification. We are depleting both our biomass and fossil fuel batteries at excessively nonsustainable rates. Obviously, we need to invent new technologies, such as highly efficient solar panels, and commit to massive reforestation to stop this massive battery discharge and sustain human civilization.

## 1.2.3   A Capital Creation System

A fourth view, the theme of this book, is that the earth is a capital creation system. It contends that humans have created a system for generating capital through capital conversion that ramped up when agriculture started. This system has enabled economic growth, increased living standards, population growth, and on the

[8]Lovelock, J. (2010). *The Vanishing Face of Gaia: A Final Warning*. Basic Books.
[9]. Alvarez, L., Alvarez, W., Asaro, F., & Michel, H. (1979). Extraterrestrial Cause for the Cretaceous-Tertiary Extinction: Experiment and Theory. *Science, 208*(4448), 1095–1108.
[10]Schramski, J. R., Gattie, D. K., & Brown, J. H. (2015). Human domination of the biosphere: Rapid discharge of the earth-space battery foretells the future of humankind. *Proceedings of the National Academy of Sciences, 112*(31), 9511–9517.

negative side, contributed to environmental degradation and social inequities. Its overall effect has been positive when comparing the quality of life of today's humans with those of even one hundred years ago, let alone tens of thousands of years in the past.

Many species are capital creators, with nests representing the most frequent output of these efforts. Nest builders include birds, mammals, amphibians, fish, reptiles, and insects. Nest building is an investment of energy and time to create an enduring structure that has reproductive advantages, such as the protection of offspring from prey and the environment.

For humans, capital creation began with the development of tools and housing (a human nest). Scientific studies indicate that prehumans were making tools around 3.3 million years ago.[11] Based upon current efforts at reproducing the fashioning of a flint hand axe, it probably took Paleolithic toolmakers about 300 h to make such a tool.[12] Once made, a flint cutting tool can accelerate the butchering of an animal and the separation of the skin from the body. A flint axe is capital because it requires a prior investment in time and energy to improve the productivity of butchering and other cutting tasks beneficial to the survival of early humanoids. Toolmaking also requires complex social interactions as the toolmaker might have had to trade with others for flint, teach others how to make a proto-knife and use it, and negotiate for time away from hunting or gathering to make tools. The toolmaker needed social capital.

Agriculture was the accelerant of the capital creation system. When humans settled in the Fertile Crescent of the Middle East about eleven thousand years ago, they set in motion a capital creation system that is the progenitor of our current lifestyle. They were able to convert the propitious natural capital of the area (cereal crops and domesticable animals) into other forms of capital.[13] They also created economic structures for capital creation, namely hierarchies and markets. We see hierarchies in the command and control structures of kingdoms and farms. Trading, an early form of a market, is at least eight thousand years old.[14] I view an economy and its component structures (such as organizations and markets) as a capital creation system that generates capital through capital conversion.

The concept of capital is a bedrock of economic thinking, and its importance was established by Adam Smith's seminal treatise on economics,[15] as he notes:

> In the following book, I have endeavoured to explain the nature of stock, the effects of its accumulation into capital of different kinds, and the effects of the different employments of those capitals.

[11]Harmand, S., Lewis, J.E., Feibel, C.S., Lepre, C.J., Prat, S., Lenoble, A., ... Arroyo, A. (2015). 3.3-million-year-old stone tools from Lomekwi 3, West Turkana, Kenya. *Nature, 521*(7552), 310–315.

[12]Stout, D. (2016). Tales of a Stone Age neuroscientist. *Scientific American, 314*(4), 28–35.

[13]Diamond, J.M. (1997). *Guns, Germs, and Steel: The Fates of Human Societies.* W.W. Norton & Co.

[14]Bernstein, W. J. (2008). *A Splendid Exchange: How Trade Shaped the World.* Atlantic Monthly Press.

[15]Smith, A. (1776). *An Inquiry into the Nature and Causes of the Wealth of Nations.* Nelson.

Further examination shows that Smith recognizes that capital, which he some-times calls *stock*, is a durable and transforming factor of production resulting from prior capital investments. Smith also notes that there are different kinds of capital and that these can be deployed in diverse ways. For example, he discerns the importance of human capital. He observes that economic activity is driven by.

... the Acquired and Useful Abilities of All the Inhabitants or Members of the Society.

Moreover, he also recognizes that a person's individual capabilities are a type of capital.[16] As he writes,

A capital fixed and realised, as it were, in his person.

He appreciates that through capital conversion, firms endeavor to increase their stock of capital. Conversion of capital from one form to another to create more capital is the foundation of all economies, irrespective of their political structure. A country or an organization's capability for capital conversion creates for it a distinctive market position. The distribution of wealth illustrates the varying facility of nations and economic structures to create capital. The earth's current social and built environment is the result of tens of thousands of years of capital conversion and creation.

Even Karl Marx, a harsh critic of capitalism, acknowledges the enduring con-tinuity of capital creation.[17] He observes:

It [capital] comes out of circulation, enters into it again, preserves and multiplies itself within its circuit, comes back out of it with expanded bulk, and begins the same round ever afresh.

While Smith and Marx have business in their sights when they discuss capital, organizations of all forms and purpose are in the business of capital creation. Universities concentrate on creating human (graduates) and organizational (knowledge and intellectual property) capital. Religions produce social (the com-munity of believers) and symbolic (prestige and authority) capital. Government agencies enable economic (e.g., highways) and organizational (e.g., regulation of electronic communication) capital creation, which in turn provides critical capital for other organizations to incorporate in their capital creation processes.

We might think of organizations as collections of capital, but it is more useful in a digital world to view them as systems through which capital flows. A balance sheet is an incomplete description of an organization because it is a snapshot of the current collection of capital, and it usually only reports economic capital, which is about 30% of the value of public company.[18] Rather than relying on a measure

---

[16]However, it was not until the 1960s that economist started to appreciate the importance of human capital investment. See Schultz, T.W. (1961). Investment in human capital. *The American Economic Review, 51*(1), 1–17.

[17]Marx, K. (1867). *Das Kapital, Kritik der politischen Ökonomie (Capital: Critique of Political Economy)* (S. Moore & E. Aveling, trans.). Progress Publishers. p. 106.

[18]https://www.economist.com/leaders/2020/02/06/what-it-takes-to-be-a-ceo-in-the-2020s.

invented in 1494, organizations need dynamic models of capital flows to understand the present and explore the future.

The capacity to convert and create capital is neither constant nor equal. The firm that requires more capital than its competitors to produce a unit of good or service receives less profit, and it will likely disappear unless it can soon match or exceed its competitors' capital creation productivity. For the last five or six decades, information systems have been the key driver of productivity improvement.[19] They have been a major agent for raising capital conversion capabilities. The underlying information technology that spawns information systems is ever evolving, and its innovative deployment changes the nature of capital conversion.

There are six foundational types of capital (Table 1.1).[20] Note that we include natural capital,[21] which some scholars omit. Irreplaceable (e.g., fossil fuels) and regenerating (e.g., forests) natural capital are a significant part of all forms of capital.[22] Natural capital was the seed capital of the birth of human civilization and continues to support capital creation (e.g., agriculture, fishing, logging, and mining). I have also extended the capital typology to consider the three broad classes of owners: individuals, organizations, and nations. Each has capital creation goals and systems, although in this book we emphasize the roles of organizations and nations in creating capital. Organizations employ individuals in their capital creation processes, and nations create a scaffolding that supports capital creation by organizations.

Some might dispute the preceding capital classification table and argue for fewer or more classes and question the definitions. There is no definitive classification, but that does not invalidate the reality of the earth's capital creation system. Feel free to revise the classifications to suit your needs for accurately representing your organization's capital creation system. It is critical to see the general nature of our society to understand the central roles of capital and capital conversion.

Capital exists at the national, organizational, and individual levels. With respect to symbolic capital, a nation has a reputation and an image. France, for instance, conjures up visions of Parisian boulevards, museums, and fine food. In India, ancient emperors created splendor around palaces and temples (e.g., Jaipur Palace, Madurai Meenakashi Temple, and Taj Mahal), which are symbols that sustain power and glue people together. Organizations can also be similarly imagined. BMW, in 2018 one of the twenty most admired companies in the world,[23] has a very recognizable logo, a reputation for finely engineered cars that are sometimes

---

[19]Stiroh, K. J. (2002). Information technology and the US productivity revival: What do the industry data say? *American Economic Review, 92*(5), 1559–1576.

[20]Dean, A., & Kretschmer, M. (2007). Can ideas be capital? Factors of production in the postindustrial economy: A review and critique. *The Academy of Management Review, 32*(2), 573–594.

[21]Hawken, P., Lovins, A. B., & Lovins, L. H. (2010). *Natural Capitalism: The Next Industrial Revolution*. Earthscan Publications.

[22]Schumacher, E. F. (1973). *Small Is Beautiful: A Study of Economics As If People Mattered*. Random House.

[23]https://fortune.com/worlds-most-admired-companies/list/.

**Table 1.1** Capital typology

| Capital | National | Organizational | Individual |
|---|---|---|---|
| Economic | Public infrastructure, both physical and informational | Financial, physical, and manufactured resources | Personal investments |
| Human | The general health, skills, knowledge, and abilities of the population | Skills, knowledge, and abilities of a workforce | Personal skills, knowledge, and abilities |
| Natural | Natural resources, living systems, and ecosystem services | Rights to use or extract natural resources, such as farming and mining | Public parks and gardens |
| Organizational | The political, economic, and legal systems, and national culture | Institutionalized knowledge and codified experience (software and databases), routines, patents, manuals, and structures | Personal planning, management, and leadership skills |
| Social | Structures for integrating and assimilating citizens within society to create broad and diverse social networks | The ability of an organization to benefit from its social connections | The ability to benefit from personal social connections |
| Symbolic | National reputation and image; and respect and admiration for a nation's institutions and culture | Organizational reputation, image, brands, and ranking within its industry | The personal honor, status, reputation or prestige possessed within a given social structure |

hailed as "the ultimate driving machine." Many individuals also accumulate symbolic capital, and it is quite common for organizations to help individuals build their social capital through public recognition, such as a company's chairperson award for innovation or the Queen of England's ennobling of those contributing to the arts.

While we can present capital as being in distinct categories, we should also recognize that national capital might be partially constructed from individual or organizational capital. Ethiopia and Kenya benefit from the individual capital of their elite long-distance runners. Germany enhances its reputation by promoting the world-class skills of its many midsized engineering firms, the German Mittelstand.[24] Similarly, a national image might be transferred to its citizens or organizations.

Individuals are ultimately the target of all capital creation activities, and thus the most important element of a capital creation system. Unless they consume the

---

[24]https://www.make-it-in-germany.com/en/for-qualified-professionals/working/mittelstand.

products and services generated, a capital creation chain fails. For example, the buggy makers nearly all disappeared with the advent of the car. There are two types of expenditures in a capital creation system. **Investment expenditures** occur when a product or service is purchased in order to create more capital, such as the typical B2B interaction. **Personal expenditure** occurs when a product or service is purchased in order to satisfy individual needs, such as the typical retail or entertainment transaction. Some expenditures can be a mix of investment and consumption, such as when a person buys a house and conducts business from a home office. Most tax systems recognize the dual nature of some personal expenditures.

The focus is on capital creation and not whether it is purchased to create further capital or to meet personal needs. I am interested in the chain of capital creation activities, their interaction, their impact on capital productivity, and the ultimate success of an organization.

I will return to a detailed discussion of each form of capital and related capital conversion processes later in this book, where there is a chapter on each type of capital and the capital conversion processes for creating it.

## 1.3   The Two Capital Creation Systems

Humboldt's massive ecosystem, Gaia, and the battery are different viewpoints on the earth's natural system, whereas the capital creation model describes a system humans have been building for hundreds of generations. Both are complex adaptive systems (Fig. 1.2). They are complex because they have many interacting components, adaptive because components can compete with each other and coevolve as change occurs among members, and classified as a system because the whole is more than the sum of the parts. Natural systems convert energy from one form to another (e.g., sunshine to sugars), and human systems create capital (e.g., spending economic capital to build symbolic capital, such as a brand).

*The state of natural systems*
As we have discovered in recent years, there are two critical measures that determine the state of our natural systems. First, the earth's temperature is determined to a major extent by the level of atmospheric $CO_2$ because it slows outgoing infrared radiation.[25] Without atmospheric $CO_2$, the earth's average global temperature would be around $-18$ °C (0 °F), and during the preindustrial period, atmospheric $CO_2$ was about 280 ppm and the average global temperature about 15 °C (59 °F). With atmospheric $CO_2$ now exceeding 400 ppm, climatologists forecast an average global temperature in excess of 19 °C (63 °F) around the year 2100. The level of $CO_2$ and the earth's average global temperature have fluctuated before, but never so rapidly, and this sharp change gives species with long gestation periods insufficient time to adjust and evolve to a changed climate.

---

[25]For a brief explanation of the effect of atmospheric $CO_2$ on average global temperature, see https://www.howglobalwarmingworks.org/in-under-5-minutes-ba.html.

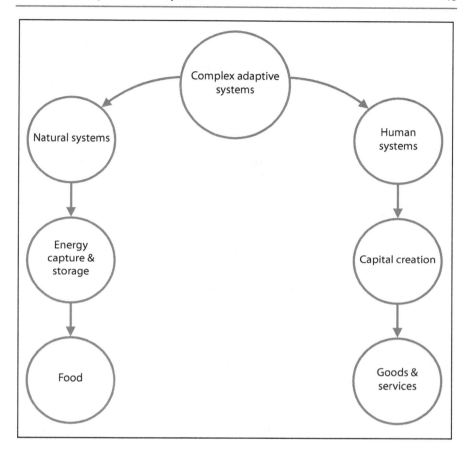

**Fig. 1.2** The dual complex adaptive system

The second critical measure is a species' population. Each species places particular demands on its environment, and massive increases in a particular species can result in environmental degradation and loss of the natural resources necessary to sustain it. In the case of humans, we are heading toward a population of 9 billion, and current estimates indicate that we can support about 2.5 billion in the lifestyle enjoyed by residents of the richest economies, such as those in North America and Western Europe. The Global Footprint Network[26] annually reports an Earth Overshoot Day, when humanity has consumed more resources than the planet can regenerate in a year. In 2020, it was August 22.

---

[26]https://www.footprintnetwork.org.

## The state of human systems

The state of the human capital creation system is determined by its capital productivity and energy efficiency. Because of the importance of these two factors, we call them C' (C prime) and E' (E prime), respectively.[27]

### C' and capital productivity

The principal interest of this book is C', the productivity of capital. Human ingenuity over the millennia, and particularly in recent centuries, has developed methods for raising C' that have transformed the quality of human life by creating a highly effective and efficient capital creation system. Long-run growth in C' has created our current world.

C' is the ratio of capital returned to capital invested:

$$C' = \frac{\text{capital out}}{\text{capital in}}$$

In order for a capital creation system, whether it be a specialized online store or a large-scale manufacturer of computer chips, to be successful, it must ultimately generate a C' at least greater than one and comparable to its competitors'. Obviously, a capital creation effort fails if the ratio is below one. It might be below one during a firm's startup or when handling a transition to a new environment, but ultimately it must reach or exceed the level of comparable investments in its industry. Usually, a firm's investors give a firm several years and several rounds of input capital to establish its anticipated C', but their impatience or lack of evidence of long-term C' viability can terminate an effort.

In the face of major environment change, such as digitization and AI, an organization's C' might dip as it tries to adjust. It will likely draw upon capital reserves to support the transition, which will be particularly difficult if it is an incumbent facing an intruder with a different organizational or technological model. In a market economy, such dips in C' are evidence of creative destruction in action. For an incumbent, the challenge is daunting because its problem's root cause is that its C' is less than its competitors and it has to use capital reserves to try to catch up to the new industry benchmark. Furthermore, the value of its capital might have been reduced because of the market change. For example, a taxi company threatened by ride hailing services can find its taxi licenses greatly diminished in value and no longer usable as collateral.

The prospect and reality of failure drives the capital creation system and contributes to the efficient allocation of capital in a free market economy.

The danger is to associate C' only with the creation of economic capital, and some societies seek to create other forms of capital. Much of medieval Europe, to varying degrees, was concerned with creating symbolic capital. Religious leaders

---

[27]The choice of the prime superscript is to stress the importance of capital productivity and energy efficiency in a capital creation system.

had high status, reputation, and influence. They used economic capital to create symbols of their closeness to God. The massive cathedrals and thousands of monasteries built during this period and the extensive religious art and music of the era are evidence of a dominance of the creation of symbolic capital. While economic growth during the European Middle Ages was essentially stagnant, the creation of symbolic capital flourished.

More recently, we see in the example of Cuba a society where the leadership put a strong emphasis on the creation and maintenance of human capital while at the same time embedding structures that limited the growth of economic capital. Following the revolution in the 1950s, the new administration made universal health care its top priority.[28] The number of doctors per 10,000 inhabitants grew sixfold from 9.2 in 1958 to 58.2 in 1999.[29] In parallel, the new government invested in education. Prior to the revolution, Cuba had one the lowest levels of literacy and basic education in the region, yet a 1998 study by UNESCO of 13 Latin American countries ranked Cuban students first in international mathematics and reading tests.[30] Health care and education are both mechanisms for maintaining and improving human capital.

The choice of what mix of capital to create is an important societal decision. An overpowering domination of one form of capital to the exclusion of others can limit the growth of other types and create a lopsided society. Thus an emphasis on the creation of symbolic capital reduces investments in economic capital that might create trade and jobs. A different balance between cathedrals and canals might have better served the bulk of Europe's population in the Middle Ages. Similarly, Cuba did not modernize its economy to take full advantage of its human capital investment.

The state of a nation's capital creation system and its emphasis on which capital to create determines the quality of life experienced by its inhabitants. Most advanced economies have opted for a relatively free market that stresses the creation of economic capital, but they vary in their approach to the maintenance and creation of human capital that a market economy requires to operate. Thus some operate national health schemes that cover all, while others have varying levels of coverage. Some have free education from kindergarten through graduate school, and others have a mix of public and private schools.

The capital creation model elevates the political discussion to the appropriate blend of the six forms of capital, so that national leaders have a holistic perspective on the goals and priorities of their national system. Governments are an integral part

---

[28]Farag, E. (2000). Ailing healthcare system produces enviable results. Cuban healthcare: An analysis of a community-based model. *The Ambassador, 3*(2). https://ambassadors.net/archives/issue8/cuba_select.htm.

[29]Sixto, F. E. (2002). *An Evaluation of Four Decades of Cuban Healthcare*. Paper presented at the Twelfth Annual Meeting of the Association for the Study of the Cuban Economy (ASCE).

[30]Cassasus, J., Cusato, S., Froemel, J. E., & Palafox, J. C. (2000). *Primer estudio internacional comparativo: sobre lenguaje, matemática y factores asociados para alumnos del tercer y cuarto grado de la educación básica. Segundo informe*. Laboratorio Latinoamericano de Evaluación de la Calidad de la Educación.

of the capital creation system because they can directly create capital, such as the transport infrastructure, that impacts the C′ of many organizations. Thus they have two key decisions related to the goals of a national capital creation system:

- What capital should a government create directly?
- What capital should a government encourage the market to create indirectly?

I will return to these important questions later in this book.

**E′ and energy efficiency**

Energy efficiency, E′, is the other critical measure for a capital creation system:

$$E' = \frac{\text{energy out}}{\text{energy in}} < 1$$

E′ measures the amount of usable energy released from an energy source and in practice is less than 1 (e.g., friction losses) because of the law of the conservation of energy. Landes,[31] in his investigation of the wealth and poverty of nations, high-lights the transformative effect of new energy sources on C′:

All economic [industrial] revolutions have at their core an enhancement of the supply of energy, because this feeds and changes all aspects of human activity.

However, he misses some key elements, and this book is based on an extension of his assertion. I propose that.

All economic revolutions have at their core an enhancement of the supply of energy, *capital conversion processes, and information processing capacity*, because these feed and change all aspects of human activity.

The extension raises three issues:

1. There is no doubt that the supply of energy is important, but the core issue is E′, the efficiency of the conversion of various energy sources. Oil is a commodity that can be purchased on the open market, but the amount of energy extracted from this fossil fuel is central to raising C′. For example, the typical internal combustion engine converts an average of 20–30% of the energy in gasoline into motion; the rest is converted into heat. In late 2017, Nissan announced that it had developed an engine with a maximum thermal efficiency of around 40%.[32] New automotive technology, in the form of electric vehicles, has effi-ciency levels as high as 97%.[33] Thus a business switching its transport fleet to

[31]Landes, D. S. (1999). *The Wealth and Poverty of Nations: Why Some Are So Rich and Some So Poor.* W.W. Norton & Company.
[32]https://www.reuters.com/article/us-autoshow-la-nissan-infiniti/new-nissan-engine-bids-to-extend-life-for-internal-combustion-idUSKBN1DO1YL.
[33]https://spectrum.ieee.org/transportation/advanced-cars/shut-up-about-the-batteries-the-key-to-a-better-electric-car-is-a-lighter-motor.

higher efficiency internal combustion engines or electrical vehicles might require less capital to operate, depending on the initial vehicle cost and annual distance traveled.

2. Economic revolutions are also driven by the enhancement of capital conversion processes, such as the factory and assembly line. The invention of the factory in the late eighteenth century restructured the cotton industry, which at that time had been the world's most significant manufacturing industry for about eight hundred years. Until around 1780, the world's cotton industry was dominated by India, but by 1860 British factories in Manchester ruled the world market. The factory, a major shift in $C'$, destroyed the cottage model of cotton manufacturing. This restructuring of cotton manufacturing, while abetted by the steam engine, was galvanized by the "dark Satanic mills"[34] that employed thousands of people and children in the mass production of cotton textiles.[35]

3. Improvements in information processing capability enhance $C'$. The Greek alphabet, the first phonemic system for recording speech, eased learning of reading and writing and facilitated the emergence of the first literate society. People gained new information-processing skills, and the widespread diffusion of literacy resulted in new forms of social organization and communication.[36] Literacy also facilitates economic development, and indeed the word *economics* derives from the Greek word *oikos*, which variously describes a family, property, or a house. For the last half century, changes in $C'$ have been primarily due to the creation of information and communication processing systems based on digital technology.[37]

Nations and organizations that fail to recognize and adapt to changes in methods of capital conversion, information processing, and the supply of energy imperil their economies and existence, respectively. McKinsey & Co, a consulting company, in 2014 released a report on the digitization of the European banking industry. It posited that digital transformation would put up to 30% of the revenues of a typical bank in jeopardy. Few businesses are likely to survive such a loss of revenue.[38] Digitization is changing $C'$ for many countries and enterprises, and the digital laggards will likely suffer relative to the fast movers.

It is not just digitization but rather, more broadly, innovations in capital conversion processes that create $C'$ shocks that continually confront the status quo. Amazon, Uber, and AirBnB are prominent examples of how digitization can change an industry's $C'$ and punish legacy players with lower performing capital creation systems. Other innovations will follow digitization that will also be $C'$ disruptive and challenge organizations to adapt or wither. Political and

---

[34]*Jerusalem,* a poem by William Blake.

[35]Beckert, S. (2015). *Empire of Cotton: A Global History.* Vintage.

[36]Goody, J., & Watt, I. (1963). The consequences of literacy. *Comparative Studies in Society and History, 5*(3), 304–345.

[37]Stiroh, K. J. (2002). Information technology and the US productivity revival: What do the industry data say? *American Economic Review, 92*(5), 1559–1576.

[38]https://www.mckinsey.com/Insights/Business_Technology/The_rise_of_the_digital_bank?cid= DigitalEdge-eml-alt-mip-mck-oth-1407.

organizational leaders must remain vigilant for such innovations and be prepared to reinvent their capital conversion processes or take on new capital conversion activities to remain relevant.

## 1.4   Systems Create Capital

There are five generic systems (Table 1.2) that organizations deploy in an integrative and multiplicative fashion to create capital. The first of these, systems of engagement, were initiated long ago when the ancestral precursors of homo sapiens were living in the savannah of Africa. The most recent, systems of inquiry, emerged more than two thousand years ago, when the ancient Greeks introduced philosophy, science, and mathematics as systematic methods for understanding the world around them.

At this stage, we will briefly describe each of these types of systems and elaborate on them in a subsequent chapter on their origins and how they support a capital creation system.

### 1.4.1   System of Engagement

A system of engagement enables humans to collaborate and coordinate to achieve their shared goals. Today, the most frequent forms of collaboration are speech, such as a conference call, or writing, such as an email to a project team. Systems of engagement are very visible in the day-to-day operations of enterprises because they are essential to coordination.

### 1.4.2   System of Framing

The purpose of a system of framing is to justify a behavior or decision, or to convince others to follow a particular course of action. It relies on language, setting, and shared culture and knowledge. For example, a CEO might likely use framing to justify an important decision or set the tone of the enterprise. If the CEO were to assemble the top 100 executives and address them at a daylong retreat, the message would likely be more impactful than an email. When Steve Jobs spoke of the importance of the customer experience, he applied a system of framing that now permeatesApple's culture in terms of the products and services it markets and its attitude toward customer privacy. Systems of framing influence behavior and can set directions for enterprises. Thus, these can be the most critical of the five systems for successful capital creation.

**Table 1.2** The types of systems

| Type | Purpose | Mechanisms |
|------|---------|------------|
| Engagement | Collaborating and coordinating activities | Touch, gesturing, speech, and writing |
| Framing | Justifying the reason for behaving in a particular way or promoting a particular opinion | The use of mental models to focus discussion, justify a viewpoint, and generalize knowledge |
| Inquiry | Generating knowledge | Use of replicable methods to justify or validate an inference |
| Production | Creating products and services | Standard operating procedures to increase efficiency and product consistency |
| Record | Recording and retrieving data | Tables, ledgers, and written reports |

### 1.4.3 System of Inquiry

The goal of a system of inquiry is to produce knowledge that makes a difference. While science is typically associated with systems of inquiry, many organizations now deploy systems of inquiry in the form of data analytics, as they have learned that the data-driven organization can have a positive influence on its $C'$. Systems of inquiry are essential for organizations to learn and adapt to a changing environment.

### 1.4.4 System of Production

A system of production is a repetitive sequence of coordinated actions that creates a product or service. An assembly line and a computer algorithm are examples of such systems. In the case of a predominately human system of production, the same set of activities is repeated by different people in a defined sequence. Each person might perform a small element of the total creation process, such as adding the wheels to a car. In a predominantly digital system of production, a set of computer codes is executed, such as processing a person-to-person funds transfer. Systems of production are usually the main, but not the sole, driver of capital creation.

### 1.4.5 System of Record

A system of record captures and recalls details of obligations and events. For an airline, a system of record is necessary for keeping track of passenger reservations by flight, date, and seat. For a manufacturer, a system of record keeps track of the products produced and resources consumed. Systems of record are essential for the management of capital and capital creation processes.

## 1.5 Capital and Systems

Every organization has the five fundamental systems in operation, in multiple and various combinations. The world, at many levels, is a system of systems. Thus an organization is a combination of multiples of the five foundational systems. The economy is a system of organizational systems.

The challenge for a nation and organization is how to integrate, elaborate, and continuously adapt each of these five fundamental systems to meet its capital creation goals on a continuing basis.

Organizational capital includes all versions of the five types of systems. It is the routines, procedures, corporate culture, and software that facilitate capital creation. Human capital, principally in the form of the people who direct an organization and who design and implement systems, is the glue that binds together capital creation and systems (Fig. 1.3). It is a very versatile cement, because it works for organizations with a wide range of purposes and capital creation goals. It is as equally sticky for those enterprises aimed at creating natural or symbolic capital as those focused on economic capital.

The purpose of this book is to describe how the capital creation system operates and provide illustrative examples so you can apply these ideas organizationally or nationally. In subsequent chapters, these goals will be addressed, providing insight into how you might improve your organization's C' and what policies a nation might adopt to help its enterprises raise their C'.

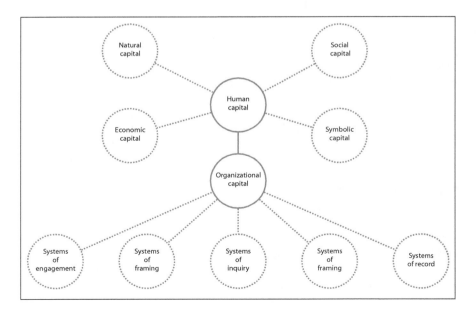

**Fig. 1.3** The interrelationship of capital and systems

## 1.6  Summary

Humans have created and embellished a capital creation system that is based on the production of six types of capital (economic, human, natural, organizational, social, and symbolic) by converting capital from one form to another. There are two capital creation systems: Natural systems create renewable natural capital by converting energy from one form to another. Human systems convert all forms of capital from one form to another. Individuals, organizations, and nations strive to raise $C'$ for the capital conversion processes most important for achieving their goals. Energy efficiency, $E'$, is a critical component of a capital creation system. There are five fundamental systems (systems of engagement, framing, inquiry, production, and record) that enable capital conversion.

# The Organization as a Capital Creation System

Human ingenuity over the millennia, and particularly in recent centuries, has developed methods for raising C′ that have transformed the quality of human life by creating a highly effective and efficient capital creation system. Organizations are the centers of innovation, because they import capital, convert it from one form to another (e.g., recruit human capital to develop an information system, a form of organizational capital), or enhance capital (e.g., educating recent graduates to market a new product) with the intention of generating capital outflows. For example, an organization might borrow funds (economic capital) to retain engineers (human capital) to develop a product (economic capital) for sale (economic capital). The general concept of capital conversion is illustrated in Fig. 2.1. Each organization has a set of capital conversion activities that are sequenced to ultimately create capital outflows. The organizational challenge is to identify and concentrate on those capital conversion processes that can generate a C′ advantage. For a mining company, the key processes are typically converting exploration data about a natural resource, such as a copper deposit, into an efficient extraction plan, executing that plan, and delivering the resulting ore to customers. Thus it converts natural capital into economic capital with the support of human and organizational capital.

## 2.1 The Prestige Car Business

The luxury car market gives us a glimpse into how a capital conversion system operates and the network of linkages between the different forms of capital. According to an industry executive, luxury cars are "12% of the volume and 50% of

© The Editor(s) (if applicable) and The Author(s), under exclusive license to Springer Nature Singapore Pte Ltd. 2021
R. T. Watson, *Capital, Systems, and Objects*, Management for Professionals, https://doi.org/10.1007/978-981-15-9418-2_2

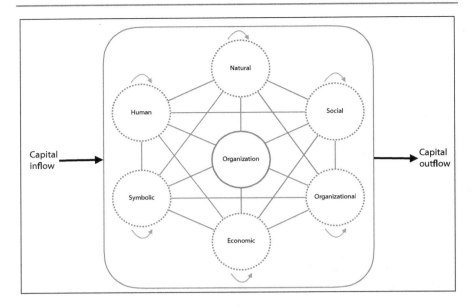

**Fig. 2.1**  The capital conversion system

the profits" for the entire car industry, with the German brands of Mercedes, BMW, and Audi dominating sales.[1]

The main capital flows and conversions for a luxury car manufacturer are depicted in Fig. 2.2. As input, the manufacturer receives funds (economic capital) from banks, shareholders, or retained earnings. It primarily invests in (1) creating a production and distribution system (economic capital) for making and distributing its vehicles, (2) its managerial infrastructure (organizational and human capital) to operate and plan its business, and (3) enhancing its brand (symbolic capital) to attract car buyers. Every car manufacturer needs to make these three investments, but the luxury car makers excel at converting economic capital into symbolic capital. The combination of the three main investments results in the production of a car that can be marketed to the luxury car segment and sold at a premium price. Some of the economic capital generated by sales is retained to continue the cycle, and some is distributed as dividends to shareholders.

There are many high-quality cars in the marketplace, and the German trio doesn't fare as well on measures such as dependability. The 2017 J.D. Powers rating has the Japanese Lexus at number one, Mercedes at five, BMW at seven, and Audi at sixteen.[2] Nevertheless, these leaders in the prestige car market have

---

[1]https://www.economist.com/news/business/21603434-japans-premium-motor-brands-are-still-far-behind-their-german-rivals-giant-carmakers.
[2]http://www.jdpower.com/ratings/study/Vehicle-Dependability-Study-%28VDS%29-by-Make/1881ENG.

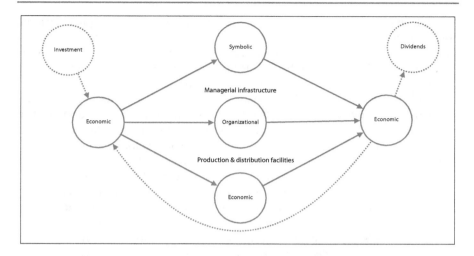

**Fig. 2.2**  The capital conversion system of a luxury car manufacturer

leveraged their ability to create symbolic capital to take a disproportionate share of the car market's profits.

Creating symbolic capital is a challenge. Volkswagen, owner of the Audi brand, tried to enter the premium car market with the Phaeton in 2002.[3] While well engineered with a luxurious interior and selling in the United States for around $90,000, it was a sales disaster in the US market between its entry in 2004 and withdrawal in 2006. It failed to create symbolic capital. Specifically, it maintained the VW badge on the front grill. One reviewer speculated on the potential embarrassment of admitting to your neighbors and friends, "I bought a $91,415 Volkswagen."[4] However, spending a similar amount on a car loaded with symbolic capital is likely to be a prestige enhancer.

## 2.2   The Red Queen Effect

The Red Queen effect argues that organisms must continually adapt, evolve, and multiply to survive in a competitive environment where all are subject to the same challenge.[5] In the capital creation system arena, it is a co-evolutionary race to raise C′, and those organizations who lag behind are likely to disappear as distinct entities.

---

[3]https://en.wikipedia.org/wiki/Volkswagen_Phaeton#/media/File:2005_VW_Phaeton.jpg.
[4]https://wheels.blogs.nytimes.com/2009/09/21/vw-reconsiders-phaeton-for-us/.
[5]Van Valen, L. (1973). A new evolutionary law. *Evolutionary Theory & Review, 1*, 1–30.

While individuals might take on some of the activities of capital creation, organizations have a scale that typically gives them a major $C'$ advantage. Indeed, the challenge for the enterprise is to manage its size to maximize $C'$. Organizations that increase their complexity by broadening their range of products and markets can face declining $C'$, as I shall discuss later in this chapter.

$C'$ is the queen of the capital creation system. Those with the highest capital productivity generate more capital that they can reinvest to create and implement new capital creation processes. Countries also face the same Red Queen challenge because a country is a capital creation system of capital creation systems. A country must establish capital creation mechanisms that enable its multitude of capital creation systems to elevate $C'$ more quickly and efficiently than other nations. Hence, the role of government is to learn what capital it should create and capital conversion activities it should undertake to support its capital creation systems. This is an issue I will return to in a later chapter.

An economy's capital conversion mechanisms (e.g., firms, governments, universities), except for failed states or failing organizations, collectively generate more output than input capital and contribute to long-run economic growth and social progress. New technologies such as 3D printing and phenomena such as digitization are opportunities for changing the methods of capital creation and uplifting capital creation productivity. The web, for example, galvanized new capital creation mechanisms that added significantly to society's capital. In a competitive economy, those whose capital conversion rates fall below industry norms will likely soon fail. Consequently, organizations need to be continually scanning the environment for new technologies and procedures that enable them to rejigger their capital creation systems for greater efficiency and effectiveness.

Every generation, except when there are major wars and disasters, inherits the prior generation's capital investments and conversion mechanisms. Over the millennia since the dawn of agriculture, this investment has been compounding at varying rates. As Einstein noted, "Compound interest is the eighth wonder of the world. He who understands it, earns it... he who doesn't... pays it."[6]

A few thousand years of compounding has produced today's world, though the distribution of capital among countries is unequal. Some countries, such as Saudi Arabia with its oil, have a natural inheritance advantage, and others have fashioned governance mechanisms and economic structures that favor the compounding effects of capital creation. However, these compounding effects are not guaranteed because chance, innovation, and the Red Queen are ceaseless interlocutors in national and organizational affairs. The depletion of a natural resource or the emergence of a substitute can destroy a natural inheritance. Alternatively, dysfunctional governments, particularly those with rigid ideologies that ignore the power of the Red Queen, can perturb a national capital creation system and shift attention from $C'$ to other issues.

---

[6]http://www.goodreads.com/quotes/76863-compound-interest-is-the-eighth-wonder-of-the-world-he.

## 2.3  Forms of Capital Creation

The organization is the main structure for capital creation, and the form it should it take is a central issue for C'. The capability to continually adapt to a changing environment is the central problem of economic organizations.[7] Alternatively, in our terms, the prime problem is to continually adapt to maintain a competitive C'. For example, we see the slow decline of US department stores, such as Sears, in the face of Walmart's superior capital conversion processes to support its mission of "everyday low prices." Now, Walmart is challenged by Amazon's ability to support new capital conversion processes, such as online shopping and home delivery, at competitive prices. While the Amazon model requires massive investment in warehouses, it does not require the same level of economic capital as the more than 4,700 stores Walmart operated in 2020.[8]

An organization has to fashion an evolvable structure and set of capital conversion processes that enable it to thwart the Red Queen. In the twentieth century, clarifying the distinction between hierarchies and markets as capital creation systems was considered a breakthrough in economic thinking, for which Coase[9] and Williamson[10] were both awarded the Nobel Prize in Economics. However, hierarchies and markets are not the only structures for capital creation. The ecosystem (e.g., Apple and its many partners involved in the manufacture of hardware and supporting software) is an additional form,[11] and the community (e.g., open source projects) is a fourth structure for capital creation.[12]

Ecosystems are not new. The global shipping system has operated as *a self-organizing ecosystem* for thousands of years. It continues to create capital by moving products from the producer to consumer, the same function performed by early traders in the Middle East at the birth of capital creation. The economic value of a product increases the closer it gets to the final consumer. Each stage of the shipping industry is designed to fulfill this purpose. While ecosystems are not new, they have recently became more prominent in capital creation—particularly a *coordinated ecosystem* built around a keystone enterprise that directs the actions of the other members.

The rise of the ecosystem is a key capital creation innovation of the last few decades. It has been facilitated by electronic networks because they enable various capital generating structures to interact in multiple and diverse ways to create

---

[7]Tadelis, S., and Williamson, O. E. (2012). Transaction cost economics. In R. Gibbons and J. Roberts (Eds.), *Handbook of Organizational Economics*. Princeton University Press.
[8]https://corporate.walmart.com/our-story/our-locations.
[9]Coase, R. (1937). The nature of the firm. *Economica, 4*, 386–405.
[10]Williamson, O.E. (1973). Markets and hierarchies: Some elementary considerations. *American Economic Review, 63*(2), 316–325.
[11]Iansiti, M., and Levien, R. (2004). Strategy as ecology. *Harvard Business Review, 82*(3), 68–78.
[12]Watson, R. T., Boudreau, M., Greiner, M., Wynn, D., York, P., and Gul, R. (2005). Governance and global communities. *Journal of International Management, 11*(2), 125–142.

capital building ecosystems. The object-oriented organization, which I will discuss in a later chapter, is transforming the creation of capital.[13] For example, Microsoft 's partners generate 95% of its commercial revenue, with more than 7,500 partners joining the ecosystem every month.[14] The launch of the Apple Watch was accompanied by the release of more than 3,500 apps for it, something Apple could not have managed within its hierarchical confines. Hierarchies have become very dependent on ecosystems to create value around their core products and extend their reach, and ecosystems compete with hierarchies. While global shipping is a self-organizing ecosystem with many autonomous members (e.g., ship owners, tugs, pilots, ports, and container terminals), most of the new breed of ecosystems are coordinated by a central hierarchy.

Today, it is rare for a firm to have the necessary specialist knowledge and managerial expertise to deliver unaided a complex product or service. Production and sales of a smart phone, for instance, require the coordinated action of multiple hierarchies to build, deliver, market, and provide telecommunication services. Coordinated ecosystems have emerged as combinations of distributed capital and capital creation capabilities that because of complexity costs are a more efficient capital creation mechanism than a self-contained hierarchy.

Complexity costs have two sources: product complexity and service spatiality. As either or both grow, a firm's organizational capital is overtaxed. As product complexity increases, a hierarchy's management is forced to address a wider variety of issues. Its capability to develop competency in multiple domains is limited. In highly complex organizations, senior managers must continually change focus to address other, and possibly quite dissimilar, issues. As firms diversify their products and reach, executives experience information asymmetries, information overload, and cognitive strain from trying to understand diverse operations.[15] They tend to focus on financial rather than strategic controls, and R&D investments are reduced.[16] It is difficult for a do-most-things hierarchy's top management team to build deep tacit knowledge across a broad domain. Thus it can be at a disadvantage relative to a coordinated ecosystem where deep tacit knowledge can be embedded in each of the specialist members. The shift to coordinated ecosystems indicates they have a C' advantage relative to a hierarchy. In other words, a coordinated collection of a-few-things-done-well organizations can outcompete the organization that tries to do nearly all things internally.

[13]Watson, R. T., Zinkhan, G. M., and Pitt, L. F. (2004). Object orientation: A tool for enterprise design. *California Management Review, 46*(4), 89–110.

[14]https://wire19.com/microsoft-commercial-revenue-flows-through-partners/.

[15]Hitt, M. A., Hoskisson, R. E., and Kim, H. (1997). International diversification: Effects on innovation and firm performance in product-diversified firms. *Academy of Management Journal, 40*(4), 767–798.

[16]Doi, N. (1985). Diversification and R&D activity in Japanese manufacturing firms. *Managerial and Decision Economics, 6*(3), 147–152.

Service spatiality refers to the variety of geographic regions in which a hierarchy wants to operate. Once it moves beyond its national market, it will likely have to deal with the heterogeneity of different legal systems, business regulations, cultural norms, and so forth. While the effects of internationalization might be positive initially, they eventually level off and become negative,[17] because as spatial diversity increases, complexity expands, management capabilities are overstretched, and coordination costs rise. The coordinated ecosystem evolved as a capital efficient mechanism for addressing service spatiality

As the complexity of technology has accelerated and become integrated within and across global products and services, the limits of managerial knowledge have imposed higher capital costs, and ecosystems are an organizational adaption to reduce these costs. Ecosystems couple together hierarchies in a capital creation network of specialized capital (e.g., chip fabrication) and capital conversion capabilities (e.g., marketing mobile electronic games in the Middle East). The members develop mutual dependencies that are hard to sever. Apple relies on Samsung to make certain components for its iPhones while competing with Samsung in the smartphone market.

The need for access to specialist knowledge and assets to effectively sell complex products in diverse and competitive markets drives the creation of an ecosystem to provide customer service (e.g., retail a product in central Asia) or consume services (e.g., engage a trade consultant for Brazil). Depending on the frequency with which foreign services are required, a hierarchy will establish a mix of continuing partnerships and service engagements.

Information and communication technology (ICT) has fostered the development of ecosystems, because digitized data lowers the friction of cooperation. Apple has become an exemplar of the ecosystem governance model with a web of relationships that include chip designers, chipmakers, electronic product assemblers, independent software developers, and music distributors. Conversely, ICT has made products more complex, as products have become smarter, connected, personalizable, and portable. Ecosystems emerged to reduce the capital creation costs of creating innovative and complex ICT-based products for global markets, and in parallel, ICT enabled ecosystems to coordinate networks of global relationships. Coordinated ecosystems and ICT co-evolved (Fig. 2.3).

While Henry Ford owned Brazilian rubber plantations to make tires for his cars, today's car manufacturer realizes that its C' will be higher if it deals with specialist tire producers who in turn get rubber from multiple plantation owners. Ford's decision was likely based on what was the best organizational structure for a high C' in the early twentieth century, and today's carmaker is focused on the same goal. It should always be about C', but while the goal is constant, the means change.

---

[17]Hitt, M. A., Hoskisson, R. E., and Kim, H. (1997). International diversification: Effects on innovation and firm performance in product-diversified firms. *Academy of Management Journal, 40*(4), 767–798.

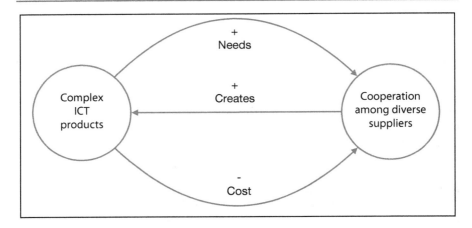

**Fig. 2.3** Co-evolution of complex ICT products and ecosystems

In a global high technology world, the coordinated ecosystem has emerged as the key vehicle for C′, but within this broad structure there are many alternative ways of sharing, separating, and coordinating capital creation processes. Each merger, acquisition, partnership, or contractual arrangement potentially reveals how a coordinated ecosystem is reshuffling the capital creation processes in pursuit of a higher C′.

## 2.4  Crucial Capital

An individual, organization, or nation has two broad classes of capital. Primary capital is central to its capital creation success, whereas secondary capital complements primary capital and contributes to its successful exploitation.

In the luxury car business, symbolic capital is the key determinant of success. Economic and organizational capital are major complementary capitals. The manufacturer must efficiently produce reliable cars and have a distribution system readily accessible to potential buyers, but symbolic capital is the C′ differentiator. As Volkswagen quickly learned, it is not enough to build a high-quality car and charge a price that is comparable to the established symbolic capital leaders.

Every industry, or sector within it, is likely to have a one or two essential capitals it must create. For example, in the mass car sector, manufacturers rely on efficient factories (economic capital) to create price competitive vehicles (economic capital) and a distribution system (economic capital) to reach a large number of potential buyers. They need some symbolic capital to attract customers, but cannot create enough to extract a luxury brand price premium. For the mass car manufacturer, the C′ differentiator is manufacturing and distribution efficiency.

For hospitals, human capital is critical. The skills of its doctors and nurses determine its ability to restore human capital. While some hospitals, such as the Mayo Clinic, have significant symbolic capital, patients seek human capital who can cure them. Silicon Valley might be more aptly described as *human capital central*, because the success of most of its high-tech firms is determined by the quality of human capital they can attract and retain.

For a politician, social capital is often the crucial asset. Former US president Bill Clinton famously had the world's largest list of contacts. Keith Ferrazi in his book, *Never Eat Alone*, describes Clinton's social capital creation mania when at Oxford University in 1968:

> [While] a Rhodes Scholar at Oxford University, he met a graduate student named Jeffrey Stamps at a party. Clinton promptly pulled out a black address book.
>
> "What are you doing here at Oxford, Jeff?" he asked.
>
> "I'm at Pembroke on a Fulbright," Jeff replied. Clinton penned "Pembroke" into his book, then asked about Stamps' undergraduate school and his major.
>
> "Bill, why are you writing this down?" asked Stamps.
>
> "I'm going into politics and plan to run for governor of Arkansas, and I'm keeping track of everyone I meet," said Clinton.
>
> Even while an undergraduate at Georgetown, Clinton used index cards to record the vital stats about everyone he met each day.

## 2.5 Competitive Success

The goal of an individual, organization, or nation is to create a competitive bundle of complementary capitals and capital conversion processes. An individual might focus on building social capital so they can create economic or symbolic capital by being a "go-to person" for resolving disputes or making connections. For example, Han Park, a Professor of International Affairs at the University of Georgia, used his social capital to harmonize relationships between North Korea and the West prior to the reign of Kim Jong-un. He has visited North Korea more than fifty times, and Dr. Park was influential in organizing former US president Jimmy Carter's trips to Pyongyang in 1994 and 2010 when relationships were extremely tense.[18]

A luxury car maker, as we have learned, has to blend symbolic, economic, and organizational capital. Its prime capital conversion process transforms symbolic capital into a price premium. It cannot ignore social and human capital, but these have traditionally been less critical to creating a competitive bundle. However, circumstances change, and nowadays the transition to autonomous electric vehicles, controlled by tens of millions of lines of code,[19] has put greater emphasis on human

---

[18]http://www.cambriapress.com/cambriapress.cfm?template=6&bid=511.

[19]https://www.technologyreview.com/s/508231/many-cars-have-a-hundred-million-lines-of-code/.

capital. Success in the auto industry will be increasingly dependent on software and the ability to recruit and nurture software engineers. Indeed, some vehicle manufacturers might already have more software than automotive engineers.

A nation must also create a competitive bundle of capital and processes. An efficient national transport network (economic capital) lowers the cost of the movement of goods. Education and health care systems create and maintain human capital. An effective political and legal system (organizational capital) facilitates productive relationships between the components of an economy. A nation also needs effective capital conversion processes. Countries that traditionally attract migrants, such as Australia, Canada, and the United States, need processes to assimilate new arrivals into their economic systems to gain full value from their skills. They need to be woven into community and business networks (social capital). Most countries have some unique features, such as their geography, culture, and local food. Natural, social, and human capital can be converted into symbolic capital to attract tourists. Alternatively, a country could use these resources to raise the quality of human capital and social capital by converting these natural resources into parks. It might promote elements of culture and cuisine to build social capital.

While most current economies are very concentrated on economic C′, this is not the only choice. Bhutan is an outlier in that it measures national happiness.[20] Its Gross National Happiness indicator measures aspects of social (e.g., interactions with neighbors) and human (e.g., quality of sleep) well-being. Bhutanese consider good governance, sustainable socioeconomic development, preservation and promotion of culture, and environmental conservation as the foundations of a happy society. Its government is required to promote these four pillars. Bhutan emphasizes capital conversion processes that do more than enable economic growth. While most other societies also fund creating and maintaining noneconomic capital, the argument for such investments is often made in terms of economic C′ because return on investment (ROI) and GDP have become measures for progress.

While this book is primarily about raising organizational C′ because organizations are the innovation engines of society, it is important to recognize that a capital creation system is a tapestry of individual, organizational, and national capital and capital conversion processes. Organizations need national governments to create organizational capital that permits various forms of economic entities to exist (e.g., the public corporation) and establish a rule of law that creates a degree of certainty about organizational transactions.

There are two essential facets of capital creation that can make it a very effective system: First, capital compounds, and capital creates capital. It is a vast accumulative collective effort. Second, the current evidence suggests capital creation works best when actors have a high degree of autonomy to self-organize within an equitable and stable social-economic-political structure. Although it has flaws, the system generally works over the long term for the benefit of many.

---

[20]https://www.nytimes.com/2017/01/17/world/asia/1.

## 2.6  Summary

Organizations are capital conversion and creation systems. There is a continual battle among organizations in the same industry to have the highest C', because this generates more capital to enable the achievement of organizational goals. The Red Queen effect requires that organizations continually adapt and evolve to survive in a competitive environment. Organizations seek to find a structure that most effectively supports capital creation. National governments can assist this search by establishing legal and regulatory frameworks for diverse organizational forms. Primary capital is central to capital creation success, whereas secondary capital complements primary capital and contributes to its success. The goal is to create a competitive bundle of complementary capitals and capital conversion processes.

# The Growth of the Capital Creation System

**3**

Agriculture society was a catalyst for capital creation. Society became more structured because a degree of continuing leadership and organization is required for farming. Farmers were entrepreneurs. They needed to plan, acquire resources, and develop procedures for seeding, harvesting, and threshing grains. In other words, they had to create organizational capital to manage their farms. The labor required for farming varies with the season, with an additional need for human capital in periods such as seeding and harvesting when the window of opportunity to create capital might be small. For example, a crop might rot if it is not gathered soon after ripening. Farmers were forced to develop procedures (organizational capital) for hiring, monitoring, and training their workforce.

Farming converted nomads to settlers, which in turn resulted in communities, towns, and nations. Within these new groupings of settlers, specialist skills developed to meet the needs of the community. Traders and merchants were needed to find buyers for a farm's output. Millers and bakers were necessary to convert cereal crops into bread. A web of interrelated specialist human capital emerged to meet the needs and consequences of farming. While preagricultural society had some specialization, such as hunter, gatherer, flint maker, and basket weaver, the adoption of agriculture and the creation of settlements fostered conditions for the acceleration of human capital specialization.

As communities grew, organizational capital for centralized control evolved. The traditional chief was replaced by a village head, town leader, or king, who ruled with the assistance of a cadre of officials with appropriate specialist knowledge (human capital) for the administration of a society, such as collecting taxes, settling disputes, and defending the city. Facilitating trade was also a key activity for a city's leaders, and this required organizational capital in the form of weights and measures, calendars, currency, and rules for fair exchange.

© The Editor(s) (if applicable) and The Author(s), under exclusive license
to Springer Nature Singapore Pte Ltd. 2021
R. T. Watson, *Capital, Systems, and Objects*, Management for Professionals,
https://doi.org/10.1007/978-981-15-9418-2_3

To strengthen their power, leaders often claimed divine connections and created rituals and customs to accentuate their supposedly god-given right to lead (symbolic capital). Grandiose buildings and garments were also deployed as symbols of power.

It also became the practice for some leaders to further cement their power by marrying their heirs to other elites (social capital). This might help prevent wars, increase wealth, and engender a solidarity among the power holders to ensure their continuity and protect their accumulated capital. They reckoned that genetic and conjugal linkages created enduring social capital, though history is peppered with tales of fratricidal disputes leading to social capital destruction.

All forms of capital existed in some embryonic form in tribal society, as we can observe today in those indigenous people allowed to live relatively untouched by modern society. For example, tribes might practice intermarriage to reduce conflict and form alliances for creating social capital. The growth of cities generated opportunities for an magnification and differentiation of these capitals.

It is possible to see various forms of capital in foraging societies, but the need to wield and sustain power over many boosted capital creation. The wealth generated by an agricultural society supplied the capital to make power amplification possible. Not everyone needed to be involved in farming, and some society members could specialize in administration or warfare. Symbols of power, such as elaborate costumes and pyramids, were established. Agriculture provided the capital and the impetus for a capital creation system, which we have now spent more than ten thousand years refining and embroidering by unleashing the competitive force of $C'$. Before agriculture, humans were a relatively rare species, and the capital creation system established by early farmers set us on the path to becoming the preeminent species on earth.[1]

## 3.1  Turning Points in Capital Creation

Innovation can be both incremental and radical. Continuous improvement programs are incremental. They appeal to the frugal who delight in cutting costs and reducing waste, and they steadily add to $C'$. Radical innovations, in contrast, can create a discontinuity in $C'$ by energizing an abrupt jump in a short period. Entrepreneurs and inventors are often responsible for ramp-ups in $C'$. Often the invention comes first, and then a host of entrepreneurs exploit it to launch an attack on the status quo. They operate as complementary forces because inventors can rarely envisage the manifold effects of their work. Consider the Internet and the massive disturbance and restructuring it galvanized, whose consequences are still rippling through the

[1]There were about five million humans in 10,000 BCE according to https://scottmanning.com/archives/World%20Population%20Estimates%20Interpolated%20and%20Averaged.pdf.

economy. Early casualties were travel agents, music stores, and booksellers, who dissolved rather quickly because of the competitive pressure of their online analogs. Traditional department stores and retailers have lingered longer, but they are reducing their physical presence. Macy's, a leading US retailer, closed more than 120 stores in the period 2015 to 2017[2] and was continuing to close stores in 2020.

Most innovations need complementary action by entrepreneurs if they are to radically change C′, because successful entrepreneurs have mastered the art of ramping up C′. Of course, the inventor and entrepreneur can be the same person if they can manage the shift in focus from product to capital creation system.

There is a continual interplay between E′ and C′ as energy is required for capital conversion. For example, the Chinese water ladder driven by two people's leg muscles can raise sufficient water to irrigate an area that will produce 30 times more energy in the form of food than energy expended on the task.[3] Human ingenuity has continued to fiddle with E′ and C′ for thousands of years to produce today's world. Sometimes this tinkering has produced major leaps in these fundamental determinants, and we are more interested in the major breakthroughs than the many incremental gains. We also want to pay more attention to the recent, and thus likely more relevant, major changes, but there are also major historical leaps that should not be ignored.

I now review some examples of C′ jumps for different types of capital so we can understand their general nature and their consequences. These are only some instances, and while all are profound, they might not be the largest C′ ramp-up in their class. Indeed, we typically lack the data to be so definitive. Some of the examples are quite old, such as the wheel, and others deal with recent inventions.

### 3.1.1 Natural Capital

Natural capital was the original kick starter for capital creation. The Middle East had the most promising natural capital to ignite capital creation.[4] There was a range of annual cereals whose seeds could be collected to create a cycle of planting and reaping that sustained permanent occupation. Furthermore, in the same area were animals that could be domesticated. Female cows, goats, and sheep could be milked. Both males and females could also be slaughtered for food. The serendipitous nature of hunting and gathering was replaced by greater control over the food supply. Of course, there were events, such as drought and pestilence, that disturbed the equilibrium, but humans gradually developed innovations, such as

---

[2]https://www.cnbc.com/2018/01/04/here-are-the-stores-macys-is-closing-next.html.
[3]Smil, V. (1994). *Essays in World History: Energy in World History*. Westview Press.
[4]Diamond, J. M. (1997). *Guns, Germs, and Steel: The Fates of Human Societies*. W.W. Norton & Co.

granaries and meat preservation through smoking and salting, that enabled them to limit the effect of environmental vagaries. The also learned to reshape their environment to make it more productive and resilient, through irrigation and dams, for example.

The ability to exert some control over the environment was the fundamental lesson learned by early farmers. They could regulate the availability of food, set aside resources to handle contingencies, and adapt the local surroundings to improve and sustain C'. Nowadays, the natural environment is modified and controlled in a variety of ways, some deleterious and some beneficial. Farms, controlled and modified natural environments, make use of arable, fertile soil to feed humans and their livestock. Today, they continue to fulfill their original role, but nature is controlled in multiple ways to enhance natural C', as demonstrated by the Green Revolution.

### 3.1.1.1  The Green Revolution

During the period 1960–2000, agriculture researchers developed high yielding varieties of many common cereal crops. The success of high yielding varieties for rice and wheat in the mid-1960s introduced the notion of a "Green Revolution." One particular success was the breeding of shorter, stiffer cereals that resulted in a plant's energy being diverting from growing stalks and leaves to producing more grain. In total, eight thousand improved, high-yielding varieties were released for eleven crops.

For the developing economies, the Green Revolution accounted for a 21% growth in yields, with about 17% of the growth occurring in the early years of the revolution. Expansion of the area seeded explains about 20% of the increase. Overall, the Green Revolution should be seen not as a one-time jump in cereal production, occurring only in the late 1960s, but rather compounding over several decades as successive generations of varieties were developed, each generating gains over its predecessors. This is the genius of capital creation. Jumps often go beyond creating new C' plateaus to establishing new slopes of incremental growth.[5]

## 3.1.2  Economic Capital

*Wheel*

The invention of the wheel and axle around 3,500 BCE reduced the amount of energy required to move goods, especially on relatively smooth surfaces. A horse can carry about 15 to 20% of its weight, and when hooked to a cart, about 120% of

---

[5]Evenson, R. E., & Gollin, D. (2003). Assessing the impact of the Green Revolution, 1960 to 2000. *Science, 300*(5620), 758–762.

its weight on a good road at walking pace.[6] A cart results in a five- or sixfold increase in load capacity compared with using a horse as a pack animal. Moving goods from farm or factory to the market is a common capital conversion process, and the adoption of the wheel was a powerful impetus to C'. The wheel is another example of the need often for complementary partners for an invention. Roads existed prior to the wheel, but it is a network of smooth roads that exploits the full power of the wheel. There was a need for a supporting specialist human capital, and these included wheelwrights, wainwrights, road builders, and innkeepers.

### 3.1.2.1 Containerization

A container ship can move at very low cost the equivalent of several large warehouses of goods with a crew of about thirteen. Since 1956, when the first load of fifty-eight containers was transported on a converted tanker from Newark, New Jersey, to Houston, Texas, the cost of shipping by both sea and land has declined rapidly.[7] For instance, the cost of transporting a kilogram of coffee from Asia to Europe is only fifteen cents, or 1% of item cost.[8] As a result of the global adoption of containerization, "It is better to assume that moving goods is essentially costless than to assume that moving goods is an important component of the production process."[9] Because of its superior cost-effectiveness compared with other forms of transport, the global shipping industry is responsible for around 90% of the world's trade.[10]

While the shipping container was an important innovation, the major innovation was the system that facilitated its global spread. The shipping of goods was transformed by a series of coordinated complementary innovations that drove freight costs to the point of irrelevance, such as illustrated by the prior coffee shipment example. There were many innovations spawned by the seed innovation of a container (Fig. 3.1). Seed innovations have ripple effects throughout a capital creation system, such as global shipping, that raise C' in many phases of capital conversion.

---

[6]http://historicalnovelists.tripod.com/equineda.htm.
[7]Levinson, M. (2010). *The Box: How the Shipping Container Made the World Smaller and the World Economy Bigger*. Princeton University Press.
[8]http://www.worldshipping.org/benefits-of-liner-shipping/efficiency.
[9]Glaeser, E. L., and J. E. Kohlhase. (2004). Cities, regions and the decline of transport costs. *Papers in Regional Science, 83*(1), 197–228.
[10]Maritime Knowledge Centre. (2012). *International Shipping Facts and Figures: Information Resources on Trade, Safety, Security, Environment*. IMO.

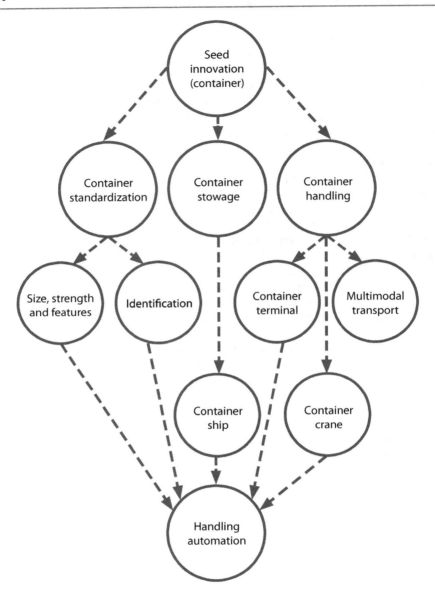

**Fig. 3.1** Containerization innovation[11]

The notion of containerization appeared as early as the eighteenth century, but it was Malcom McLean who created a low-cost transport system by inventing the

---

[11]Ripley, D. (1993). The Little Eaton Gangway and DerbyCanal. Oakwood Press.

container ship and crane.[12] The container was the seed idea that germinated other innovations that were necessary to make containerization a global phenomenon. Initially, as shipping companies converted to containers, efficiency was blighted by the many different container sizes and both intra- and intermodal incompatibilities. It was not until the mid-1960s that standardization was completed in the form of ISO 668.

The visible evidence of systems-wide innovation is seen in the form of containers, ships, and cranes, but other innovations were also required, especially in standardization and governance, to ensure safety and interoperability globally. Governance is the less visible side of many innovations, but it is frequently required to promote industry wide acceptance. New regulations need to be created and old ones revised or rescinded. With standards in place, inventors can focus on efficiency within a physical component, such as a ship, and across components, such as ship to crane, to ensure efficient interoperability. Container and governance standardization energized a movement that also produced efficiency gains in multimodal transport and encouraged the automation of container handling.

Maersk, the world's largest container shipping company in 2018, was a late-comer to the container business. It overcame the advantages of the early movers due to the new skills it developed in financial, managerial, and information systems[13] that were necessary to fund, manage, and operate a large fleet of ships annually moving millions of containers. In other words, Maersk understood the deep structure of the transformation of the shipping industry's capital conversion processes. The evolution of the shipping industry by a series of related and interdependent innovations changed physical capital conversion processes, such as moving goods from exporter to importer, but also other capital conversion processes, such as raising funds to build ships and created new processes, such as tracking the movement of containers on a global basis.

The container launched a stream of innovations in a variety of areas that radically changed global shipping over half a century. The cost of shipping goods was reduced from as high as 25% of the cost of the good moved to around 1%,[14] accompanied by productivity improvements of as much as 40-fold.[15] Containerization was a major leap in $C'$ for the shipping industry.[16]

---

[12]Levinson, M. (2010). *The Box: How the Shipping Container Made the World Smaller and the World Economy Bigger*. Princeton University Press.

[13]Levinson, M. (2010). *The Box: How the Shipping Container Made the World Smaller and the World Economy Bigger*. Princeton University Press.

[14]MacMillan, D. C., & Westfall, T. B. (1960). Competitive general cargo ships. *Transactions SNAME*, 68, 836–878.

[15]Levinson, M. (2010). *The Box: How the Shipping Container Made the World Smaller and the World Economy Bigger*. Princeton University Press.

[16]The section draws heavily from Watson, R. T., Lind, M., and Haraldson, S. (2017). *Physical and Digital Innovation in Shipping: Seeding, Standardizing, and Sequencing*. Paper presented at the HICSS. https://scholarspace.manoa.hawaii.edu/handle/10125/41741.

### 3.1.3  Human Capital

Every employer prefers to have healthy workers who rarely miss a day due to illness and have the education and skills to excel at their job. The national health care and education systems are the foundation for establishing productive human capital. The first maintains human capital and the second creates it.

#### 3.1.3.1  Public Health

In the United States in the late nineteenth and early twentieth centuries, the mortality rate fell more rapidly than in any other period in its history.[17] Prior to this decline of about 40% between 1900 and 1940, those who lived in urban areas had a higher mortality rate than those in the countryside. In our terms, there was a ramp in the $C'$ for human capital, which was mainly due to a decline in infectious diseases.

In 1900, waterborne diseases accounted for about 25% of the mortality from infectious diseases in major US cities. The introduction of systems for filtering and chlorinating water were responsible by 1936 for about a 75% reduction in infant mortality and about a 65% decline in child mortality. Analysis of the costs and benefits of clean water technologies implemented during the period indicates that every $1 spent gave a return of $23, based on valuing a person's life at $500 per year in 2003 dollars—a very impressive human $C'$ change for what seems to be an extremely conservative estimate of the value of life.

Clean water technology exemplifies the returns of investments of preventative measures, such as immunization and other disease reduction actions, that a public health system can generate. This is not new knowledge, but an underinvestment in public health systems means that neglected knowledge lowers a nation's human $C'$. Health care systems are the key factor in maintaining the quality of human capital. All things considered, a healthier population will contribute to the overall national $C'$.

### 3.1.4  Public Education

The industrial revolution in Britain resulted in the division and specialization of labor. It also created urban slum housing and took advantage of child labor. Both of these sets of factors contributed to the emergence of a state system of education. Factory owners needed employees with some basic literacy and numeracy skills to work in their vast factories. Education also socializes people for employment by developing punctuality and skills in following instructions, for example. Politicians accepted that they should alleviate the conditions of poor children. Thus Peel's Factory Act of 1802 specified that the first four years of a seven-year apprenticeship should include daily instruction in reading, writing, and arithmetic in an area set aside for education, but it did not specify how long. By 1816, nearly 60% of

---

[17]Cutler, D., and Miller, G. (2005). The role of public health improvements in health advances: The twentieth-century United States. *Demography, 42*(1), 1–22.

children received some form of schooling, usually about a year in total. State involvement in education slowly advanced, and in 1839 the first British government education department was created. By 1851, schooling attendance had risen to two years, and in 1861 some 90% of children received some form of schooling, though of mixed quality.[18]

If we consider the period from the 1750s, the dawn of the Industrial Revolution, to the eve of World War I in 1914, the spread of industry and the rise of mass education co-evolved. The Industrial Revolution sparked prolonged, rising rates of productivity, first in Britain and then in western Europe, the northern United States, and around the Great Lakes region of Canada.[19] The creation of economic capital, the preeminent goal of the Industrial Revolution, required improved human capital. The mass of farm laborers migrating to the city could perform the most basic tasks, but the Industrial Revolution created a need for mechanics, accountants, managers, and a range of other new jobs that required some education. For the Industrial Revolution to continue, it needed higher-quality human capital. As a result, it transformed schooling from a cottage industry of varying quality into a massive hierarchical, standardized, state educational system. Private schools continued to operate, but the state set the broad curriculum. The Industrial Revolution set in process the human capital revolution that transformed society and initiated the educational investment that enabled today's high tech society and high standard of living. The rise of public education created a massive resource of human capital in the newly industrialized economies and kick started innovation, invention, and scientific discovery.

In India, the midday meal scheme which started in Chennai, in the state of Tamil Nadu, played a crucial role in improving the health of malnourished children and in fostering substantial growth in school enrollment and attendance.[20] The initiative first began by Chennai Corporation in 1920, aimed to help poor students enrolled in schools. Since the British Government refused to support this project from the Elementary Education Fund, the midday meal scheme had to wait till 1956 when the then Chief Minister of Tamil Nadu decided to support the scheme and expand it across the state. Subsequently the mid-day meal scheme not only expanded Tamil Nadu, but also across India. The Government of India developed it as a program to improve the nutritional standing of school-age children. Arguably the largest program in the world serving school children, economic surveys on this program have shown a positive impact on enrollment, attendance, retention, and the nutrition of school children.[21] The midday meal scheme thus served to develop human capital for the country, especially benefiting poor and marginalized children.

The introduction of public education systems unleashed a broad-based human capital creation system that had two significant and persisting outcomes: First, once

[18]Gillard, D. (2011). *Education in England: A Brief History*. London.

[19]Madrick, J. (2002). *Why Economies Grow*. Basic Books.

[20]Ramakrishnan, T. (2020). Tracing the history of Tamil Nadu's mid-day meal scheme. The Hindu, https://www.thehindu.com/news/national/tamil-nadu/tracing-the-history-of-tamil-nadus-mid-day-meal-scheme/article30874858.ece.

[21]Khera, R. (2013). Mid-day meals: Looking ahead. *Economic and Political Weekly*, 48(32).

human capital is abundant, it grows readily as skilled people combine their talents to create other forms of capital, in addition to expanding their personal human capital. The venture capital model is highly dependent on the mixing of diverse and creative human capital, and we see it flourishing in areas rich in human capital. Second, building human capital is also an investment in maintaining human capital. Well-educated people tend to be healthier and fitter and also more willing to invest in the education of their children. Education shapes the opportunities of those who invest in it and their offspring, and it is an enduring benefit to society and capital creation. It might well be the most important factor in their joint success.[22]

### 3.1.5  Organizational Capital

Governments, through the legal system, legitimize and regulate the range of economic structures that can exist within their economy. They can stifle innovation when they forbid certain forms of organization, such as we saw in China prior to Deng Xiaoping's economic reforms that permitted new forms of organizations.

Organizations need to create and continually refine a structure that enables them to adapt to changing competition and consumer desires. Structure is a critical determinant of current and future C′ performance.[23] Although major innovations in organizational structure are rare, they can have a profound influence on C′ because they set the scene for the capital conversion within an organization and the economy when a particular type of structure ramps up C′. Let's consider one of these innovations.

A joint stock company issues shares that can be bought and sold, and a shareholder's portion of the ownership is determined by their relative percentage of total shares issued. While there is evidence of this form of organizing existing more than one thousand years ago, the British East India Company, established in 1600 and lasting around 250 years, popularized the model when it demonstrated its C′ advantages. The company at one stage accounted for half the world's trade in commodities such as cotton, silk, salt, tea, and opium. It has been described as "the corporation that changed the world."[24]

Initially, the advantages of a joint stock company were not readily apparent to potential investors. According to court records, initial average share prices varied between £100 and £300, and not a single shareholder invested more than £1,000. Indeed, the company repeatedly used the Privy Council to force investors to pay for their allotted shares.[25]

---

[22]Keeley, B. (2007). *Human Capital: How What You Know Shapes Your Life*. OECD. https://www.oecd.org/insights/humancapitalhowwhatyouknowshapesyourlife.htm.

[23]Chandler, A. D., Jr. (1962). *Strategy and Structure: Chapters in the History of the American Industrial Enterprise*. MIT Press.

[24]Robins, N. (2006). *The Corporation That Changed the World: How the East India Company Shaped the Modern Multinational*. Pluto Press.

[25]Chaudhuri, K. N. (1965). *The English East India Company: The Study of an Early Joint-Stock Company 1600–1640* (Vol. 4). Frank Cass.

The joint stock company gained acceptance, despite the concerns of early investors, because it has several advantages. First, it is a platform for raising finance for new ventures that restricts the liability of the investor to the amount invested. It was an innovation in risk management. Second, it resulted in the separation of ownership from management. Professional managers are usually better at capital creation than investors, and the ongoing nature of a joint stock company gave them career continuity. It was an innovation in the deployment of human capital.

The joint stock company, now generally known as a *public company*, continues to be a dominant organizational form in advanced economies. The nature of its internal structure has evolved, such as the hierarchy being recast as a matrix in some firms and the use of options to give employees a stake in its future.

When the Industrial Revolution started in the 1750s, Britain had in place an organizational structure to support financing, managing, and growing new enterprises. A capital creation system requires a set of interlocking mechanisms that complement one another. The entrepreneurs that could foresee the opportunities created by combining steam engines, factories, and mechanical looms needed national organizational capital that enabled them to fund and manage their vision. The joint stock company was an on-ramp to the Industrial Revolution.

## 3.1.6  Social Capital

*Service organizations*

Rotary International was the first of the so-called service organizations. Others include Lions and Kiwanis. Established in Chicago in 1905, Rotary International now has 1.2 million members, around 35,000 clubs, and operates in more than 200 countries. Rotarians meet at least twice a month, and if they miss a regular meeting of their local club, they can make up by attending the meeting of another Rotary club.[26] This policy encourages members to interact with other Rotarians when traveling.

Service organizations, despite the name, are foremost about creating social capital. The regular meetings and the strict attendance policy ensure regular interaction among the members, who typically are drawn from the local business and professional community. Regular meetings and service projects create social bonds that sustain long-term relationships. A Rotarian moving to a new town can quickly join an existing social network. Even when traveling, members have a strong incentive to extend their networks by interacting with the members of another club.

Since 1979, a major Rotary service goal has been the global eradication of polio. Other Rotary service themes include literacy, peace, water, and health. In general, service projects are directed at raising human $C'$. Lions, for instance, has a strong focus on preventing blindness.

---

[26]https://www.rotary.org/.

Rotary and its ilk focus on creating social capital. One particular blog reinforces this goal by questioning whether Rotary's social capital is in decline. The blogger responds to a Rotary International president's goal of increasing member retention rates by opining, "It stopped growing because its leaders assumed it was in the business of supplying humanitarian services rather than in the business of creating Rotarians; they were product oriented instead of member oriented."[27] The writer goes on to assert that retention rates are a measure of the effectiveness of clubs in creating social value and optimizing the collective value of the Rotary network.

Another case is the growth of India's IT industry, which grew from a meager USD 1 billion in 2000 to USD 191 billion in 2020.[28] Exports to the United States have distinctly defined the growth of the industry. A key facilitator of outsourcing between India and the US is the Indian diaspora,[29] which consists of social forums of Indian-Americans who play a key role in many US organizations. Social capital created by diasporas in one part of the world enable economic capital creation in their native country.

For many professionals, joining a service organization accelerates the growth of social C'. These clubs have served this role effectively for over a century, and they have the secondary effect of raising human C', but it seems imperative that they remember their fundamental capital creation goal to continue to attract and retain members. This is an orientation that all organizations must keep in mind. They must clearly understand their prime capital creation purpose and nurture it continually.

### 3.1.7  Symbolic Capital

*National TV networks*

By late 1950s, the United States had three dominant national TV networks (ABC, CBS, and NBC), who reached many households in the country, either directly or through affiliates. They created national known figures and brands that many people might be exposed to multiple times in a week, if not in a day with some brands. They created for many illusions of face-to-face relationships with presenters, actors, or performers[30] and high recognition and respect for some brands.

Nightly news readers and commentators became familiar household names and were widely admired. They had very high levels of symbolic capital. Walter Cronkite, the anchor for the *CBS Evening News* for nineteen years, was often described as "the most trusted man in America," based on a 1972 poll.[31] On his death, then current president Barack Obama, eulogized, "He was someone we could

---

[27]https://zone34retentioncentral.blogspot.com/2015/07/is-rotarys-social-capital-in-decline.html.
[28]https://www.nasscom.in.
[29]Elias, A. A., & Mathew, S. K. (2015). Offshore IT outsourcing between India and New Zealand: A systemic analysis. *Pacific Asia Journal of the Association for Information Systems*, 7(3).
[30]Horton, D., and Richard Wohl, R. (1956). Mass communication and para-social interaction: Observations on intimacy at a distance. *Psychiatry, 19*(3), 215–229.
[31]https://www.cbsnews.com/news/walter-cronkite-dies/.

trust to guide us through the most important issues of the day; a voice of certainty in an uncertain world. He was family. He invited us to believe in him, and he never let us down. This country has lost an icon and a dear friend, and he will be truly missed." A national TV network gave Cronkite the opportunity to create massive symbolic capital, because he could reach millions of Americans every evening.

Similarly, large corporations discovered that national TV networks were a platform for enhancing their reputation and that of their brands. An outstanding example is *General Electric Theater*, which was broadcast on Sunday evenings during 1953 to 1962 and helped create the national image of GE. After only four months on the air, it was television's most popular weekly dramatic program. GE established its identity with the weekly message that "Progress is our most important product." Its advertisements in fall 1954 promoted topics such as the "Kitchen of the Future," "Lamp Progress," "Jet Engine Advancement," and "Atomic Safety Devices." According to the Gallup-Robinson pollsters, *General Electric Theater* was "the leading institutional campaign on television for selling ideas to the public."[32]

In September 1954, Ronald Reagan became the host of *General Electric Theater* and continued until 1962. The show gave him a national forum for demonstrating his charm, communication skills, and vision for the United States. His weekly prominence resulted in invitations to speak at a variety of forums throughout the country. The symbolic capital he created was certainly a very valuable asset in his successful quest for the US presidency.

When you are part of the home every night or once a week, there is an opportunity to build symbolic capital on a previously unprecedented scale. The intimacy of the home television and a national network was an expansion of the capacity to create symbolic capital.

*The age of cathedrals*

Societies have generally focused on the creation of economic capital. There might be short periods when other capital goals are accentuated, such as in China following the Mao-led revolution, but these tend to be for short periods, followed by a reversion to economic $C'$ dominance. There is one period, however, where for a major part of the world and for several hundred years, symbolic capital was preeminent.

Religious practices are full of symbols, because they are the language of myths and beliefs. The indefiniteness of ultimate reality, the creation of life and the afterlife, is the fundamental concern of all religions. They all have a creation story and beliefs about life beyond death. Religious practices rely heavily on analogies or parables, metaphors, poetry, art, buildings, rituals, and costumes to augment language and represent the special role of religion in human life.[33] A religion needs to build and maintain its symbolic capital to retain and attract adherents, and they can have breakout periods of symbolic $C'$ growth.

---

[32]http://www.museum.tv/eotv/generalelect.htm.
[33]Eliade, M., and Adams, C. J. (1987). *The Encyclopedia of Religion* (Vol. 12). Macmillan.

The great time and place of symbolic capital was Europe in the period 1000 to 1400, where religion dominated life and was the major cultural force in music (e.g., Gregorian chants[34]), art (e.g., the *Apocalypse Tapestry*[35]), and literature (e.g., Dante's *The Divine Comedy*). It was the age of the cathedrals. They were expensive and lengthy projects, especially given the general poverty of the period, and consumed a large portion of a region's wealth. Their cost and scale surpassed everything else, including defensive castles, parliaments, and government buildings. One estimate is that in Europe at that time, there was a chapel for every two hundred inhabitants.[36] These massive symbols of the Catholic Church were the great dominating buildings around which cities were reborn. They were magnetics for wealth and trade.[37] They were not intended to promote economic growth, and trade was incidental to their religious purpose and the creation of symbolic capital.

In Europe, symbolic capital reigned divinely until its gradual displacement by the Industrial Revolution's reinstatement of economic capital as the prime shaper of society. Symbolic capital reestablished its role in society in the form of brands.

### 3.1.7.1   The Age of Brands

In most markets, the ability to differentiate is a key determinant of profitability and thus C′. Hence it is not surprising that organizations look for means of creating a distinctiveness beyond the features of their products and services. They look to create symbolic capital that helps them stand out from the hoi polloi in crowded market places. Brands have become an important form of symbolic capital because of their potential differentiating power. Brand building and management is for many organizations a key performance differential. In the commercial space, brands can enable premium pricing. In the not-for-profit arena, a brand can attract support and donations. Individuals, organizations, and countries use symbolic capital to facilitate goal attainment.

## 3.2   Summary

Capital has waves of incremental and radical growth. Many organizations have continuous improvement projects to maintain their competitiveness through gradually raising C′. The gentle lapping of improvement is occasionally perturbed by a tsunami innovation that wipes out established forms of capital creation and ramps up C′ overall or for specific types of capital. Incremental growth allows an organization to adjust to its competitors' actions and changes in consumer demands. There is an opportunity for organizations to co-evolve when change is slow-paced. A radical innovation requires rapid response and reinvention or quick (e.g.,

---

[34]https://en.wikipedia.org/wiki/File:Gaudeamus_omnes_-_Graduale_Aboense.org.

[35]https://en.wikipedia.org/wiki/Apocalypse_Tapestry.

[36]McIntyre, A. (2008). Cathedrals and the birth of freedom. *IPA Review* (July), 51–52.

[37]Duby, G. (1983). *The Age of the Cathedrals: Art and Society, 980–1420*. University of Chicago Press.

bookstores) or slow (e.g., department stores) demise. The threat typically comes from new technology deployed by nontraditional competitors. Over the last five decades, information and communication technologies have produced multiple tsunamis that have fueled new capital creation forms and sidelined others. Digitization is the latest example of how the capital creation system morphs over time to raise its productivity. It is not the first ramp up, as illustrated multiple times in this chapter, and it will not be the last. Thus it is important for individuals, organizations, and nations to recognize that they need a dual strategy of ongoing incremental and occasional radical $C'$ to remain competitive.

# Systems for Creating Capital

4

## 4.1 The Systems Imperative

Humans[1] are a biologically evolved social species with advanced cognitive skills. While there are a number of social species, such as ants, humans are the most sophisticated in terms of creating societies. All species have some cognitive skills (e.g., a plant senses sunlight and orientates toward it), and some have very specialized skills (e.g., echolocation in bats). Humans, however, have the most advanced cognitive skills. We have jointly applied our social and cognitive skills over millions of years to create the sociotechnical systems that dominate today's world and are responsible for our capital creation system.

*System* is perhaps the most frequently applied term to the many instances of a network of interlocking complex mechanisms (such as a transport system, a financial system, and in our case, a capital creation system) that make the multidimensional tapestry of our globe. All these systems maintain their essential identity under varying local conditions and over time, while subject to change, evolution, and the infusion of technology. Humans have been designing, building, operating, and disrupting systems, particularly natural systems, for millions of years. It has been a long, exponentially explosive growth in terms of numbers, complexity, and interactivity.

This chapter was seeded by a short commentary[2] by Geoffrey Moore identifying two types of systems: systems of record and systems of engagement. The author of an influential business book, *Crossing the Chasm*, Moore attracted considerable attention in the industry press, including mentions in *Forbes* and *Information Week*,

---

[1]When we use the term *humans*, we also include some of our direct ancestral species.
[2]Moore, G. (2011). *Systems of Engagement and the Future of Enterprise IT: A Sea Change in Enterprise IT*. AIIM.

© The Editor(s) (if applicable) and The Author(s), under exclusive license to Springer Nature Singapore Pte Ltd. 2021
R. T. Watson, *Capital, Systems, and Objects*, Management for Professionals, https://doi.org/10.1007/978-981-15-9418-2_4

and he made multiple conference presentations based on his commentary. His thoughts resonate with industry, but as this chapter will show, they err on several perspectives: (1) there are more than two types of systems; (2) the evolution is not from systems of record to systems of engagement, but rather the reverse; and (3) thinking of systems as distinct entities fails to alert managers as to their critical interplay. Moore stimulated our thinking about the origins of information systems because notions such as systems of record and systems of engagement embrace both the past (clay tablets and gesturing) and the present (big data and social media).

An analysis of critical prior events can be foundational to studying the present and the near future. Thus I identify critical episodes in the history of systems that will help you understand their origin and, more importantly, how they interconnect in a capital creation system.

## 4.2  Foundational Ideas

This chapter draws on general systems theory and research in evolutionary psychology and sociology, and it serves to present key concepts before we delve into the five types of systems.

### Systems
The systems concept is very influential in organizational thinking. Many aspects of the human-made environment are systems, such as the road system and the Internet. Human systems are the scaffolding of today's environment, and the economy is a complex system of capital creation systems. It is our ability to understand how these systems operate, interact, and evolve that determines our success in managing organizations and economies.

The systems concept was initially transferred from the sciences to the social world in the form of General Systems Theory, with the notion that a system is, according to the *Oxford English Dictionary*, "A group or set of related or associated things perceived or thought of as a unity or complex whole." The term has wide applicability in describing today's world. A more expansive term, *complex adaptive system* (CAS), has also been transferred from the natural to the social world to chronicle the essential nature of many systems. In this book, I use the broad term *system* with the understanding that systems are typically complex, interrelated, and adaptive.

Theories from chemistry, biology, and physics can explain the origin and operation of natural systems, but how do we explain the origin of human-made systems? Working with the notions that (1) a system is a set of interrelated objects forming a whole, and (2) systems are adaptive and interconnected, I proceed to identify five types of systems that humans created over millions of years and are, propose, the conceptual building blocks of other systems developed by humans yesterday and today (and those yet to come). These systems also help us understand the development of humans as a cognitive social species, but first we need to review some evolutionary psychology theory on the modular mind.

**Modular Mind**

Modular mind theory[3] asserts that the human mind consists of a massive number of functionally specialized and independently evolved modules that have domain-specific cognitive skills, resulting from specific environmental and social pressures faced by our prehistoric ancestors. Modules are best defined in terms of the specific operations or functions they perform.

Similarly, the human body evolved multiple specialized physiological systems, such as the heart and lungs, to enhance environmental and biological fitness. Notably, while humans don't differ markedly in our physiological systems compared with other mammals, our cognitive modules give us distinctive and dominant ecological advantages over other species.

A module's functionality is determined by how it processes information. Thus the visualization module processes a limited range of electromagnetic frequencies detected by individual rods and cones in the retina. The ears detect variations in air pressure and transmit these as impulses to the hearing system, some of which might be processed by the speech module. For prehistoric humans, it was essential to be able to distinguish tribal members from others, because misidentification could be lethal. Not surprisingly, the brain has a facial recognition module, which consists of about two hundred cells, with single neurons (submodules) for handling separate facial features, such as hairline width, which are then combined to create the image of an encountered face.[4]

Modern humans have inherited a multitude of modules forged long ago to promote survival in the African savannah, when humans lived in bands or tribes and rarely interacted with strangers. Keep in mind that this legacy set of modules evolved to solve a set of environmental challenges very different from many of the issues facing today's humans. For example, in their ancestral setting, humans evolved a fast-acting inference module that generates strong intuitions for survival. This same module in today's world, however, can produce a confirmation bias.[5] We are programmed to strongly defend a previously formed opinion or belief by accepting confirming evidence and ignoring that which suggests otherwise. This bias, which worked well for our ancestors because it promoted their survival, is not well-suited for the open, evidence-based contemplative decision-making typically

---

[3]Kurzban, R. (2012). *Why Everyone (Else) Is a Hypocrite: Evolution and the Modular Mind.* Princeton University Press.
[4]Chang, L., & Tsao, D. Y. (2017). The code for facial identity in the primate brain. *Cell, 169*(6), 1013–1028, e1014.
[5]Nickerson, R. S. (1998). Confirmation bias: A ubiquitous phenomenon in many guises. *Review of General Psychology, 2*(2), 175.

necessary for organizational survival today.[6] We have to recognize the shortcomings of our legacy modules and fashion mechanisms to subvert them, like playing the devil's advocate.

### Systems Classification
In biology, a tree is used to depict evolutionary linkages, with the tips typically showing the lineage's living descendants. The key challenge in creating a tree is to decide when a species splits, but forking is not abrupt but rather a gradual process. In my case, I recognize that a system is distinguishable from its ancestor(s) when it emerges to fulfill a distinct purpose. Human systems are purposive. They are evolving designs intended to serve a distinct function. Early human systems were reactions to survival problems, and later systems were designed to solve the problems of early civilizations. At the same time, emergent systems were likely deliberately reshaped by humans to more effectively serve their functions, and human-designed systems were modified over time to more effectively meet their original goals or serve new goals. Thus classifying human systems by their purpose makes sense.

## 4.3   A Typology of Systems

By examining humanity over a long period, I have identified five fundamental human-made systems that facilitated the development of society by the most advanced cognitive social species. These systems, I contend, are the building blocks of all societies. We see them today in a digital guise, but their deep roots are evident. For your convenience, I repeat the overview of these five types of systems (Table 4.1) presented earlier.

### Systems of Engagement
The ability of our ancestors to survive was dependent on cooperation—for instance, in aggressive scavenging and when building shelters. Understanding the perceptions and intentions of others is fundamental to cooperation, and humans have created unique processes of cultural learning and engagement based on shared intentionality. We evolved to cooperate to achieve shared goals through social coordination mechanisms. Cooperation is an innate human motivation. It requires that the parties have a shared intentionality,[7] and they need a *system of engagement* for creating and achieving common goals.

---

[6]Warning: The authors of most nonfiction books are subject to a confirmation bias. As such, we present facts and arguments to confirm our understanding of the nature and operation of a capital creation system, though in writing this book we did have to change our minds a few times when the evidence contradicted initial thinking.

[7]Tomasello, M. (2008). *Origins of Human Communication*. MIT Press.

**Table 4.1**  Five types of systems

| Type | Purpose | Mechanisms |
|------|---------|------------|
| Engagement | Collaborate and coordinate activities | Touch, gesturing, speech, and writing |
| Framing | Justify the reason for behaving in a particular way or promoting a particular opinion | Use of a mental model to focus discussion, justify a viewpoint, and generalize knowledge |
| Inquiry | Generate knowledge | Use of replicable methods to justify or validate an inference |
| Production | Create and transport products and services | Standard operating procedures to increase the efficiency of product and service creation, lower transport costs, and enhance transport consistency |
| Record | Record and retrieve data | Tables, ledgers, and written reports |

Humans uniquely have developed a system of engagement that requires parties to share chunks of information to enable the creation of a joint goal; then they must cooperate to achieve that goal. Thus *a system of engagement is a set of shared symbols that enables two or more humans to share intentions and achieve their common goal*. It includes all mutually understood symbols that can be used to communicate, such as an upright palm, a soft touch on the shoulder, or a shout of warning.

Initially, systems of engagement were likely founded primarily on gestures (visual symbols, such as the movement of hands, limbs, and body, and facial expressions) and touch (haptic symbols, such as stroking, pulling, and pushing another's body). Gestures can, for example, indicate directionality (e.g., pointing) and action (e.g., beckoning), whereas touch can express emotion through what is touched and how it is touched, and also direction by guiding or pushing another. As we become acculturated by our parents and peers, we learn our society's particular gestures and touches.

Based on an analysis of phonemic diversity, speech (aural symbols) originated solely in southwest Africa about 50,000–100,000 years ago, before the African diaspora.[8] Speech did not suddenly appear, but rather evolved. Speech elaborated the system of engagement beyond a few basic sounds that might have served to express various levels of agreement. Humans linked basic sounds, phonemes, to create words and then started to develop a syntax and grammar, which reduced ambiguity, to fashion a language which has proved to be a highly effective system of engagement when the parties share the same understanding of a sequence of sounds (i.e., a language) but quite useless when they do not, in which case humans often resort to gestures such as pointing. Haptic signals are still a feature of a system of engagement. A limp handshake sends a quite different message compared to a strong hug.

---

[8]Atkinson, Q. D. (2011). Phonemic diversity supports a serial founder effect model of language expansion from Africa. *Science, 332*(6027), 346–349.

Writing (visual symbols) subsequently enabled systems of engagement to overcome distance. Manufactured writing, the printed book, increased the size of the audience a person could engage. In the digital world, systems of engagement are still the foundation of collaboration. We now rely on coding visual or aural symbols into digital format, transmitting them electronically, and then decoding them into visual or aural symbols. There is limited support for the digitization of haptic signals at this stage, though they are present in operating systems such as iOS.

A system of engagement enhanced the reproductive success of early humans because it enabled them to cooperate on activities essential to survival, and we are the descendants of those with the "cooperative" gene[9] and those with the cognitive capacity to participate in a system of engagement. A certain level of cognitive processing, however, is required to interpret the meaning of a series of connected symbols and enact the interpretation. Evolution favored those with the "cognitive" gene who could understand what others were trying to communicate and thus share in the fruits of collaboration. Thus a system of engagement requires a motivation to share intentions and the cognitive ability to interpret another's communication of these intentions.

Once created, a system of engagement is not exclusively confined to survival tasks. It is a capability that (as early humans understood) can be used for other purposes, such as to entertain through miming or storytelling. A system emerging or designed to support one goal can be reinvented to serve other uses. Thus systems of engagement likely evolved as humans discovered other applications for gesturing, touching, and speaking. New symbols were added that supported nonsurvival activities and went beyond sharing intentionalities. The emergence of speech created a more powerful system of engagement than gesture or touch. For the vast majority of humans, our main form of engagement is our native tongue. A system of engagement for socialization also created the circumstances for other fundamental human systems to emerge.

### Systems of Production

Humans have been making tools for more than three million years, and the earliest evidence suggests that these tools were used for flesh removal and marrow access.[10] While there are differing interpretations of the archaeological data on whether early humans were big game hunters or opportunistic scavengers,[11] it is clear that they developed tools for removing meat. Furthermore, both hunting and scavenging were likely more successful when humans cooperated. Early humans mixed the languages of gesture and touch to collaborate to acquire meat, and then developed

---

[9]Sober, E., & Wilson, D. S. (1998). *Unto Others: The Evolution and Psychology of Unselfish Behavior.* Harvard University Press.

[10]McPherron, S. P., Alemseged, Z., Marean, C. W., Wynn, J. G., Reed, D., Geraads, D.,... Béarat, H. A. (2010). Evidence for stone-tool-assisted consumption of animal tissues before 3.39 million years ago at Dikika, Ethiopia. *Nature, 466*(7308), 857–860.

[11]O'Connell, J. F., Hawkes, K., Lupo, K. D., & Jones, N. B. (2002). Male strategies and Plio-Pleistocene archaeology. *Journal of Human Evolution, 43*(6), 831–872.

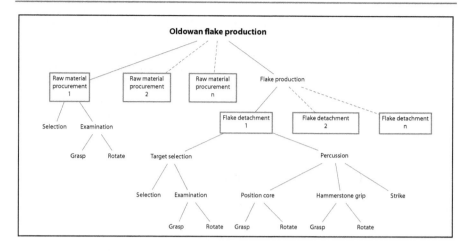

**Fig. 4.1** Oldowan flake production process (Stout, D. (2011). Stone toolmaking and the evolution of human culture and cognition. *Philosophical Transactions of the Royal Society of London B: Biological Sciences, 366*(1567), 1050–1059)

tools to remove flesh from bones and access the marrow. A system of engagement was necessarily in place before toolmaking emerged.

Some of the earliest stone tools, proto-knives, are attributed to the Oldowan industry,[12] where sharp stone flakes were made by striking one rock, the core, with another, the hammerstone. Archaeologists have experimentally reconstructed the Oldowan process for making a stone tool (Fig. 4.1).[13] Reenacting this process minimally requires two steps: (1) the procurement of the raw materials and (2) flaking. Procurement involves selecting core and hammerstone rocks of appropriate size, shape, and composition. Flaking involves examining the core rock to select the target point for the hammerstone, then appropriately positioning the core, deciding how to grip the hammerstone to deliver an accurate strike, and taking percussive action (see the following figure). Other flake production processes can be similarly represented as sequences within a hierarchy. In summary, *a system of production is a repetitive sequence of coordinated actions that might be divided among actors to achieve a goal.*

More than three million years ago, humans had developed a reproducible process for making a simple cutting blade. They had used a system of engagement to create a system of production. This early system of production was probably based

---

[12]Semaw, S. (2000). The world's oldest stone artefacts from Gona, Ethiopia: Their implications for understanding stone technology and patterns of human evolution between 2.6 and 1.5 million years ago. *Journal of Archaeological Science, 27*(12), 1197–1214.
[13]Stout, D. (2011). Stone toolmaking and the evolution of human culture and cognition. *Philosophical Transactions of the Royal Society of London B: Biological Sciences, 366*(1567), 1050–1059.

on gestures and touching, just as today's sports coaches use both gesture and touch in teaching the process for hitting a tennis ball, for example.

The Oldowans might have practiced division of labor by breaking up knife-making into procurement and production. The skilled stone finders and flake producers would have also had to train others in their skills. Notice how one process, toolmaking, creates another process, training toolmakers. Furthermore, the prototype knife was a tool for butchering a carcass, another process to be refined and sustained through training within a tribe.

It is likely that archaeologists cannot deconstruct primitive tool making and use into layers of technological interdependencies, but the opportunity was certainly there for early humans to discover the principles of a system of production, and then it was just a matter of applying them over a few million years to eventually fashion assembly lines, oil refineries, and digital algorithms.

## Systems of Framing

Before discussing systems of framing, we need to consider what we know about human reason, "the faculty that makes humans knowledgeable and wise,"[14] and how it has created two distinct types of systems: systems of framing and systems of inquiry.

There are two types of reason: *justificatory* and *argumentative*.[15] The justificatory viewpoint proposes that reason is about producing and evaluating justifications and arguments through discussion with others. It differs from the argumentative perspective, which maintains that the function of reasoning is to raise the quality of the comprehension of a situation or phenomenon and associated decisions. Based on this dichotomy, I focus on justificatory interactionist reasoning as the foundation for systems framing. Later I will return to examine argumentative reasoning as the basis for systems of inquiry.

As I discussed earlier, evolutionary psychology maintains that the mind evolved to give humans specialist modules for specific tasks essential for biological fitness. One of these modules generates inferences from environmental inputs without simultaneously developing a reason for the relationship between the inputs and inferred conclusions. This module is not exclusively human, as many animals also automatically make inferences, such as what to eat and when to flee. This innate inference module operates spontaneously, intuitively, and unconsciously without motivation and guidance, because there were certain situations that our ancestors faced where survival was dependent on fast and instinctive action. Reasoning is biased toward survival in the African savannah, and *constructive paranoia*, a strong desire to avoid seemingly low probability dangers, is reported among today's forest dwellers in New Guinea.[16]

---

[14]Mercier, H., & Sperber, D. (2017). *The Enigma of Reason*. Harvard University Press.
[15]Mercier, H., & Sperber, D. (2017). *The Enigma of Reason*. Harvard University Press.
[16]Diamond, J. (2013). *The World Until Yesterday: What Can We Learn from Traditional Societies?* Penguin.

Given the pace of evolution, this inference module was very likely operating well before the emergence of speech. Humans had already managed to traverse several million years of life in a challenging environment, and speech was a late addition to their repertoire of survival tools. Reasoning is perhaps the clearest evidence that humans' cognitive capability and speech added a rich and expressive channel to their system of engagement, compared with gesturing and touch. Speech complemented the inference module by giving humans a conduit for justifying their innate responses and actions. Speech was adopted for after-the-fact rationalization to convince others to think and act as the speaker suggested. It became a tool for persuasion to align innate inferencing and group coordination. We tend to account for our actions to meet our self-interests, fit the circumstances, and the information or beliefs shared with the listener. Accurately tracing the origin of a decision is frequently sidelined by vindication and persuasiveness.

We craft reasons to justify to others our thoughts and behavior so we can convince them to adopt our beliefs or a suggested course of action. Reason can also be used for building symbolic capital, because it can signal both intelligence and creativity.

Today, speech-based justification dominates, because eloquent speakers can present distinctions and nuances that are often invisible to others.[17] When reasoning matters, it is often conducted verbally, such as in legislative assemblies, courts of law, and board meetings. The application of speech to justify innate inferences created a system of framing.

Imagine a human of 60,000 years ago whose inference engine generates an insight about a potential threat facing her band. What means beyond speech does she have to justify her insight and argue with those around her? There are no data or topic experts, but only words to convey her concern, but words, their selection, and the order or presentation are very important because they establish a frame of reference. The combination of speech and an inference module laid the foundation for systems of framing, which greatly influences our interpretation of our surroundings and societal action. *A system of framing justifies the reason for behaving in a particular way or promoting a particular opinion. It intertwines language, setting, and shared culture and knowledge for justifying and attracting adherents to a viewpoint.* The development of this system commenced when humans interlaced inferences and speech to create a means of influence.

Consider global warming, which has been framed in multiple ways. In the United States, some Republican leaders speak of unsettled science and the economic cost of the shift from fossil fuels. On the Democratic side, the stress is on looming catastrophes (e.g., polar ice cap melting, mass extinction of species, tipping points). A group of Evangelical Christians frame the global climate change in terms of religious morality, whereas the business press touts the commercial opportunities in areas such as renewables and energy efficiency innovation.[18] Each

---

[17]Fairhurst, G. T. (2010). *The Power of Framing: Creating the Language of Leadership* (Vol. 290). John Wiley & Sons.
[18]Nisbet, M. C., & Mooney, C. (2009). Framing science. *Science, 316*(Apr 6), 56.

group is presenting a justification for certain actions or inactions to influence public opinion and political will.

Humans, whether our deep ancestors or today's citizens, have difficulty understanding the world they witness and their experiences within it. To efficiently process new signals from this world, they apply interpretive frames to classify information and give it meaning. Framing is the mechanism by which people develop a particular understanding of, or attitude toward, an issue. A frame is often set by someone who initiates a dialogue because they want to influence opinion on a topic. Setting the frame can be critical, because a small change in the presentation of an issue can generate large changes in opinion.[19] As a noted political communicator and pioneer of framing as a political campaign strategy indicates, "It's not what you say; it's how you say it."[20]

Humans have an innate drive to understand the natural and social world in which they live. A desire to see purpose and design in their world led humans to frame geological formations, astronomical features, and natural catastrophes as the outcome of some purposeful agent. For example, if a volcano were spewing hot rocks (realism), then there must be someone (an invisible supernatural) heaving them out of the caldera. Many legends and myths are similarly an explanation of an event that blends realism and the supernatural. Some myths can be linked to prior natural events in space and time. For example, an Australian Aboriginal legend and Native American story have been correlated with massive volcanic explosions 37,000 and 7,700 ago, respectively.[21] Sun gods appear in many myths, but they vary in their purpose and traits because each originator had a different *mental camera*,[22] a device for framing and recording a scene.

Framing has two drivers: first, the desire to convert intuitive inferences into action via persuasive speech, and second, to comprehend the observed world by inferring purpose. Without a system of inquiry, prehistoric humans relied on a system of framing to address these two drives. Hence, we can think of framing as originating as purpose-driven reasoning to influence or explain. Later, a system of inquiry emerged as an explanatory mechanism.

## Systems of Record

The rise of agriculture in the fertile crescent of the Middle East kindled the need for a system of record. Farming changed the temporal relationship between production and consumption. The hunter-gatherer consumes what is produced in a short period, but a farming society has to adapt to the seasonal production of some crops and the

---

[19]Chong, D., & Druckman, J. N. (2007). Framing theory. *Annu. Rev. Polit. Sci., 10*, 103–126.

[20]Luntz, F. (2007). *Words That Work: It's Not What You Say, It's What People Hear*. Hachette Books.

[21]Masse, W. B., Barber, E. W., Piccardi, L., & Barber, P. T. (2007). Exploring the nature of myth and its role in science. *Geological Society, London, Special Publications, 273*(1), 9–28. https://www.economist.com/science-and-technology/2020/02/27/an-australian-legend-may-be-the-worlds-oldest-datable-story.

[22]Barber, E. J. W., & Barber, P. (2005). *When They Severed Earth from Sky: How the Human Mind Shapes Myth*. Princeton University Press.

steady consumption of daily meals. There is a need to store grain to support consumption until the next crop. Long-term obligations are created, such as when a farmer stores a crop in another's granary, and there is a need for a corresponding record of this transaction. The emerging agricultural economy created a need for a long-lasting and unique record, first with clay tokens and then later using cunei-forms. These technologies externalized the memory of obligations so that the various parties had a long-lasting and verifiable record of their agreement. There was a parallel need for an information system to make sense of these recordings (reading) and teach others how to make them (writing), and this capability could be extended beyond commercial transactions to other events that needed to be remembered. Broadly, *a system of record is a mechanism for recording and recalling details of obligations and events.*

A system of record is essential for humans to move beyond simple bartering to accommodate the new temporal relationship between food production and con-sumption. As the economy developed, so did systems of record. For example, tables appeared fairly soon in the cuneiform system because they supported counting. Clay tokens representing obligations could be traded rather than the product itself, and thus agricultural society abstracted the exchange of a value into a generalized obligation, which we call *money.*

Once developed, a system of record moved beyond its clay tokens and com-mercial transaction origins. Different representation methods appeared, such as alphabets and ideograms; the medium evolved (e.g., papyrus, vellum, and paper); and most importantly, the purposes multiplied. For example, starting in the eighth century BCE, Babylonian astronomers over the next several centuries recorded around 330,000 celestial observations.[23] In doing so, they created the foundation for a system of inquiry.

The Greek alphabet, building upon earlier Semitic writing systems, was a major development for systems of record. It is founded on a phonemic system in which each letter represents a sound. This made it easier for people to learn to read and write compared to earlier scripts. As the first largely literate society, Greece nur-tured systems of record. For example, Hippocrates ( $\sim$ 460–375 BCE) established a medical school and the practice of detailed case reporting to create a system of record for illness. As a result, his graduates were able to predict the course of an illness, but they usually had only limited ideas on how to cure it.[24]

**Systems of Inquiry**
The purpose of inquiry is to produce knowledge that makes a difference. For example, Jenner's discovery of immunization for small pox is an example of knowledge that made a difference. Of course, we have to be careful of judging when a difference occurs. Some knowledge has a delayed impact because the problem it solves has not yet emerged or an existing problem has not been asso-ciated with established knowledge. George Boole, for example, developed in 1854

---

[23]Fara, P. (2009). *Science: A Four Thousand Year History.* Oxford University Press.
[24]Fara, P. (2009). *Science: A Four Thousand Year History.* Oxford University Press.

the logic that became central to digital computing about a century later. Thus systems of inquiry produce knowledge, and their impact is determined by the nature of the domain in which the inquiry system is embedded. Thus, in pure mathematics, little attention is given to making a difference, whereas in medicine, intention is almost exclusively focused on curing or treating a disease. In business, a system of inquiry is typically expected to have a short- or medium-term impact on profitability. A system of inquiry generates knowledge by applying replicable methods to justify or validate an inference. Its findings should be reproducible and explainable.

Systems of inquiry have their origins in ancient Mesopotamia, where Babylonian scholars developed expertise in mathematics, astronomy, and medicine. Because they had established a system of record, Babylonian astronomers were able to discern repetitive patterns and forecast the future position of the sun, moon, and the observable planets.[25] They had, however, no satisfactory explanation for these regularities. They applied a system of framing and invoked supernatural causes to explain their observations.

Ptolemy, in the second century of the common era using the same set of observations, looked for a cause and effect relationship, the basic template of a system of inquiry. He constructed a geocentric model, a theory, to predict the behavior of the planets with reasonable accuracy. Even though his geocentric model was later shown by Galileo to be incorrect, the more important issue is that he applied a system of inquiry and moved beyond resorting to supernatural explanations to explain observations. Ptolemy provided a rationale based on describing cause-effect relationships. In brief, *a system of inquiry is a mechanism for converting observations into general statements about cause and effect.*

A system of inquiry first processes data to create information, which is then generalized as knowledge. Theories, frameworks, or models are often used to present knowledge. Ptolemy constructed a physical model of his geocentric theory.[26] The second step is the validation of generalized knowledge, typically through robust empirical testing in a variety of settings to establish the shortcomings and limits of the frame. When a frame fails, it should be discarded or refined based on repeating the discovery and validation phases. A system of inquiry is an "endless approximation" of successive frame improvements to advance the meaning and explanation of a phenomenon.[27] Sometimes a frame can be poorly anchored, and no amount of adjustment can overcome its shortcomings; in these cases, a system of inquiry needs to start with a new foundation and proceed on the next journey of reality approximation. After a century of research, for instance, theoretical physicists are trying to reconstruct quantum theory because there is little consensus among them as to the relationship between quantum theory and reality.

---

[25]Fara, P. (2009). *Science: A Four Thousand Year History.* Oxford University Press.

[26]See   https://en.wikipedia.org/wiki/Ptolemy#/media/File:Ptolemy_1476_with_armillary_sphere_model.jpg.

[27]Churchman, C. W. (1971). *The Design of Inquiring Systems: Basic Concepts of Systems and Organization.* Basic Books.

There is an interplay between a system of inquiry and system of framing. A system of inquiry creates a parsimonious model of nature, human behavior, and their interaction. It socially constructs knowledge by applying the principles of a system of framing because the frame makers are trying to influence and persuade others of their frame's validity. They will typically use an accepted system of inquiry (e.g., data analytics) so that they can apply the system of inquiry methodology, such as statistical analysis, to influence their audience. While verbal reasoning was the original mainstay of a system of framing, a system of inquiry augments it with methods designed to boost validation.

Each discipline accepts a number of different systems of inquiry, and these can be combined in one or multiple studies to generate knowledge. Each of these systems incorporates a way of validity checking. For the medical field, a clinical trial is a key validation check. For organizations, the many methods that fall under the general rubric of data analytics have become the mainstay of organizational systems of inquiry. It is common to split a data set and process one data set to create knowledge (e.g., a time series forecast model) and validate it with the other data set.

## 4.4   Classification Completeness

For all taxonomies, such as the five foundational systems, the key validation issue is the exhaustiveness of the taxonomy. In this case, are five systems enough? As a starting point, I turn to two commonly used frameworks employed by organizations for delineating their critical features, the value chain,[28] and business model canvas,[29] and mapped them onto the foundational systems.

### The Value Chain

A value chain is the set of activities that an organization performs in order to create value for its customers (Fig. 4.2). While activities vary by industry, the primary feature, the lower portion in the diagram that follows, is the production of a good or service. This production sequence is supported by another set of services, the upper portion of the diagram. As can be seen, each of the elements of the diagram can be mapped to generally one, and at most two, fundamental systems. Primarily, the elements describe systems of production, which is not surprising since the value chain is about organizing for the creation of economic capital.

Marketing and sales map into systems of framing and systems of engagement, respectively. Marketing establishes the framework within which sales occur because it decides, among other things, what to produce, key product features, market segments and channels for each product, and how to position a product or firm. These are all framing problems. For example, positioning a firm is about

---

[28]Porter, M. E. (1985). *Competitive Advantage: Creating and Sustaining Superior Performance.* Free Press.
[29]Osterwalder, A., & Pigneur, Y. (2010). *Business Model Generation: A Handbook for Visionaries, Game Changers, and Challengers.* Wiley.

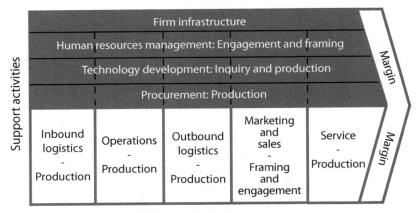

**Fig. 4.2** Value chain and foundational systems

framing how it is perceived by potential customers. Walmart's "Everyday low prices" is an example of successful framing, as is Apple's well publicized focus on the "customer experience." Framing is more than a pithy statement of purpose, but also includes issues such as the public presence of an organization. Compare Walmart's suburban big box stores with Apple's central city stores in prestigious locations. These retail location choices echo each firm's framing.

Once the key frames are established, the sales department has a responsibility to engage the targeted customer segments through the range of marketing channels defined by the framing or marketing strategy. An organization with a failed system of framing significantly handicaps its system of engagement. Its sales personnel may face trying to engage customers with the wrong product, through the wrong channels, and with a flat or unenticing message.

### Business Model Canvas

The business model canvas is a methodology for designing a business model (Fig. 4.3). A mapping of the foundational systems shows that it is more engagement-oriented than the value chain. This is not surprising, as these tools originated in different periods. The value chain describes production-centered organizations of the 1980s and earlier. In comparison, the business canvas model reflects the business environment of the early twenty-first century, where ecosystems have emerged as a major form of marshaling resources and require building relationships with key partners and customers. A manufacturer is typically a hierarchical command and control structure, where engagement can mean sending an order to a supplier. In contrast, an ecosystem might have a keystone firm and many partners. Maintaining tight interconnections is necessary for coordinating partners' actions to produce a composite product. For an ecosystem, engagement is about

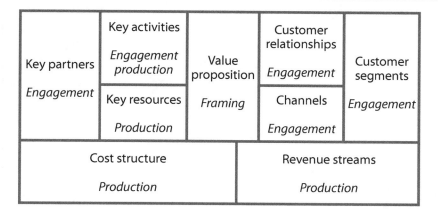

**Fig. 4.3** Business model canvas and foundational systems

building social capital that enables the ecosystem to deliver a jointly created customer experience.

Customer engagement is very different in the ecosystem era because firms no longer control the framing of their image and brands.[30] Social media allows customers to actively engage, sometimes on a virally large scale, in shaping the public perception of a firm and its reputation. When United Airlines mishandled and broke a passenger's guitar and failed to respond with a replacement, the guitar player released a song that humorously excoriated United. More than 150 million people have viewed "United Breaks Guitars" by David Carroll and his band.[31] Organizations have relinquished the high level of framing control they once had. Customer engagement is become critical to building symbolic and social capital, as I will discuss later.

Noticeably, the central focus of the business model canvas is the value proposition, a framing of what the organization does for its customers. This is a key distinction between the value chain and the business canvas. It also accords with our recognition of the central role of the system of framing for every organization, as I now highlight in the following discussion on the interrelatedness of systems.

---

[30]Pitt, L. F., Watson, R. T., Berthon, P., Wynn, D., & Zinkhan, G. M. (2006). The penguin's window: corporate brands from an open-source perspective. *Journal of the Academy of Marketing Science, 34*(2), 115–127.
[31]https://www.youtube.com/watch?v=hWb4VGG5ZPI.

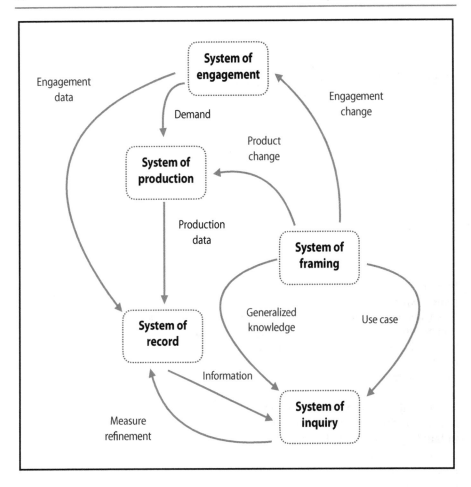

**Fig. 4.4**  Virtuous interrelationship among systems (an example)

## 4.5  The Interrelatedness of Systems

Systems are often composed of subsystems (the steering system within an auto-motive system), and systems can be part of supersystems (an organization within an economy). Within an organization, the foundational systems need to be highly interrelated to achieve both effectiveness and efficiency and sustain the organization.

We can trace these interactions and their effects (Fig. 4.4). We take a typical main route and don't consider all the possibilities offered by each system. For example, with a system of engagement, we consider only engagement with the customer and not other stakeholders.

Following the example of the business canvas model, we start with the system of framing. An organization's system of framing should facilitate a reflective analysis of its purpose, what products and services it will produce, and how it will engage with its stakeholders. For example, Tesla has framed itself through three claims: "Quickest acceleration. Longest range. The safest cars ever." It has dispensed with the traditional dealership model and engages directly with customers through its stores and galleries.

A system of engagement fulfills demand for an organization's products, typically through sales and orders, and in the process identifies demand patterns and preferences that fuel its system of production. It also includes activities such as advertising, public relations, and handling customer interaction. As a result, a system of engagement also generates data, particularly with the advent of social media, that can be captured in a system of record.

A system of production produces the products that customers demand. It might respond directly to or anticipate demand. Tesla operates an order-taking model, whereas most vehicle manufacturers produce in advance of demand and sell through dealerships. It is rather ironic that car manufacturers have lean just-in-time manufacturing to produce vehicles to sit on dealers' lots for months before selling.[32] Most vehicle manufacturers have a system of framing for customer engagement that no longer makes sense, but regulation shackles them to the last century. When an organization loses control of its system of framing, its ability to raise C′ is compromised.

A system of production generates data for a system of record. It will typically incorporate details of units produced and resources consumed for a time period. With the advent of digital technology and the IoT, the breadth and depth of a system of record can be expanded. When every production asset is connected and reports its current status, a system of record has more potential value.

A system of record, composed of data from the systems of engagement and production, provides the raw fuel for a system of inquiry. Of course, a system of inquiry should also incorporate relevant external data. As the volume and variety of data grow, they open up opportunities for applying technologies such as machine learning and data mining to extract more and deeper knowledge, which can enable the data-driven enterprise to be more successful than its competitors who ignore this opportunity to learn.[33] A system of inquiry can create knowledge that might ultimately lead to refinement of existing product systems and redesign of existing products or new customer services.

While a system of inquiry can produce a vast volume of information, its output needs to be filtered and compressed into a form that executives can process. These are typically theories, frameworks, and models. Theories might not be as elaborate as in a scientific setting, but could be represented as a series of conjectures or

---

[32]In 2017, the average new vehicle sat on the dealer's lot for seventy days according to CNBC (https://www.cnbc.com/2017/04/25/cars-are-sitting-on-the-lot-longer-even-as-dealers-sweeten-the-offers.html).

[33]Brynjolfsson, E., Hitt, L., & Kim, H. (2011). *Strength in Numbers: How Does Data-Driven Decision-Making Affect Firm Performance?* Social Science Research Network.

recommendations. Making general sense of a system of inquiry's results is critical to realizing their value so that they can be processed by the organization's system of framing.

The organizational system of framing is continually receiving information from both its internal system of inquiry and multiple external systems of inquiry. It tries to interpret these and decide how it should adjust its current system of framing. It might test some potential reframing by specifying expected common queries to run against its system of inquiry (e.g., if we did X, what might be the consequences?). Typically, an organization will make minor framing adjustments by tweaking elements of the systems of production, engagement, and inquiry. It might change the product mix, introduce new services, or adjust customer engagement protocols. There is less likelihood of a major reframing of mission and value proposition unless the system of inquiry indicates an existential threat, and even that might be denied because of the persisting strength of the current frame. For instance, when the Japanese automotive industry entered the Californian market in the early 1970s, Detroit executives ignored the growing evidence of a consumer preference for well-made small cars. By the time Detroit's system of framing had absorbed the need to change, the Japanese car companies were well-established.[34] Similarly, some politicians are so strongly anchored in their ideological frames that they ignore extensive evidence, such as climate change, that should provoke a major frame shift.

The nexus between an organization's system of inquiry and system of framing is, I posit, the most important linkage between systems. In a changing global, political, economic, and competitive environment, very rarely can a system of framing remain static. The most powerful organizations are humbled when they realize their system of framing—their purpose, market offerings, and forms of customer engagement—is no longer attractive. Frame destruction probably occurs most rapidly in the high-tech area, and examples include Blackberry and Nokia. Of course, a high-quality system of inquiry might not save a company if it does not have the resources and mind-set to define and populate a frame with its products. However, to have a minimal system of inquiry or to ignore its outputs is a path to the past. Countries potentially face the same fate when they sideline their national systems of inquiries, such as research labs and universities, and stick with a discordant ideological frame. An advantage of a free market economy is that it continually challenges existing organizational frames and impels systems of framing to respect systems of inquiry, but poor choices for the national frame can handicap many organizations in their efforts to raise $C'$ beyond the level of their foreign competitors.

The purpose of organizational design is to fashion the five foundational systems to create a virtuous set of interrelationships that create a long-lived $C'$ advantage. There is no denying that the model strips aside much complexity because it is a landscape for comprehension rather than detail. The detail comes in designing, for example, the multiple systems of engagement represented in the diagram by a single

---

[34]Arthur, W. B. (1990). Positive feedbacks in the economy. *Scientific American, 262*(2), 92–99.

box. There will likely be a need for separate systems of engagement for customers, investors, creditors, governments, the general public, and so on. Similarly, a large firm will have multiple systems of production. While the instances of a particular version of a foundational system will differ in detail, their essential purpose will be the same. All systems of production create something.

There will be differences based on the dominant $C'$ of an industry. With its focus on human capital, a university will manage different systems of engagement for students, faculty, alumni, donors, and governments. Its systems of production will vary for undergraduate and graduate students, and research and teaching faculty. A luxury products firm's $C'$ is dependent on both the symbolic capital it generates and the quality of the economic capital it markets. It might thus have an overall system of framing and coordinated product line systems of framing (e.g., one for marketing clothes and another for luggage), as well as diverse systems of production for each of the product lines.

## 4.6   Efficiency and Effectiveness

All organizations face the dual challenge of being efficient (doing things the right way) and effective (doing the right thing). Effectiveness requires a continual reexamination of the goals and needs of each stakeholder. While these tend to change gradually, there can be major disruptions caused by new technology or market entrants. Tesla's entry into the car industry with electric cars and a showroom model is a major disturbance for an industry that has relied on the internal combustion engine and a dealership model for decades. For many auto makers, the shift to electric motors might be simpler than dismantling their current dealership model. Effectiveness requires the use of internal and external systems of inquiry to continually monitor the environment and identify patterns that indicate significant change is afoot. The system of framing, typically the domain of the senior management team, needs to refresh its frames to adjust to the change. Thus many car companies have started to mass produce electric cars, though the distribution model is intact. A system of framing represents an organization's decision on how to be effective.

Once a system of framing for effectiveness is in place, the focus needs to shift to efficiency. Systems of engagement, production, and record are the engines of an organization, and they must run smoothly and efficiently because they typically handle high volumes. A system of engagement might contact thousands or millions of customers everyday (e.g., a retailer emailing customers about its latest offerings), a system of production could make a multitude of products in a year (e.g., a smart phone manufacturer), and a system of record can store and retrieve thousands of customer transactions every few seconds (e.g., an airline's record of customers' future flights).

## 4.7   Summary

There are five fundamental systems that humans developed over millions of years. These were all in place in some rudimentary form at least two thousand years ago, and have been refined, combined, and interconnected within and between organizations over the course of centuries to create today's global economy. Effectiveness is determined by systems of inquiry and framing. Efficiency is grounded in systems of engagement, production, and record.

# Energy for Capital Creation

5

Capital creation is dependent on energy. Thus, civilization has long sought to find ways of increasing energy efficiency in order to raise capital productivity. E′ is a critical input to the quality of human life.

## 5.1 Measuring E′

Before we start considering the influence of E′ on capital creation, we need a clear idea of how it is measured. A synonym for E′ is *energy return on investment* (EROI), though I prefer E′ because it reinforces the fundamental impact of energy efficiency on human societal development. I use C′ for the same reason.

The availability and pricing of energy can directly and indirectly influence an economy's performance and quality of life.[1] It is, however, not just the modern world that depends heavily on the availability of energy. Humans, like all species, have always been dependent on energy to survive, and we have increased this reliance over tens of thousands of years.

E′ measures the ratio of the energy available (energy out) to the total energy required to capture and extract this energy (energy in). As a result of the conservation of energy law, E′ is always less than one because of inefficiencies (e.g., friction) during the capture and extraction processes. We measure energy in and out in the same units, such as kilojoules or calories. Determining E′ also requires that we can measure direct and indirect costs, though accounting for indirect costs is challenging.

---

[1]Tainter Joseph, A. (1988). *The Collapse of Complex Societies*. Cambridge University Press.

© The Editor(s) (if applicable) and The Author(s), under exclusive license
to Springer Nature Singapore Pte Ltd. 2021
R. T. Watson, *Capital, Systems, and Objects*, Management for Professionals,
https://doi.org/10.1007/978-981-15-9418-2_5

Consider the case of the extraction and processing of oil. An examination looking at direct costs would likely consider the energy involved in

- Exploration
- Extraction
- Refining
- Transport to point of use

One analysis considering the direct costs of the previous list estimates that 100 MJ of extracted oil delivers 58 MJ at the point of use.[2] These figures exclude infrastructure costs, such as roads and bridges, to transport oil, which is estimated to consume about 37.5 MJ, reducing the amount remaining to be consumed to 20.5 MJ. Much of this is likely used in internal combustion engines for cars and trucks, which have an efficiency of about 20%. Thus, 100 MJ of oil generates about 4 MJ of applicable energy for vehicle transport.

Missing from the preceding costs are environmental degradation caused by oil extraction, such as the Mexican Gulf oil spill in 2010, or air pollution from gases and particulates emitted by burning fossil fuels that appear in health costs, and the impact of $CO_2$ on global warming, with its many costs for society. Many of the indirect costs are often carried by society because regulations and taxes fail to fully account for the externalities of the oil industry. Indeed, in many countries fossil fuel–based industries are subsidized to a larger extent than renewables.

The preceding breakdown of the energy input costs of an oil-based and internal combustion engine economy suggests we have an E′ of at most 0.04. Such a low return for so much effort and environmental impact is astonishing. Surely we can do significantly better with a switch to renewables and electric motors? Certainly, the bar is set very low.

While there are several measures[3] for computing E′, the most appropriate approach should be based on long-term societal considerations, as society ultimately bears the full cost of policies.

## 5.2  Foraging for Energy

When humans emerged as distinct species, they subsisted by foraging. Plants and animals were their source of energy. They needed to collect sufficient food to ensure survival. Based on the observation of societies that continue to forage today, hunting and gathering might require only fourteen to twenty hours a week. Additional time is required for food processing. Foraging has not always been such a leisurely pursuit. There was a major bump in E′ when humans learned to cook.

[2]Hall, C. A. S., Lambert, J. G., & Balogh, S. B. (2014). EROI of different fuels and the implications for society. *Energy Policy, 64*, 141–152.
[3]Hall, C. A. S., Lambert, J. G., & Balogh, S. B. (2014). EROI of different fuels and the implications for society. *Energy Policy, 64*, 141–152.

The calorific benefits of cooking are significant.[4] Cooking (1) increases the digestibility of starch and protein, (2) reduces the digestion costs of cooked versus raw meat, and (3) reduces the costs of detoxification and defense against pathogens. The pounding of food prior to eating can also provide energy gains because broken fibers are more digestible. Cooking raised the E' of the forager because it enabled more energy to be extracted for the same level of energy expended on hunting and gathering. The consequences are important for human evolution, as a higher level of energy in the form of food improves body mass, raises rates of reproduction, and improves health. Improvements in the E' of foraging conferred survival and reproductive advantages. Spending less time on finding food gave humans more time for leisure, invention, and the creation of capital. It is difficult to find time to invest in learning how to make a proto-knife when you need to spend most of your waking time hunting and gathering.

## 5.3  Farming for Energy

The beginning of farming was the next ramping up of E'. Agriculture resulted in the concentrated growing of crops that produced high-energy yields. By clearing land and planting cereal groups, farmers focused the sun's solar energy on digestible biomass. Consequently, more human or animal fuel could be produced from a cultivated plot than an equivalent area of natural landscape.

Agriculture also strengthened the relationship between capital and energy. Farming has always been capital intensive because it requires clearing land to create fields, along with planting, harvesting, and storing crops. A farmer typically has to invest at least for several months before getting a return, but a well-managed farm is a mix of natural and economic capital that can produce returns for generations.

Cereal crops, such as wheat, rice, and maize,[5] are good stores of economic value. They have high energy value and can, with appropriate care, be kept for long periods. Thus a farmer can cash in a crop immediately upon harvesting or keep the seeds for conversion to cash at a later stage.

Agriculture also embraces animal husbandry. Animals are a source of energy for farming and food. The presence of a range of domesticable animals was a decided advantage of the Middle East and contributed to its emergence as the birthplace of agriculture.[6] Early farmers could use cows to carry loads and plow fields, and goats and sheep were a source of milk and meat. In addition, cows, goats, and sheep provided raw material for clothing. From a C' perspective, oxen increase a farmer's plowing productivity, and thus the ability to convert a field and seeds into more

---

[4]Carmody, R. N., & Wrangham, R. W. (2009). The energetic significance of cooking. *Journal of Human Evolution, 57*(4), 379–391.

[5]These three grains currently provide about 50% of the world's nutritional energy, according to Weissenbacher, M. (2009). *Sources of Power: How Energy Forges Human History.* ABC-CLIO, p. 19.

[6]Diamond, J. M. (1997). *Guns, Germs, and Steel: The Fates of Human Societies.* W. W. Norton & Co.

seeds (economic capital). Furthermore, the stalks and stems that could not be digested by humans were food for cattle, goats, and sheep, thus raising the level of energy that could be extracted from a farm for human use, either directly as grains, or indirectly as meat.

Fruit trees were not domesticated in the Fertile Crescent until about 4,000 BCE, possibly because growing fruit requires more capital. Whereas a cereal group can produce a return in a few months, a fruit tree will typically not be productive for several years. Capital is always a scarce resource, and likely was particularly scarce when civilization was dawning. Early societies transitioning from foraging to farming needed quick returns, or they might have starved.

Farming creates energy for human and animal consumption by systematically harnessing sunshine to grow selected high-energy yielding plants. More recently, this energy has been converted into liquid fuels, such as ethanol, to power machines.

The superior capital of farmers enabled them to displace foragers in many parts of the earth. Agriculture supported a higher population density, and thus more warriors (human capital). It also resulted in the creation of superior tools and technology (economic capital), and the development and ongoing operation of formal hierarchies to manage resources (organizational capital). Agricultural society quickly gained a numerical and technology advantage in disputes with hunters and gatherers.

## 5.4  Animal Husbandry for Energy

There are limits to the rate of human energy conversion. We can convert about 20–25% of the food we digest into energy, and we don't like to expend all our energy on work. Thus humans were motivated to find other sources of energy for farming. Hence, while animals were initially domesticated for their meat and skins, early farmers eventually realized that they could also be a source of energy for agricultural work. Cattle are particularly suited for farming because they are around three times as powerful as humans, and this strength can harnessed with a yoke. Sheep and goats could have presumably been used as pack animals to move farm produce. Later, horses, donkeys, and camels were domesticated and employed to work for humans.

The energy provided by domesticated animals raised farming's $C'$. More importantly, it implanted the idea that there were alternatives to human energy that could reduce the manual labor required by farmers and raise their farms' output. Thus we see the parallel development of tools and methods for productivity gain.

## 5.5  Energizing the Industrial Revolution

The Industrial Revolution required energy and factory workers, but with the bulk of the population required to produce food, factory workers were in short supply. In the 1820s, 71% of workers were in the agricultural industry.[7] Nowadays, it is about 1%. The factory worker problem was partially solved by the potato.

Potatoes provide more calories, vitamins, and nutrients per hectare than other staple crops. The introduction of the potato into Europe from South America is reckoned to have been responsible for about 25% of its population growth and urbanization between 1700 and 1900. Potatoes were a positive E' ramp for Europe. They decreased the need for agricultural workers, and those displaced were a workforce that could be employed in urban factories.[8] The potato is another food example of a shift in E'.

Watt's improvement of Newcomen's 1705 steam engine arrived in 1768, about half a century after the introduction of potatoes to Europe. Watt's design used about 75% less fuel than Newcomen's engine. It took another 15 years to modify the engine to support rotary motion and provide the E' productivity shock that set the Industrial Revolution in motion.[9]

These two major changes in E', potatoes and Watt's steam engine, fueled the workers and provided the power, respectively, to enable the Industrial Revolution. This was a major and maybe defining event in the evolution of the capital creation system.

### The Electric Motor

Another key advance in E' was the electric motor, which is more efficient than either steam or internal combustion engines. In the United States in the period 1920–29, there was almost total electrification of mechanical power in manufacturing, with the replacement of old steam-based equipment and the implementation of new electrified plants. Electricity demand grew at 10.4% per annum while nonelectrical sources declined at 0.2% per year.[10] Ubiquitous access to electricity came when the electrification of the advanced economies started in the 1930s and was essentially complete by the 1960s.[11] National or regional electric grids were developed to transmit reliable and standardized power to factories, offices, and homes.

---

[7]Abramovitz, M. (1956). *Resource and Output Trends in the United States since 1870*. NBER, pp. 1–23.
[8]Nunn, N., & Qian, N. (2011). The potato's contribution to population and urbanization: evidence from a historical experiment. *The Quarterly Journal of Economics, 126*(2), 593–650.
[9]Landes, D. S. (1999). *The Wealth and Poverty of Nations: Why Some Are so Rich and Some so Poor*. W. W. Norton & Company.
[10]Helm, J. L. (1990). Energy: Production, Consumption, and Consequences. The National Academies Press.
[11]Bakke, G. (2016). *The Grid: The Fraying Wires between Americans and Our Energy Future*. Bloomsbury Publishing.

Electric motors currently comprise the single largest demand for electricity, more than twice as much as lighting. They account for around 45% of all global electricity consumption. They also provide an outstanding opportunity for an E' bump to the industrialization of the world, with the potential to improve energy efficiency by roughly 20% to 30% and reduce total global electricity demand by about 10%.[12]

## 5.6    The Shift to Renewables

We are now in the early stages of the renewable energy ear, and there is another E' jump in progress. In early 2020, new solar and onshore wind systems are the cheapest source of electricity for at least two-thirds of the world's population. The global benchmark levelized cost of electricity (LCOE) for onshore wind and utility-scale solar has fallen 9% and 4%, respectively, since the second half of 2019. They are now USD 44/MWh and USD 50/MWh, respectively. The benchmark LCOE for battery storage is USD 150/MWh, half the price of two years ago. For natural gas importing countries, new battery storage systems are the cheapest technology for peak power support (up to two-hours of discharge duration).[13]

Most renewables are in the early stages of the learning curve with respect to R&D, manufacturing, and installation. Furthermore, rooftop solar on households, factories, and retail establishments offers local production opportunities that avoid distribution losses and costs. Thus there is some promise of a significant E' improvement in the next few decades as the world converts from fossil fuels to renewable energy generation.

## 5.7    The E' Opportunity

Perhaps the greatest E' opportunity is improved energy efficiency, as some two-thirds of energy generated in the United States is wasted, according to the Lawrence Livermore National Laboratory.[14] Energy efficiency is the invisible fuel. We need a dual strategy in the form of (1) a shift to lower-cost and non-carbon-emitting energy sources, and (2) an investment in raising E' for all energy sources.

---

[12]Waide, P., & Brunner, C. U. (2011). *Energy-Efficiency Policy Opportunities for Electric Motor-Driven Systems*. International Energy Agency.
[13]https://www.forbes.com/sites/mikescott/2020/04/30/solar-and-wind-costs-continue-to-fall-as-power-becomes-cleaner/#48f6bd97785f.
[14]https://flowcharts.llnl.gov.

Energy consumption in the United States is currently relatively flat at about 97 quads[15] and estimated to grow by 5% in total from 2016 to 2040, which would return it to the peak levels at the beginning of the twenty-first century.[16] While a flat growth rate would seem worth lauding, the American Council for an Energy-Efficient Economy (ACEEE) asserts that there are opportunities to raise E' that collectively could reduce 2050 energy use by 40% to 60% relative to current forecasts.[17] The US Energy Information Agency reports that in 1990, 9,000 BTUs (9.5 MJ) were consumed for each real dollar of US economic growth. In 2017, it was 6,000 BTUs, and the agency predicts by 2050 it will be 3,000 BTUs.[18] Given the current level of energy wastage, such predictions appear reasonable, and their achievement would also contribute significantly to the C' of every US enterprise because energy is an unavoidable cost of business. National government initiatives to raise E' will increase a country's global competitiveness.

## 5.8 Looking Forward

We need to continue to find ways to raise E' to build an energy-efficient society based solely on renewable energy and nonfossil fuels. Energy efficiency reduces the cost of many capital conversion processes and also reduces the need to invest in additional capital. These are different approaches to raising E'.

### 5.8.1 Generation of Electricity

Electricity will be primary form of energy in a sustainable society. Since the creation of a sustainable society implies the cessation of burning fossils fuels, R&D needs to be focused of raising the E' of the various forms of renewable energy.

**Photovoltaic Cells**

The photovoltaic effect, whereby photons can create electrons, was discovered by Edmond Becquerel in 1839. Bell Labs developed silicon solar cells in the 1950s. Now, solar cells are a competitive alternative to burning fossils for electricity production, and there is a clear trend of continuing efficiency improvements and declining costs.

The E' of experimental photovoltaic cell is about 46%.[19] In other words, nearly half of the incident solar energy is converted to electrical energy. SunPower

---

[15]A quad is $10^{15}$ BTU, or $1.055 \times 10^{18}$ joules (1.055 exajoules or EJ).
[16]https://www.eia.gov/outlooks/aeo/pdf/0383(2017).pdf.
[17]https://aceee.org/research-report/e1502.
[18]https://www.eia.gov/outlooks/aeo/pdf/AEO2018.pdf.
[19]https://www.ise.fraunhofer.de/en/press-and-media/press-releases/press-releases-2014/new-world-record-for-solar-cell-efficiency-at-46-percent.

Corporation reports 21.5% efficiency for the solar panels it currently ships.[20] If current research results can be commercialized, then we could expect a doubling of solar panel efficiency.

In addition to raising the E′ of solar panels, society also needs to reduce the cost of manufacturing panels. Swanson's law states that with every doubling of the shipment of solar panels, there is a 20% reduction in cost.[21] Between 2010 and 2020, the cost of utility scale solar per kWh dropped by a factor of five.[22] Once installed, solar energy is essentially free because of the low maintenance costs of solar panels.

The combination of energy conversion improvements and manufacturing cost reductions have made solar energy competitive with fossil fuels, without subsidy for even those countries in the high latitudes. Incidentally, global fossil fuels receive an annual subsidy of about USD 5 trillion,[23] whereas for renewable subsidies were about USD 140 billion worldwide in 2016.[24] A shift to renewables will release capital for national infrastructure investments to raise C′. In addition, because solar generation can be distributed, there is likely to be less need to invest in regional or national grid systems.

**Wind Power**

According to the wind power experts, larger turbines now under development will further reduce the cost of wind energy on land and offshore. Their best guess is that the cost of land-based wind will fall by, on average, 24% by 2030 and 35% by 2050. Experts also foresee fixed-bottom offshore platform cost declines of 30% by 2030 and 41% by 2050.[25]

**Handling Intermittency**

Wind and solar are subject to the vagaries of the weather and daily rhythms, and thus their energy supply is intermittent. Demand can also be intermittent, but supply and demand do not always coincide for precise matching. Germany, for instance, has more than 66 gigawatts of renewable capacity that on an overcast and calm day can generate negligible power. Conversely, on a sunny windy day, the grid can be stressed because it was not designed to handle such a load.

---

[20]https://us.sunpower.com/solar-panels-technology/x-series-solar-panels/.

[21]http://blogs.scientificamerican.com/guest-blog/smaller-cheaper-faster-does-moores-law-apply-to-solar-cells/.

[22]https://rameznaam.com/2020/05/14/solars-future-is-insanely-cheap-2020/.

[23]https://www.eesi.org/papers/view/fact-sheet-fossil-fuel-subsidies-a-closer-look-at-tax-breaks-and-societal-costs.

[24]International Energy Agency (IEA), 2017, World Energy Outlook 2017, International Energy Agency (Paris, France).

[25]https://emp.lbl.gov/news/future-wind-energy-part-3-reducing-wind.

Resolving the intermittency problem will be a critical step in creating a carbon neutral society with a high $E'$ based on renewables. Bill Gates has opined that intermittency is the major problem for a renewables-based economy.[26] Another entrepreneur, Elon Musk, in late 2017 demonstrated that we are on track for a solution. After suffering several price spikes and grid outages, South Australia accepted Musk's offer to install a lithium ion battery farm to manage fluctuations in demand and supply, which can be quite large for a state that generates more than 40% of its energy from wind. The USD 50 million installation was completed on November 23, 2017.[27] Almost a month later, the vast battery was tested when a coal-fired power plant in the adjacent state of Victoria tripped and went offline. The battery delivered 100 MW into the national electricity grid in 140 ms. A local alternative power station would have taken thirty to sixty minutes to start up and stabilize the market.[28]

Batteries are one element of the intermittency solution. Because there is a least a 10% energy loss when a battery is charged or discharged, it is better to use electricity as it is generated. Thus a comprehensive solution should aim to using pricing and demand/supply shifting to balance supply and demand (Fig. 5.1). Intermittency can create situations of over and under supply, the mirrors of under- and overdemand.

In the case of oversupply:

- Prices can be lowered to stimulate demand.
- Production rights can be purchased to reduce supply, which implies paying generators not to produce.
- Deferrable electricity uses can be activated, such as charging cars.
- Batteries can be charged.

In the case of undersupply:

- Prices can be raised to dampen demand.
- Consumption rights can be purchased to reduce demand, which implies paying customers not to consume.
- Deferrable electricity uses can be deactivated, such as charging cars.
- Batteries can be discharged.

[26]https://www.theatlantic.com/magazine/archive/2015/11/we-need-an-energy-miracle/407881/.
[27]https://www.vox.com/energy-and-environment/2017/11/28/16709036/elon-musk-biggest-battery-100-days.
[28]https://www.sciencealert.com/elon-musk-s-south-australian-battery-responded-in-just-140-milliseconds-after-a-coal-fired-power-plant-failed.

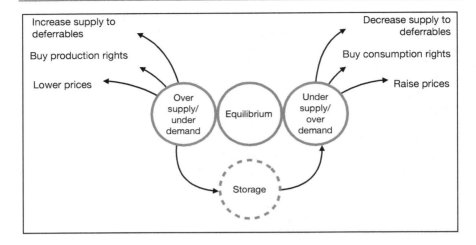

**Fig. 5.1** Operational choices for grid equilibrium

**Demand Response Systems**
Demand Response (DR) programs address intermittency by using data-based decisions of incentives and penalties to influence consumer behavior, essentially to balance electricity demand and supply. These programs act on information by reducing consumption during peak loads or shifting these peak loads to off-peak hours. DR systems capture data pertaining to the behavior of consumers, which forms a key input to DR Business Intelligence & Analytics (BI&A). Information received as output from BI&A in a DR system is further used by DR management to positively influence the behavior of consumers.[29] The Energy Resource Institute (TERI) examined various business models of off-grid electricity services and suggests that electricity tariffs should be based on the willingness to pay by the rural consumers, which is determined by factors such as trust, proximity to payment points, and quality of customer service. These objectives of maximizing social welfare can also be achieved through DR programs.[30]

**Approaching an E′ Ramp**
If we consider the elements of the emerging energy environment, we can envisage a future of inexpensive clean energy and higher E′. The key developments are

[29]Sangeeth, S.L.R., & Mathew S.K. (2018). Information processing and demand response systems effectiveness: A conceptual study. In *Proceedings of the 51st Hawaii International Conference on System Sciences (HICSS)*, Hawaii. ISBN: 978-0-9981331-1-9.
[30]Bhattacharyya, S., Palit, D., & Sarangi, G. K. (2015). Towards scaling-up of electricity access-summary and policy recommendations from OASYS South Asia project.

- **Low cost renewables**. As discussed earlier, based on recent unsubsidized prices, hydro, solar, and wind are the cheapest forms of energy.
- **Battery farms**. Advances in battery technology make large battery farms technically and economically feasible with current lithium ion technology.
- **Electric vehicles (EVs)**. A number of nations have announced that they will ban the sale of cars with internal combustion engines in the next decade or so. China, the world's largest car market, has plans to phase out gasoline and diesel powered vehicles.[31] Similar actions are anticipated by California, the largest US car market.[32] EVs convert about 60% of electrical energy to motion, whereas conventional gasoline vehicles only convert about 19% of the fossil energy to motion.[33] A shift to EVs is a massive gain in E′ that will pass through into reducing the cost of many product and services.

**The Internet of Things (IoT)**. Advanced economies are sensitizing their assets and instrumenting their production and ecological environments. Billions of network sensors will create smart cities, smart grids, and smart organizations. The proponents of Energy Informatics demonstrate that Energy + Information < Energy.[34] An IoT will provide the data necessary to make a myriad of smarter resource management decisions that will raise E′ in areas such as energy production, distribution, and consumption and many other aspects of the economy. It will also enable more effective cooperative resource usage and move the sharing economy beyond sharing rooms and cars to a host of other resources. More sharing increases C′ and lowers the demand for production of the shared products. Some extreme estimates suggest that a car-sharing economy based on autonomous EVs might shrink the car industry by 90%.[35] In Norway, an all-electric ferry introduced in 2015 has cut greenhouse gas emission by 95% and operational costs by 80% compared to its fossil-powered counterparts. Fjellstrand Shipyard, the ship's builder, has a reported backlog of fifty-three additional ferries.[36] Increases in E′ drive increases in C′.

---

[31]https://www.economist.com/news/business/21728980-its-government-developing-plan-phase-out-vehicles-powered-fossil-fuels-china-moves.

[32]https://www.theverge.com/2017/9/27/16373778/california-internal-combustion-ban-emissions-carb.

[33]https://www.fueleconomy.gov/feg/evtech.shtml.

[34]Watson, R. T., & Boudreau, M.-C. (2011). *Energy Informatics*. Green ePress; and Watson, R. T., Boudreau, M.-C., Li, S., & Levis, J. (2010). Telematics at UPS: En route to Energy Informatics. *MIS Quarterly Executive, 9*(1), 1–11.

[35]https://www.economist.com/news/leaders/21726071-it-had-good-run-end-sight-machine-changed-world-death?frsc=dg|e.

[36]https://electrek.co/2018/02/03/all-electric-ferry-cuts-emission-cost/.

## 5.9  Summary

Gains in energy efficiency, whether gradual or abrupt, provided the foundation for improving the quality of human life, from cooking food to solar panels. While many see the move to renewables as a necessity for a sustainability society, we view the transition as also a necessity for an increased standard of living. The air will be cleaner, climate change slowed and eventually reversed, and goods and services will be cheaper.

# Objects

6

## 6.1 Humans as Objects

To a computer scientist, an object is something that can send and receive a set of standardized digital messages. Your maps app is an object. It can receive a message containing the latitude and longitude of your current location from a GPS app and then send a message to your map app to show your position on a map. Software is a collection of communicating objects, with each object performing a specialized function or coordinating the action of other objects through messaging.

The introduction of digital communication systems, such as the Internet and cell phone networks, gave people object-like characteristics. We can send and receive digital messages. Amazon was one of the earliest organizations to realize the potential of *objectivated*[1] humans. Its initial online bookstore was dependent on customers (objects) sending digital messages to order and pay for books. It relied on another object, a book warehouse, to fulfill the order, and another object, a credit card company, to handle payment. The foundational core of Amazon is software to coordinate the actions of connected objects.

Many of the start-ups emerging since the commercialization of the Internet implicitly treat people as objects. For example, in the UK, Betfair replaced the local bookmaker with a system for digitally connecting people who wanted to make and take bets. Whereas the traditional bookmaker took a cut of about 15% of a gambler's wager, Betfair reduced its share to 5% of the winner's take. In 2004, four years after launching its website, Betfair was the world's largest betting exchange.[2]

---

[1] A term we introduce to describe humans who have digital devices that enable them to send and receive electronic messages and thus behave like active objects.

[2] Davies, M., Pitt, L. F., Shapiro, D., & Watson, R. T. (2005). Betfair.com: five technology forces revolutionize worldwide wagering. European Management Journal, 23(5), 533–541.

An object-oriented (OO) enterprise raises C' by getting objects, such as customers, to work for free. The online book buyer does the work of a bookstore's clerk. The online gambler does the work of a bookmaker's turf accountant. In addition, the OO organization is not shackled by geography. Netbank, a pioneering online bank in Atlanta, attracted depositors from across the entire United States and grew accounts by a compound 275 per annum during the period 1997–2001. Its value proposition, higher rates for depositors, was facilitated by the lower cost of online transactions (USD 0.13) compared to bank tellers (USD 1.08) or ATMs (USD 0.27).[3] When humans were willingly objectivated, they let loose new forms of value propositions that rendered a C' improvement based on OO principles.

## 6.2   Framing the Value Proposition

Every organization strives to increase C'; otherwise it soon disappears. All enterprises need a strategy for long-term survival. The first step is to design a business model centered on a value proposition that appeals to key capital input providers. A value proposition is the crux of the system of framing. It defines succinctly how the organization presents itself to society and guides the design and operation of other systems. For example, Zara's value proposition is to rapidly deliver fresh fashion at reasonable prices to young urban women. This framing means it manufactures small lot sizes using automated cutting machinery, outsources local assembly, and operates a centralized distribution system. There is also frequent digital communication between stores and designers, so Zara's system of framing can continually fine-tune the value proposition.[4]

Typically, a value proposition aims at attracting customers and the creation of economic capital through sales of a product or service. For a university, its value proposition must entice human capital, both students and faculty. An art gallery might have two concordant value propositions—one that appeals to visitors and another to patrons. I recommend that you create a business model canvas[5] for defining your business model because it pays particular attention to defining the value proposition and the elements required for its achievement. It provides a starting point for designing an organization to execute the value proposition.

[3]Rothstein, C., & Watson, R. T. (2004). NetBank: The conservative Internet entrepreneurs. *Communications of the AIS*, 14(10), 1-24.

[4]Almquist, E., Bovet, D., & Heaton, C. J. (2004). What Have We Learned so Far? Making CRM Make Money—Technology Alone Won't Create Value. In A. H. Kracklauer, D. Q. Mills, & D. Seifert (Eds.), *Collaborative Customer Relationship Management*, pp. 7–22. Springer.

[5]Osterwalder, A., & Pigneur, Y. (2010). *Business Model Generation: A Handbook for Visionaries, Game Changers, and Challengers*. Wiley.

## 6.3   Object-Orientation: Achieving the Value Proposition

Many organizations now accept the advantages of the ecosystem model, and they are concerned with how to fashion an ecosystem-based capital creation system. The principles of object-orientation (OO), which are widely used for software design and development, provide a set of concepts and vocabulary for the design of an ecosystem. It is an innovative framing of organizational design that is appropriate for the digital age.

One of OO's several key advantages is modularity, which speeds up the writing of software because libraries of existing modules can be reused. Java, one of the most widely used OO programming languages, owes part of its popularity to the over 250,000 source files available to programmers,[6] who can construct a new application by making extensive use of existing chunks of code packaged as objects.[7] Java programmers have created a vast repository of shared organizational capital that facilitates the productive creation of more organizational capital. These shared libraries are readily accessible from GitHub, a web-based hosting service mostly used for computer code. The Java libraries, and those for other programming languages, showcase how digital connectivity facilitates the persistence of capital creation as programmers maintain and extend open-code libraries.

The fundamental concepts of object technology are transferable to the design of capital creation ecosystems. OO thinking can help organizational designers quickly assemble a new organization by extensively reusing existing objects (i.e., organizations). The computer science perspective on OO program design closely parallels the purpose of enterprise design. Indeed, the following quote by a computer scientist illustrates the generality of the concept beyond software development.

> The goal of OO design is to identify accurately the principle roles in an organization or process, assign responsibilities to each of these roles, and define the circumstances under which roles interact with one another.[8]

As the preceding quote illustrates, OO principles are applicable to the design of software, enterprises, and other products. They are general tenets for design.

Today's economy is founded on global, highly interlinked electronic networks that enable real-time digital data exchange and the design and operation of coordinated ecosystems. It has enabled the production and delivery of products and services to be disaggregated and distributed among cooperating objects. For many organizations, the ecosystem it coordinates, such as Apple, or the ones to which it belongs, such as the chip supplier Intel, determine C'. Some organizations, such as

---

[6]https://blog.takipi.com/the-top-100-java-libraries-in-2017-based-on-259885-source-files/?utm_source=twitter&utm_medium=maintweet&utm_content=topjava2017&utm_campaign=java.
[7]This section draws upon Watson, R. T., Zinkhan, G. M., & Pitt, L. F. (2004). Object orientation: a tool for enterprise design. *California Management Review, 46*(4), 89–110. For a similar perspective, see Davenport, T. H., Thomas, R. J., & Desouza, K. C. (2003). Reusing intellectual assets. *Industrial Management, 45*(3), 12–13.
[8]Pancake, C. M. (1995). The promise and cost of object technology: a five-year forecast. *Communications of the ACM, 38*(10), 33–49.

Samsung, are both coordinators and ecosystem members. Understanding how to operate as part of an ecosystem has becomes critical to C'. OO provides a framework for such comprehension.

## Key OO Concepts

OO technology was introduced to accelerate the building and maintenance of software by writing reusable code based on existing objects or modules. OO incorporates the fundamental capital creation logic in that prior investments are the foundation for future investments. For example, if an app needs to process a credit card, then incorporate an existing object that has been tested for Payment Card Industry Data Security Standard (PCI) compliance. A program can be written in the same way a stereo system might be configured by combining items from various manufacturers.

Objects are self-contained units containing data describing the object and the actions (called *methods* in OO parlance) that it can perform. OO is supported by several key concepts. As I discuss each of these concepts, I position them within the context of an organization (Table 6.1). OO is based on seven key ideas, but I will discuss only those relevant to a capital creation system.

Some adaptation is needed to re-imagine computer science concepts and apply them to organization. I first describe the computer science OO notion and then redefine to fit an organizational context.

**Table 6.1** OO concepts

| Concept | Computer science | Organization |
|---|---|---|
| Object class | A group of objects with similar properties | A group of organizations (e.g., banks) or individuals (e.g., car drivers) with similar properties |
| Object | A program containing data and methods | An organization with databases and business processes (organizational capital) |
| Message | Objects request services from each other by exchanging messages | Organizations request services from each other by exchanging messages |
| Encapsulation | All processing that changes the state of an object is done within that object | An organization is an autonomous unit and external bodies cannot interfere in its operations |
| Reuse | A new application can be built from existing objects Computer code must be written to exchange messages between objects | A new organization can be built from existing organizations Procedures must be developed for exchanging messages between organizations |

**Object Classes and Instances**
A class is a group of objects with similar properties, and an object is a member of a class. For our needs, a class can be thought of as a group of organizations in the same industry or individuals with similar roles. A bank is an example of a class, and instances of that class would include the Industrial and Commercial Bank of China and a local community bank. Furthermore, this class has methods or services such as accepting deposits or facilitating payments. Clearly, organizational objects do not have the same level of uniformity as computer science objects. Nevertheless, all objects in an organizational class share many common features, and customers will have a clear idea of what services they can expect from organizational objects in a class. In other words, all banks offer much the same set of services.

**India Facilitates the Age of Objects**
In 2009, the government of India established the Unique Identification Authority of India (UIDAI), with the goal of issuing every resident with a unique twelve-digit identity number, known as Aadhaar, that is based on a person's biometric data. It is the world's largest biometric ID system.

Aadhaar—meaning "foundation" in Hindi—is intended to (1) reduce identity theft through biometric authentication, particularly in relation to claims for government benefits; (2) address the problem of multiple identities such as voter ID and ration cards that are functional in nature and could be created simultaneously in different States and exploited by individuals; (3) provide all Indians with a unique, verified identity which simplifies many financial transactions; and (4) cut shopkeeper fraud by allowing beneficiaries to choose the supplier of their government-subsidized rations.[9]

The government has encouraged citizens to link their Aadhaar numbers to its services, SIM cards, bank accounts, and retirement funds.

Connected objects, including people, need to be uniquely addressable in order to receive messages and be identified as senders. Having a single national identifier creates organizational capital that facilitates the development of new organizations, particularly those based on OO principles.

**Encapsulation**
Encapsulation means that all data processing that changes the state of an object (i.e., changes the value of any of its data) is controlled by the object. An object's data are shielded from actions by other objects. In organizational terms, organizational units are independent entities and their internal operations are insulated from others. For

---

[9]https://www.ft.com/content/53a2c11a-0b2f-11e8-8eb7-42f857ea9f09.

example, a UPS customer cannot specify how UPS moves a parcel from A to B—
just that it will happen within a defined period at a specified price.

For software systems, encapsulation is the rule, but there is a cost. While each
object may be optimal in terms of its purpose, a program resulting from a combination of objects is likely to be suboptimal. Ease of software coding and maintenance are exchanged for suboptimality. If systems performance is poor, then
pertinent objects might be internally inspected and rewritten to improve overall
efficiency. Encapsulation is then restored as the modus operandi.

Similarly, in organizations there might be occasions where the efficient operation
of an enterprise requires greater integration between business units to reduce suboptimality costs. Giving up encapsulation, however, increases coordination activities. Costs are incurred in coordinating the activities of the cooperating objects to
ensure that the entire operation is efficient. The senior management of a hierarchy
has the power to interfere in internal business units to enhance efficiency, but this is
often resisted by divisional leaders who prefer autonomy and encapsulation.

Ecosystems, whether self-organizing or coordinated, can be viewed as a set of
encapsulated objects. However, societal expectations often require infringement of
the encapsulation principle. Thus, some clothing and technology companies who
have outsourced systems of production have learned that key stakeholders expect
that they know what happens in their partners' factories.[10]

There are four layers of encapsulation—know-what, know-how, know-why, and
care-why—which parallel the types of human capital investment discussed in
Chap. 14 on the measurement of capital. I consider only the first three since the
highest level, self-motivated creativity or care-why, is more akin to a state of mind
than a form of encapsulation.

### 6.3.1  Know-What

Know-what defines what services an organizational object can provide and what
specific data must be supplied to receive a particular service. Know-what enables
one organizational object to make use of the services of another. Organizations
interact with each other at the know-what level. A merchant, for example, knows
that its credit card processor can authenticate a credit card and approve or reject a
transaction, given the presenter's card number and authenticating information (i.e.,
name, card expiry date, and card security code). Encapsulation is based on
know-what.

---

[10]For example, see https://www.fastcompany.com/40444836/escalating-sweatshop-protests-keep-
nike-sweating.

### 6.3.2   Know-How

Encapsulation is broken when an external object needs to know how another operates. An object's internal operational black box is opened for inspection and possible redesign. Some organizations will share know-how so that their joint operations can be more tightly integrated to raise $C'$. For instance, an electronics company might have separate partners for assembly and maintenance. By inspecting how the assembly process occurs, it might be able to institute changes that reduce maintenance costs.

### 6.3.3   Know-Why

When organizations cooperate across a supply chain, understanding how the complete end-to-end process operates can lead to beneficial $C'$ gains for many of the participants. Know-why, or ecosystem-wide knowledge, enables an organizational unit, usually the keystone of a coordinated ecosystem, to transform the processes of some objects to reduce the suboptimal effects of encapsulation by integrating or coordinating some processes across systems. For example, a personal computer manufacturer might learn that one of its major retailers increases its product's value proposition by installing several applications prior to offering the product to customers. The personal computer manufacturer has to install an operating system, so it makes sense for it to run a single install that also adds the required applications each retailer requires. Two processes are integrated. Another possibility is to work with the supplier of the internal hard disk drive to further integrate processes by doing a single install of the disk drive management system, operating system, and applications software during the final stages of disk drive assembly.

While de-encapsulation can provide benefits, it is not costless. It takes time to learn how a partner operates and even longer to identify the cost-reducing integration opportunities of an ecosystem. Such learning should only take place with the intention of improving the efficiency or effectiveness of the partnership or ecosystem. For many business units, maintaining know-what knowledge is adequate and may be all the partner is willing to reveal. Once changes have been implemented, encapsulation is often restored. The levels of encapsulation can also be viewed as types of coordination devices, with each layer representing a more costly coordination mechanism. In other words, know-how is more costly than know-what.

For startups, gaining customers is often the priority, and therefore unless de-encapsulation contributes to this goal, it should not be pursued. For an established organization operating in a price competitive market, de-encapsulation should be sought if the indications are that it will result in a net reduction in costs. In a fast-changing technological environment, encapsulation can reduce managerial complexity and increase response, and seeking these advantages might be more fruitful than seeking efficiency gains from de-encapsulation.

*Apple De-encapsulates to Drive Down Costs*
To drive down costs, Apple has reportedly taken control of the procurement of some parts for its laptops. Previously, suppliers had complete discretion on the selection of suppliers for nonkey components, such as screws, metal parts, and plastic pieces. Under the new policy, Apple will negotiate directly with third-party suppliers and dictate the price and volume to partners, who previously made these decisions. The change is likely to eliminate a 10–15% markup on the purchase prices taken by partners. While reducing costs, the new policy should also increase Apple's control over the quality of some components.[11]

## Message Passing

Provided it knows the appropriate protocol, an object can send a message to request a service from another object. Message passing, in organizational terms, means that enterprises communicate by exchanging data. For example, a vessel nearing a harbor could send a message to the piloting service to request a pilot at a certain time and location to guide it into the harbor. Another message might go to the tug company for assistance in berthing. Today's digital economy can be viewed as a vast network of objects using electronic messaging to request and provide services. Since the introduction of the Internet, electronic message passing has become the foundation of coordination and synchronization.

## Reuse

A design for a new app will often have features found in many existing apps, such as a spell checker. Therefore, programmers will search existing open libraries for these features rather than writing them from scratch. The reuse of existing software objects speeds up coding and debugging.

In terms of organizations, reuse is an important OO concept to migrate from computer science to enterprise design. A new organization can be built by assembling existing organizations (objects) and instituting a communication system for passing messages between them so that the new organization's goals are achieved. This idea is illustrated by examining a ride-sharing business.

---

[11]https://appleinsider.com/articles/18/06/04/apple-grabbing-control-of-non-crucial-parts-for-new-macbooks-to-reduce-costs.

## 6.3.4  Ride-Sharing

A ride-sharing service is built upon reusing three key existing objects: drivers, cars, and riders. Let's examine a typical sequence of events:

- Using a ride sharing app, a rider sends a message to the coordinating object, the ride sharing service, requesting transport from A to B at some specified time. The message will include the rider's ID, the GPS coordinates for A and B, and the requested time of the service.
- The rider receives a confirmation message of the ride request and approves credit card payment for the service.
- A driver receives a message to collect a passenger at location A, take the person to location B, and follow route C.
- The rider receives messages tracking the driver's progress to A.
- If necessary, the rider and driver can message each other when there is some imprecision for the rider's location, which can happen with airport pickup points.
- Upon arriving at location B, the rider receives a message asking for a rating of the driver and can add a tip to the previously approved credit card transaction.
- The driver receives a message asking for a rating of the rider.

We can also explore the ride-sharing business via an object diagram (Fig. 6.1).

A ride-sharing service electronically coordinates existing objects. Drivers, people who have access to a suitable vehicle, and riders, those needing transport, are existing objects. They can be dynamically linked by message passing. Credit card processors already exist and, given appropriate information about a rider and a driver, can process an exchange of funds while extracting a slice for the ride-sharing service. Similarly, third-party mapping services can be accessed from the ride sharing app to provide a route to the driver for customer pickup and delivery. The same mapping service can show the pickup location and the progress of the driver toward this point. The entire OO design is supported by another object, a mobile phone company, that facilitates message passing between objects.

A ride-sharing service is based on human capital (drivers) having economic capital (cars) that they are willing to use to drive a rider for economic capital (fares). Economic capital (investment funding) is needed to create symbolic capital (branding and advertising) to recruit drivers and make potential riders aware of the service and its value proposition. Economic capital is also required to create organizational capital, mainly in the form of systems and procedures, to implement the capital creation model. This organizational capital supports the operations of the coordinating object of the ride sharing service, the central object of the preceding figure. Primarily, it includes apps to enable the drivers and riders to connect for a trip. The capital tree is show in Fig. 6.2.

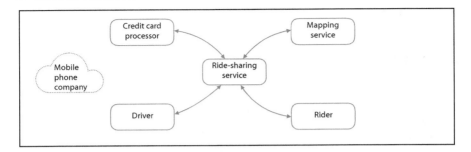

**Fig. 6.1** An OO view of ride sharing

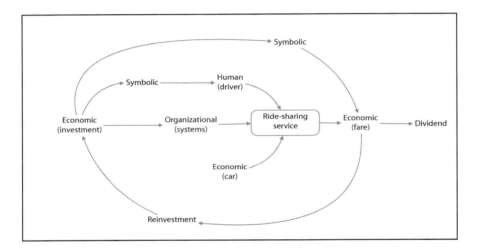

**Fig. 6.2** A capital tree model of ride sharing

The next step is to add systems to the ride sharing capital tree. Drivers must be recruited (engagement) and trained (production). For each driver, personal data and details of their recruitment and training are captured in a system of record. A system of engagement, mainly advertising and incentives, is used to develop awareness among potential riders. Again, there will be a system of record to capture the actions and outcomes of various systems of engagement's actions. To create a trip, the generator of economic capital, a system of engagement, is required to match a rider and driver. For riders, a publicly available app is used to indicate the details of a pickup and trip. A corresponding driver app matches a driver to the rider. Collecting riders and taking them to their destinations is the production system. Finally, there are systems of engagement for rating and tipping the driver, and for the driver

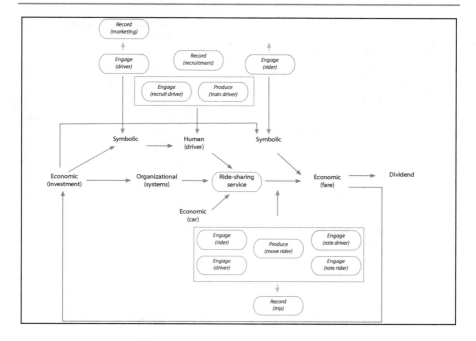

**Fig. 6.3** A capital tree model of ride sharing with the systems layer

to rate the rider. Details of the entire trip are captured by a system of record. The systems layer is depicted in Fig. 6.3.

A trip requires messaging with a credit card processor object, and this occurs in two forms. First, a rider's credit details need to be authenticated when they register with the app. Second, whenever a rider engages for a trip, approval is required for the cost of the trip. Also, there is messaging with the mapping service object to direct the driver to the rider's pickup point and then to the rider's destination.

## 6.4 New Capital Creation Systems

The capital creation system continually creates new objects that provide new services. Furthermore, new technologies are created for connecting objects more efficiently in more places. The Internet, for instance, was a major shift in enabling object connectivity. Amazon, with an initial investment of near USD one million, was among the first to exploit this opportunity and illustrate the power of OO thinking. The day it launched its website, Amazon was an immediate competitive threat to Barnes & Noble, which at that stage had a nationwide chain of four hundred stores with annual sales of USD two billion. Amazon was able to use an OO business model to greatly leverage its small starting capital.

The OO approach demonstrates the accumulating power of the global capital creation system and the accelerating effect of information and communication technologies. It illustrates that creating a new organization is about identifying how to connect existing objects in a novel way to create a new capital creation method. Most of the objects for creating a new organization already exist in advanced capital creation systems. Entrepreneurs find innovative ways to combine objects to deliver existing services better, such as ride sharing compared to taxis, or new services, such as route scheduling that dynamically adjusts for traffic congestion.

As the ride-sharing example illustrates, the processing of fares can be handled entirely by a credit card processor, and available mapping services can handle navigation. Most importantly, the technology, in the form of smart phones and mobile telecommunications, already exists for connecting rider and driver objects and synchronizing their actions.

**OO Design and Competition**
An OO design can be highly scalable when it recruits objects to handle the physical tasks, such as making and delivering products and coordinates these activities. Because it essentially provides the software to coordinate physical systems, such an OO design can be extended sufficiently quickly to enhance the initial offering and maybe forestall imitators. As we see with Lyft and Uber, the OO ride sharing model is easily replicated. Drivers, autonomous objects, often work for both companies as well as taxi firms. There does not seem a way of binding riders to a particular firm, as is usually the case with the traditional taxi business.

Amazon's model can be cloned, as Jet has shown, but it is a challenge because Amazon was able to establish network effects through its reviewing system. It has become the place to learn about customers' reactions to a product because it typically has more reviews for any product than its competitors. Thus OO designers need to think about how they can create network effects, or get customers to create value for other customers, so that they create a barrier for imitators. AirBnB's review system appears to give it some stickiness and inhibits replication. Consumers want more information when they are renting a place for a few days compared to the short duration and commodity nature of a ride-sharing service.

For entrepreneurs, I suggest the following five-step process:

1. Identify a novel combination of objects that is an enticing value proposition for an identified market and sketch out the OO and business canvas[12] models.
2. Convert the OO and business canvas models to a capital creation system.
3. Add the systems layers to the capital creation model.
4. Implement and attract customers.
5. Make the value proposition enduring.

---

[12]Osterwalder, A., & Pigneur, Y. (2010). *Business Model Generation: A Handbook for Visionaries, Game Changers, and Challengers.* Wiley.

While the preceding list makes the process appear linear, the reality is likely to be considerable iteration and revision among the steps to discover what combination of objects and systems generates a value proposition that persists in attracting customers. Developing the various elements in parallel provides a crosscheck to ensure that key components or relationships are not omitted. Once a capital creation system is operational, the management team needs to ensure that its systems of inquiry feeds information into its system of framing so that it is continually refocusing to ensure its value proposition remains attractive.

## 6.5  Mature Capital Creation Systems

OO thinking offers the mature organization a means of reducing complexity and focusing its core competencies on raising $C'$. One of the salient features of today's information age is the deluge of data. Data, once rare, is now abundant, overflowing, and often unexamined. Managers can easily become disoriented by this avalanche, and need to develop coping strategies. When faced with a data overload, an organization can reduce the need for data processing or increase its capacity to process data. Creating autonomous objects, such as self-contained divisions, spinning-out parts of an organization, or outsourcing are means of reducing data processing needs. Creating additional data processing capacity is more than adding computers, but rather is more about adding managers who can identify what information is necessary to address a problem, can make sense of this information when extracted from databases or reports, and can make high quality decisions.

Organizations wishing to simplify and focus attention can start with creating an OO model of their existing enterprise by breaking it into objects that could feasibly operate autonomously and exchange standardized messages with other such objects in the business. If we return to Henry Ford's days of owning rubber plantations and tire factories, these are candidates for objects. For example, a rubber plantation can be a separate object that processes messages for the supply of rubber. Indeed, it would be far better to have multiple rubber plantation objects so there is competition and resiliency in the supply system.

Once an object model has been created, then identify the objects that are critical to success. The beauty of AirBnB is that it realized it could be in the travel accommodation business without owning any rooms and without the managerial overhead of a hotel chain intent on providing a consistent customer experience for each of its brands. The key for AirBnB is having human capital who can create organizational capital to link owners/renters and travelers.

Of course, for a capital creation system that has a large investment in economic capital, reinventing itself around a core of human and organizational capital will be a challenge. Consider New York City, where you need one of nearly 14,000 medallions to operate a taxi. These medallions can be traded, but the entry of ride-sharing destroyed this monopoly. In 2014, a record price of USD 1.3 million was paid for a medallion. In January 2018, seven medallions sold for under \$200,000.[13] When an OO model enters a market, it can reduce the C' of existing organizations, and thus make it hard for them to reinvent themselves or mimic the OO model because of the loss of value of their existing economic capital.

It is essential that the core object executes those procedures that preserve an organization's ability to compete. In an information-age economy, the core object should generally fully retain the systems of record, inquiry, and framing. Systems of production are potential objects for outsourcing. Systems of engagement might be split between parties. For instance, most athletic shoe firms outsource their system of production. They also typically have independent retailers as one of their systems of engagement, and they operate other systems of engagement for marketing directly to consumers and shoe retailers. Cooperative and coordinated systems of engagement between a firm and its retailers reduces the economic capital a firm requires to grow and maintain its reach.

By focusing on a core set of key processes, an organization can become highly knowledgeable and skilled. It is focus that generates expertise, not diversity of operations. If you need a hip joint replacement, seek out a surgeon who does multiple such operations each week and avoid the surgeon who is a head-to-toe generalist.

OO organizational design, either for creating a new business or redesigning an existing enterprise, is a digital connectivity facilitated adaptation of the capital creation system to handle increasing complexity. Organizations have learned that they need to simplify and focus attention in order to raise C'.

An organization's collection of capital informs you of its past success. Its capital creation capabilities, its systems, are an indicator of future success. Many startups based on OO principles attract high valuations because they have a C' advantage over incumbents, such as the Amazon and Barnes & Noble situation.

## 6.6  Maturity Levels

To gain value from the ideas in this book, you need to move beyond a nodding agreement, or head-shaking disagreement, to take action. We've developed a five-stage maturity model for adopting and implementing a capital creation perspective within an organization or across an ecosystem (Table 6.2).

**Conceptual**
If the ideas in this book are to help your organization improve its C', then you need the leadership team to accept that it operates a capital creation system. Furthermore, it must clearly articulate the distinct set of capitals appropriate for its industry or organization. I have suggested six types of capital, but this is not dogma. You might start with these six and then combine and divide as appropriate for your needs.

---

[13]https://www.wsj.com/articles/is-the-market-for-new-york-taxi-medallions-showing-signs-of-life-1516228199.

**Table 6.2** A capital creation maturity model

| Level | Title | Description |
|-------|-------|-------------|
| 1 | Conceptual | Senior management recognizes it operates a capital creation system, there are multiple types of capital, five fundamental types of systems, and the digital world consist of connectable objects |
| 2 | OO models and capital trees | The organization has created one or more high-level OO models and capital trees to understand capital creation within its organization |
| 3 | System sequences | The organization has mapped the sequencing of systems in each major capital creation process |
| 4 | Measurement | The organization has refined and applied metrics and processes to measure outcomes (capital) and means (systems) |
| 5 | Exploitation | The organization has a process in place for revising OO models, capital trees, systems sequencing, and measurement to increase C' |

A renowned finding in psychology indicates that humans can generally remember $5 \pm 2$ things,[14] so don't get carried away with defining different forms of capital. You need useful differentiation, not exhaustive precision. The five foundational systems are fixed based on their historical emergence as described in Chap. 4, but they need to be interpreted broadly to fit with specific circumstances.

### OO Models and Capital Trees

I introduced the OO model capital tree as a means of envisioning and communicating capital creation systems. Your thinking on capital creation will advance in maturity when you go beyond reading about the concept to applying it in a familiar situation. It will force you to understand the core nature of your organization and how various forms of capital interact to create value. Developing OO models and capital trees is probably best undertaken as a leadership group exercise to develop a consensus. You might find a facilitator beneficial for leading the process and asking challenging questions.

OO models and capital trees should be widely shared internally so that all employees understand how your capital creation engine operates. This should assist with a broad goal alignment and the recognition of opportunities to improve C' by modifying the tree.

### System Sequences

A branch of a capital creation tree converts capital from one form to another via a series of systems. Each of these systems needs to be identified by type, charted at a high level following business modeling standards, and stored in an organizational

---

[14]Miller, G. A. (1956). The magical number seven, plus or minus two: some limits on our capacity for processing information. *The Psychological Review, 63*(2), 81–97.

repository. Opportunities for simplifying within systems and standardizing across the organization should be investigated.

**Measurement**

Measurement maturity implies there are established and validated measures of capital and systems (see Chaps. 14 and 15), with a corresponding system of record. A system of inquiry extracts information for managers and corporate governance structures to ensure that there is a high level of transparency of the current and likely future state of an organization's capital creation system.

**Exploitation**

To facilitate exploitation, decision makers must deeply understand the organization's capital creation system. Additionally, there are processes in place for revising OO models, capital trees, systems sequencing, and measurement systems to increase $C'$. A virtuous interrelationship between the various types of systems is operating effectively to ensure that incremental and radical reframing actions are identified and implemented in a timely manner.

## 6.7   Summary

Imagining the world as a series of digitally connected objects was galvanized by the advent of the Internet. It stimulated the dot com revolution and dramatic changes in $C'$ for many industries. Older models for capital creation with lower levels of $C'$ were eliminated, greatly diminished in market share, or entered a phase of slow decline. People's willingness to be objectivated, mobile devices, and digital network advances continue to fuel the development of OO alternatives to traditional organizations. To fully grasp the potential of the interplay among capital, systems, and objects, organizations need to consider a multiphase adoption process that successively develops the level of sophistication with which you can address the realities of operating a capital creation system in today's and tomorrow's worlds.

# The Future

7

Forecasts of the future are often wildly wrong, so this chapter is short to avoid making too many errors.

## 7.1 Capital

The capital creation system will persist, but the focus on what capital to create will change, as it has in the past. Nevertheless, I doubt that the present focus on creating economic capital will diminish significantly.

### 7.1.1 Economic

The metrics for national and organizational success are directed at the production of economic capital. GDP, despite some misgivings about its usefulness,[1] dominates national economic decision-making. Growth in GDP will likely continue to dominate assessment of an economy's performance, and total GDP and GDP/per capita will remain key measures for comparing economies. For firms, earnings and profit will endure as the dominant performance measures. Nonprofit organizations are typically focused on the creation of other forms of capital, but most will still rely on economic capital inputs, such as donations and grants.

---

[1]Pilling, D. (2018). *The Growth Delusion: Wealth, Poverty, and the Well-being of Nations*. Tim Duggan Books.

## 7.1.2  Human

There will be growth in the investment in human capital, because of the increasingly central role it plays in capital creation. In a knowledge society, organizations rely on healthy educated employees to raise their C'. As we invest more in lifelong education, the benefits of highly skilled and healthy employees working a few more years will boost C'.

We will need to address two major human C' problems: the continuing growth in the proportion of funds spent on health care and education. Unless societies find ways to escalate C' for health care and education, we will eventually run out of funds or have to institute major rationing of access to these services.[2,3]

Some of the growth in the costs of health care may be attributed to increases in life expectancy, which has risen in OECD countries by ten years since 1970.[4] In the United States, despite the highest health care expenditure per capita, life expectancy gains have been smaller relative to the OECD group.

Nearly every new information or communication technology, from radio to tablets, has been touted as offering an educational breakthrough. So far, the promises have been minimally achieved, as a review of recent proposed saviors such as the one-laptop-per-child project and MOOCs reveal.

The digital revolution has so far failed to provide a major C' jump for health care and education, yet we depend on human capital to drive the digital revolution in all areas of the economy. The continually rising cost of maintaining and enhancing human capital will be a drag on the capital creation system.

The growth in the importance of human capital will also likely have some impact on governance structures. Organizations composed essentially of human capital, such as professional service firms and universities, usually operate as cooperatives. Organizations relying heavily on economic capital tend to have an investor-driven governance structure. Giving employees equity is a bridge between these two governance options for organizations that are roughly equally dependent on human and economic capital. Thus one potential trend is an increase in the share of cooperative governed organizations as human capital's importance to capital creation increases.

## 7.1.3  Natural

With increasing urgency, we need to create and restore natural capital to mitigate and reverse global climate change. Many major organizations have adopted emission reduction strategies to slow the growth in atmospheric $CO_2$, and with widespread imitation of such actions, we could reverse the growth in atmospheric

---

[2]https://www.healthsystemtracker.org/chart-collection/health-spending-u-s-compare-countries/
#item-since-1980-gap-widened-u-s-health-spending-countries.
[3]https://nces.ed.gov/fastfacts/display.asp?id=76.
[4]http://www.oecd.org/newsroom/healthier-lifestyles-and-better-health-policies-drive-life-expectancy-gains.htm.

greenhouse gas levels. We also need to invest in other natural capital restoration activities, such as reducing biodiversity loss. The restoration of our natural inheritance is the challenge of this century. As global warming is a reality not uniformly acknowledged, it is a formidable test of organizational, national, and global leadership.

The technology trends are moving in the right direction, and energy efficiency has momentum. Renewable energy technologies, as discussed earlier, are now competitive with $CO_2$ emitting sources in most situations, and even more so if subsidies for the fossil fuel industry are eliminated. The cost of batteries is declining rapidly, and the price of electric cars will likely fall within a decade, making them cheaper than those equipped with an internal combustion engine. It is, however, difficult to predict the friction effects of vested interests on the speed with which we can reduce $CO_2$ emissions.

### 7.1.4  Organizational

The use of computers for improving organizational performance started in 1951 with J. Lyons & Co, a British food and catering company.[5] Ever since, organizations have been developing software, organizational capital, to raise C'. We now live in a software dominated world and are touched by its effects many times in our daily lives. Software is the means by which human capital is converted into organizational capital. Lyons used its computer to calculate the value of its bakeries' output, previously a human task. Now we use AI and machine learning to convert high-level human skills, such as diagnosing an illness, to create organizational capital.

AI has become a third factor in the creation of capital. First, solar energy created natural capital, and then humans become capital creators. Now, we see computer scientists applying tools, such as deep learning, to create applications, organizational capital, for a range of complex tasks once performed by humans. For the last five or so decades, software programmers and robotics engineers have been converting human into organizational capital. Now AI is creating organizational capital.

Currently, AI can produce results that often exceed human decision-making accuracy, but it is too often a black box and does not provide a rationale for its decision. Over the next decade, we are likely to see algorithmic transparency open this box so that decision makers are provided with an explanation for a recommendation. This should give them more confidence in adopting a particular AI model. When humans and AI co-decide, usually a superior approach for complex situations, the availability of an AI explanation will enable humans to factor in information not included in the AI model's input.

---

[5]https://warwick.ac.uk/services/library/mrc/explorefurther/digital/leo/story/.

### 7.1.5  Social

Social capital will always be important, as we are a social-cognitive species. In less than two decades, the emergence of social media has had a profound effect on many countries and lives. The current disillusionment may be transitory, and new social media technologies may see a new wave of social capital creation. Many of the impacts on the creation and application of social capital were not anticipated, so maybe the best advice is to be vigilant and reactive.

### 7.1.6  Symbolic

In recent years, China has illustrated that as societies become richer, the consumption of symbolic capital tends to increase. In 2008, Chinese consumers accounted for 12% of global luxury spending. In the eight years since 2008, an estimated more than 75% of the total growth in global luxury spending was by Chinese consumers, either at home or abroad.[6] The price paid for luxury brands includes a symbolic capital premium in the range of 20% to 200% for well-designed, engineered, and crafted goods not available in the mass market.[7] Unless there is a major and sustained economic downturn, symbolic capital creation will probably continue to grow in importance as organizations pursue branding as a differentiation strategy.

There is, nevertheless, an interesting development, as Amazon has entered the branded product market with 76 private-label brands across a range of consumer products, with half of the brands attached to clothing.[8] Ranked the number one brand in 2018,[9] Amazon yokes its immense symbolic capital to affordability, rather than a premium price. Given its resources and tech know-how, Amazon could enter the largest luxury market, autos, with an affordable electric car. No market should be viewed as an Amazon-safe haven.

## 7.2  Systems

### 7.2.1  Systems of Engagement

For most organizations, their systems of engagement are critical. For a business, they determine what it sells, what it makes, and its profitability. It can be argued

---

[6]https://www.mckinsey.com/business-functions/marketing-and-sales/our-insights/chinese-luxury-consumers-more-global-more-demanding-still-spending.

[7]Silverstein, M. J. & Fiske, N. (2003). Luxury for the masses. *Harvard Business Review, 81*(4), 48–57, 121.

[8]http://www.businessinsider.com/amazon-private-label-brands-list-2018-4.

[9]https://www.inc.com/business-insider/amazon-google-most-valuable-brands-brand-finance-2018.html.

that systems of engagement ultimately determine strategy because a firm must find a means of delivering a value proposition that attracts sufficient customers to generate an industry competitive C'. The combination of product, price, and systems of engagement determine sales.[10] New ICT is an occasion for experimenting with novel systems of engagement, as we have seen with the Internet and smartphones. The looming opportunity is wearables, where smartwatches have a foothold, and we can expect further inroads with smartglasses, clothes, and shoes. Humans will be multi-objectivated because their wearables will be reachable by authorized systems of engagement. We can anticipate over the next decade a bevy of attempts to combine wearables and systems of engagement. Nonprofits are likely to trail business in exploring new systems of engagement, but they would be wise to consider the full gamut of developments.

## 7.2.2  Systems of Framing

As bandwidth and communication speeds continue to increase, there is likely to be an increase in data speed and breadth among connected systems. There is a danger of systems of inquiry flooding systems of framing with a lot of noise and too little signal. At the same time, decision makers have the opportunity to react quickly when they can detect a true danger signal. Responding rapidly with an incremental reframing, such as a minor software fix, is unlikely to be problematic. The danger is in radical reframing before the validity of alerting signals has been examined, the consequences of reframing carefully explored, and some deep thought given to potential unintended outcomes.

In terms of the technology, incident rooms supporting systems of framing are likely to become more sophisticated, process a wide range of real-time digital data streams, and use more AI-based analytics. The humans processing the information provided and trying to make sense of it will likely face greater complexity, more information overload, and a heightened sense of urgency. One solution is for top management teams to practice complex and time-pressured decision-making. While this might seem *unrealistic given* the current fragmented and high-velocity nature of managerial decision-making, it seems the only way to create the capabilities for an effective system of reframing under duress. It also emulates the role-playing exercises utilized by defense forces to prepare and practice for circumstances when battle plans need to be reframed dynamically.

## 7.2.3  Systems of Inquiry

Earlier, some major forms of systems of inquiry were discussed: R&D, white papers, digital twins, and data analytics. I envision that these will remain dominant

---

[10]Cespedes, F. V. (2014). *Aligning Strategy and Sales: The Choices, Systems, and Behaviors That Drive Effective Selling*. Harvard Business Review Press.

and will require more investment by many companies to remain competitive by continually raising C'. Currently, data science is mainly based on long-established techniques, such as regression, clustering, and visualization, whose output is readily interpreted by decision makers. AI methods, such as deep learning and neural networks, are less popular.[11] AI is held back by a lack of algorithm transparency. It needs to be reworked to generate explanations. There is evidence that the next generation of AI tools will add this functionality, and then we are likely to see AI advance more rapidly.

### 7.2.3.1   The Problem of Rigid Ideologies

Every country has a right to decide what mix of capital is appropriate for its citizens and circumstances. This mix is rarely constant, and ossification around a specific mix is likely to be detrimental. Unfortunately, the world has seen, and continues to witness, too many nations that get into a capital creation rut because their systems of inquiry wither.

As an example, over the last few hundred years, Russia has had several major ideological determinants, including tsarism, communism, Stalinism, democracy, and Putinism. Except for a brief period of democracy, the country has been led by omnipotent and often ruthless autocrats. Systems of inquiry do not do well in such an environment because, if they flourish at all, they frequently produce results that challenge the prevailing system of framing. Rather, they get co-opted by the system of framing and relinquish their objectivity to present a fake facade. These Potemkin systems of inquiry are just as illusory as the portable villages erected by Grigory Potemkin along the banks of the Dnieper River to deceive Empress Catherine II about the reality of the Russian countryside. If key findings of systems of inquiry are rejected by systems of framing, then a capital creation system's capacity is diminished. For instance, consider the effects of ignoring global warming, failing to immunize children against polio and other preventable diseases, and protectionism

Thomas Carlyle, a Scottish writer and philosopher, derided political economy as "a dreary, desolate, and indeed quite abject and distressing [science]; what we might call... the dismal science."[12] This is a dismal science, in my view, when some economists identify themselves with an ideology and view the world not with a clear eye but with a cataract left or right eye. When any discipline's systems of inquiry are subjugated to a system of framing, it is dismal, and it is not science. A system of framing should not suffocate systems of inquiry. To the contrary, the purpose of a system of inquiry is to ventilate with evidence the stale air of a system of framing to keep capital creation systems competitive and relevant.

---

[11]https://www.kdnuggets.com/2017/12/top-data-science-machine-learning-methods.html.
[12]https://www.economist.com/node/8401269.

## 7.2.4  Systems of Production

The trend of automating systems of production is most likely to continue because of advances in AI, automation, and robotics. Automation means labor disappears as a key cost determinant, and this facilitates a return of manufacturing to developed economies driven by the advantage of being closer to consumers. Robotics permits greater production flexibility and, combined with market proximity, means local manufacturing can respond more rapidly to trends.

Solar panels and wind farms will also result in some localization of energy production, the most localized being solar panels on a dwelling's roof that feed a household battery. The shift to renewables with some localization potential is a threat to the systems of production of fossil fuel extractors, their distributors, electricity generators, and grid operators.

We foresee a major reshuffling of systems of production as organizations relocate their resources and redesign supply chains as a result of the options provided by robotics and renewable energy technologies. Such a restructuring will have many repercussions and unforeseen outcomes, and yet it seems absent from political agendas

## 7.2.5  Systems of Record

Systems of record continue to grow at about 40% or so per year. Much of the growth is due to the volume of unstructured data generated by people posting photos, videos, and text. There are no indications that this growth will slacken, and it will likely increase as the IoT expands. Most organizations will remain data-rich and information-poor, because they simply lack the human capital to turn data into information, make sense of it, and implement appropriate decisions.

New technologies for recording data change efficiencies related to data storage and processing will emerge. Currently, relational database technology and Hadoop distributed file systems are commonly used for data management. Blockchain, whose proponents promise much, is in the hype stage, and there is still some concern about its applicability. In particular, caution is expressed about its scalability to handle large volumes of transactions. Blockchain supports management of a shared distributed ledger, or database, across a public or private network. Thus, it is a good fit for self-organizing ecosystems because members can share encrypted data without the need for centralized controlled. For coordinated ecosystems, the keystone player might be the appropriate manager of data that need to be shared within the ecosystem, and it could do this selectively to protect the competitiveness of its members. Blockchain will gain some traction, but how much will be determined in the next three to five years.[13]

As organizations rely increasingly on data to define and satisfy stakeholders' goals, changes in data availability and timing influence their ability to raise $C'$ through new products, services, or processes. As organizations adopt IoT and convert their economic capital to stream real-time data about their current status, more data become available more rapidly. There is the potential to create a digital data stream, a real-time system of record, for every asset and sharpen the speed and value of decision-making. For example, every parking space in a city can now be online and its price managed dynamically based on demand patterns to maximize revenue. Real-time systems of record reduce the latency of data capture, developments in edge computing reduce analysis latency, and remote control of assets through the IoT reduces action latency. Real-time streaming of systems of records has implications for the other foundational systems, and can give organizations faster reflexes.[14]

A digital twin can mirror with high-fidelity the reality in which an object or process exists. It requires a system of record that is a precise mathematical model of the behavior of the physical product. Similarly, we can expect digital twins of processes to be created, such as the Maserati assembly line.[15]

IoT, digital data streams, and digital twinning are changing the nature of systems of record. They will also change capital creation processes by speeding up decision-making and potentially enabling customization unique to a person, location, and time.

## 7.3  Objects

The IoT and wearables will introduce more objects into the environment, and objects will vastly outnumber humans. We already live in a world of objects that can be connected in a multitude of ways through standardized electronic messaging. The vast and growing variety of combinatorial options will create many opportunities for new forms of capital creation and the destruction of old forms. Furthermore, because so many objects will be available, the time and cost of creating a new organization will likely be lower because capital creation will be mainly about

---

[13]For balanced assessment of the current state of blockchain, see https://www.mckinsey.com/business-functions/digital-mckinsey/our-insights/blockchain-beyond-the-hype-what-is-the-strategic-business-value?cid = other-eml-alt-mip-mck-oth-1806&hlkid = d2c58d1171ab41a8a16e22859260e7cf&hctky=1443659&hdpid=6a0817ff-c71d-4a97-be68-b9b733f3d39f.

[14]This paragraph is based on Pigni, F., Piccoli, G., & Watson, R. T. (2015). Digital data streams: creating value from the real-time flow of big data. *California Management Review, 57*(4). 5-25.

[15]See https://www.youtube.com/watch?v=Hk__pjSe3a8.

novel object connection. Cloud computing is a further facilitating resource. Indeed, think of the cloud as just a collection of usable objects, as can be confirmed by a visit to the Amazon Web Services site.[16]

## 7.4   Conclusion

Speculating on the future of the capital creation system as a whole and an organizational system as one of the many parts is an often barely fathomable jigsaw faced by leadership teams in nearly every setting. In this chapter, I waved a lantern around on a few areas that I consider salient, but a brief illumination is not enough. Rather, I encourage you to periodically shine a light brightly on your most important capital, systems, and objects, so you might comprehend your organization's future as an object-oriented capital creation system.

---

[16]https://aws.amazon.com.

# Part II
# Capital Creation Mechanisms

The prior chapters established the case for viewing the world as a vast capital creation system and recognizing that every ongoing organization is a capital creation system. Now, we need to learn how the capital creation process works, so that you can apply this thinking to your organization. Consequently, this section consists of six chapters, each dealing with one form of capital and describing how each of the forms of capital interact. For example, the next chapter describes six different capital interactions for creating economic capital. The examples across the next six chapters span a wide variety of situations to illustrate that capital creation is everywhere and in many forms. In total, thirty-six mechanisms are reviewed and illustrated with one or more example cases, as depicted in Table 1. The cases vary from old to new organizations, from small to large, include profits and nonprofits, and range across more than fifteen countries. We hope you find them a source of inspiration and imagination. Please make contact if you identify conversion examples that you think we should share through the book's website.[1]

When one capital interacts with another, there are two possible outcomes. First, an input capital creates output capital. For example, a manufacturer sells its product to another company. This is economic → economic capital conversion. Second, an input capital can raise the productivity of capital. For instance, when an insurance company introduces robotic process automation (organizational capital) for simple claims, it gives its claims assessor (human capital) more time to focus on complex claims and fraud detection.

---

[1] rwatson@terry.uga.edu.

**Table 1** Capital creation options and examples

| Input | Output | | | | | |
|---|---|---|---|---|---|---|
| | Economic | Human | Organizational | Natural | Social | Symbolic |
| Economic | Stella Artois & Transaction Alley | KPMG | Lifebuoy soap | Oconee River Land Trust | Go-Jek | Guggenheim Museums |
| Human | Bristol Tennessee Essential Services | Georgia State University | Robots learning from human | Agroecology in Malawi | Aussie Rules footy | Dos Equis |
| Organizational | UPS | Woodside | 3M | Renault Trucks & Daiseki | Dreamforce | Johnnie Walker Whisky & The Sino-Danish Center in Beijing |
| Natural | GoldCorp | Outward bound | Shinkansen bullet train | Chernobyl and the Korean DMZ | Citizen science | Yellowstone National Park |
| Social | KakaoBank | EY | DeWalt | Let's Do It! | ClassPass | All England Lawn Tennis and Croquet Club |
| Symbolic | Top tourism sites | Apple Design Studio | Arup | Pope Francis | Porsche travel club | Athensmade |

This section uses the "capital tree" as a representation of the main features of a capital creation system (Fig. 8.1). A capital tree defines the main features and capital conversion processes of an organization. The representation method is simple and can easily be drawn on a whiteboard. Because of the format of a book page, we show trees in a left-to-right style, but feel free to use a more treelike top-to-bottom depiction.

# Economic Capital

When most people hear the word *capital* they usually think of economic capital and, in particular, its financial forms such as of cash, equities, and bonds. More broadly, economic capital also includes tangible assets, such as commercial buildings and factories. It is the most measurable of capitals because there are usually markets for buying and selling these assets. Thus economic capital is usually the most convertible of all capital forms because it can be turned into cash and then used for another purpose because of the fungibility of money. Of course, there are stranded assets which are no longer part of a capital conversion system, such as Swedish shipyards that cannot not compete with those of China, Japan, or South Korea. Their value is reduced to scrap metal. Nations create economic capital when they build transport systems and physical infrastructure, such as a broadband fiber optic network. Individuals also have economic capital, usually in the form of investments, homes, and cars.

The creation of economic capital is the dominating activity of modern economies. Indeed, we measure their success in terms of its creation through metrics such as GNP and GDP. We'll return to the measurement issue in a later chapter.

We now consider the various capital conversion paths for creating economic capital.

## 8.1 Economic → Economic

The conversion of economic to economic is very common, and it is usually executed through a sale, auction, lease, rent, or some usage fee. The usual conversion results in money being used to pay for capital or received for capital. Occasionally, bartering will be a method of capital exchange. Because the characteristics of some forms of economic capital can be well-defined, such as commodities and equities, markets have been created to facilitate the assembly of buyers and sellers. Nowadays, many of these markets support electronic participation, such as the London

R. T. Watson, *Capital, Systems, and Objects*, Management for Professionals, https://doi.org/10.1007/978-981-15-9418-2_8

Metal Exchange and Dutch Flower Auction, so that geography does not limit participation. When the buyers are most likely to want to inspect a product, such as a used car, economic exchanges remain physical, such as Manheim Auctions, which has more than one hundred wholesale auto auction sites in eleven countries.[1]

**Stella Artois**

Digitization creates an opportunity to increase the value of economic capital by managing its value more precisely. Bus stop shelters, for example, can be used to advertise products and events. The value of this advertising space is not constant. It might be worth more on a sunny day or sporting weekend. In London, some bus stop shelters now have flat panel displays that can be remotely managed. Stella Artois has discovered that sales of its Cidre beverage are significantly higher when the temperature is above average. Because bus stop advertising space is now digital, Stella Artois can selectively advertise when the temperature exceeds a certain level during certain hours of the day.[2]

We can understand the process of capital conversion using the five systems framework. As a starting point, Stella Artois needs a system of record for sales of its products. Ideally, this is spatial-temporal data that indicates the where and when for each sale and other useful facts. These records could be merged with London weather data from the UK Met Office's system of record for the nation. A system of inquiry can then identify good times and weather to advertise to increase sales, and finally a dynamic poster, a system of engagement, on bus stop shelters can target potential customers. The display of each advertisement can generate another digital data stream to augment the system of record to enable the monitoring of advertising impact.

*Record → Inquiry → Engagement*

In the digital age, all physical economic capital is a candidate for joining the IoT. Some cities have put their parking spaces online so they can measure demand and implement revenue management to maximize the value of each parking space. Every organization needs to carefully consider all its assets, even minor ones like bus stop shelters, and the potential to enhance their economic return through digitization. As we have noted before, digitization is a tool for raising $C'$, and in the bus shelter case, both Stella Artois and Transport for London (TfL) gain.

---

[1]https://publish.manheim.com/en/about-manheim.html.
[2]http://liveposter.com/portfolio/stella-artois-cidre-weather-activation/.

**Transaction Alley**

If you use a credit card in the United States, it's likely your transaction will be handled in Transaction Alley, the moniker given to the concentration of FinTech companies in Atlanta, which is headquarters for three of the top five credit processing firms. Almost 70% of the USD 5.3 trillion in US credit and debit payment card annual transactions are processed in Transaction Alley. The industry employs 40,000 people in Georgia and 105,000 people globally.

As the following figure demonstrates, credit processing links five systems together (Fig. 8.1). It starts with a store's system of engagement when a customer, enticed by a product or sales pitch, presents a credit card, which is then processed through four systems of production to get approval from the bank that issued the card. The approval then flows back through the same four systems of production. A receipt is printed in the store for the customer, where a salesperson executes the store's system of engagement script for handing over the transaction record and thanking the customer for her business.

Credit card processing is essential for converting economic to economic capital. A product (economic capital) is converted to a deposit in a bank (economic capital). It is one of the most common capital conversion processes in the world, occurring a myriad of times every day in a matter of seconds for

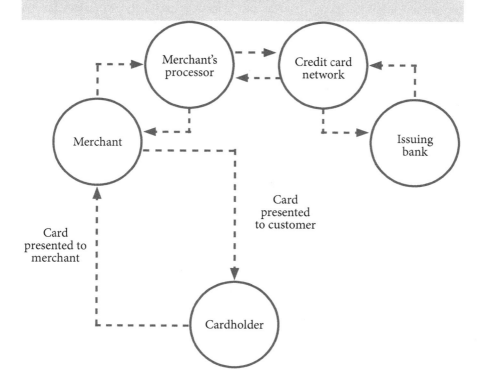

**Fig. 8.1** Credit card processing

each transaction. Each system of production will take a small fee for processing a transaction. It will also create a system of record. The card's issuing bank's system of record, for example, will be used to prepare each card holder's monthly bill. Because it is standard practice in the digital world to have a system of record generated by each system of production, I omit them to focus on the essential aspects of the conversion process.

In simple form, the process starts with engagement, has four sequential production systems, which each generate a system of record, and finishes with engagement.

*Engagement → (Production → Record) {4} → Engagement*

## 8.2  Human → Economic

In this section, we illustrate using the automotive industry how the role of human capital in the creation of economic capital changed over time, leading to the general recognition that the future of advanced economies is highly dependent on the quality of their human capital. They rely very much on a highly educated and healthy population to compete with developing economies.

The migration of farm workers from the countryside to cities provided the labor for the industrial revolution, whose factories were vast mechanistic organizations that required semiskilled workers to produce goods (economic capital). Most unskilled agriculture laborers could with a small amount of instruction gain sufficient skills to undertake factory work. Most factory owners operated on the principle that human capital was expendable and easily replaced.

In 1909, Henry Ford famously offered his customers, "a car painted any color that he wants so long as it is black."[3] Mass production of a single model in one color was not a major human capital challenge, and Ford focused on economic capital as the prime success factor. This emphasis is embodied in the River Rouge Complex, which was, when completed in 1928, the world's largest integrated factory employing at its peak around 100,000 people. For Ford, human and organizational capitals were complementary (Fig. 8.2), and his system of production, the assembly line, was the central concern.

In 1923, Alfred Sloan became president of GM when it acquired his ball-bearing company. He reorganized the company into separate autonomous divisions that were subject to strategic direction, and financial and policy controls from a small headquarters staff. He created the widely emulated multidivisional corporate model that is still a common way of organizing human capital.

---

[3] Ford, H. & Crowther, S. (1922). *My Life and Work*. Garden City Publishing. p. 72.

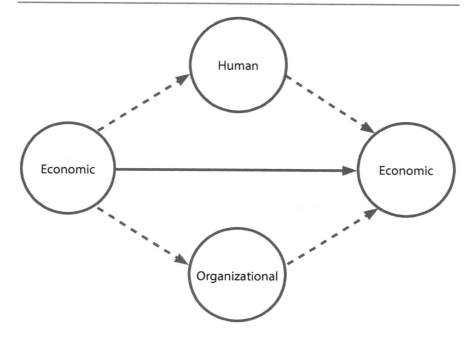

**Fig. 8.2** Ford's capital creation tree

Sloan's aim was to produce a car "for every purse and purpose,"[4] and annually each GM model was revised to meet changing needs and also to ensure that models did not compete with each other. Thus the Chevrolet division manufactured and marketed to those buyers seeking an inexpensive car, whereas Cadillac catered for the most affluent. When Sloan took over at GM, Ford had some 60% of the market, compared with GM's 12%, but in 1927 GM's sales overtook and exceeded Ford, as is still the case.[5]

Sloan acquired a skilled management team to run his multidivisional organization and determine what models to produce for each market segment. He still needed human capital to assemble cars, but his more complex organization and annual strategic planning required the creation of organizational capital. He recognized that this was the core competency of his economic capital creation system when he said, "Take my assets—but leave me my organization and in five years I'll have it all back."[6] In the case of Sloan, human and economic capitals complemented organizational capital (Fig. 8.3). Sloan forefronted the system of framing. Annually, his strategic planning meetings defined the market in terms of models

[4]Sloan, A. P. (1964). *My Years with General Motors*. Crown Business. p. 512.
[5]http://www.economist.com/node/13047099.
[6]Alfred P. Sloan in the 1920s, cited in Bateman, T. S., & Snell, S. (1999). *Management: building competitive advantage*. Irwin. p. 276.

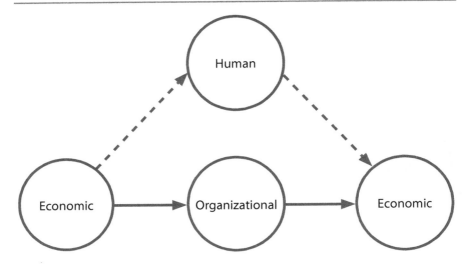

**Fig. 8.3** Sloan's capital creation model

and their features, and differentially marketed to the various target segments (purpose and purse). GM's organizational capital operated a very successful system of framing that enabled it to quickly surpass Ford.

In the 1970s, Ford and GM were outsmarted when Japanese carmakers, in particular Toyota and Honda, entered the US car market with a different capital conversion model for the automotive industry. Their model enabled them to offer consumers a better deal in terms of quality and cost.[7] While lean production certainly played a part, there was another key factor: human capital.

An analysis published in the 1980s,[8] around the time Toyota and Honda were establishing themselves in the United States and Europe, reports that Japanese companies aim to maximize the utilization of their human resources, resulting in higher productivity, lower turnover, and less absenteeism. They focus on recruiting quality workers who will assimilate readily into the company culture and encourage them to stay. They create a strong lifetime social bond between employees and the firm, which facilities teamwork and cooperation. The emphasis on human capital includes the continuous development of employees' skills. The Japanese automakers demonstrated that high-quality human capital could build more reliable and durable cars at a lower cost. Assembly line workers could be trained in advanced manufacturing techniques, such as lean production and quality control, and execute with precision. High productivity and high quality could be jointly achieved with highly developed human capital. The best Japanese auto workers

[7]Holweg, M. (2008). The evolution of competition in the automotive industry. In *Build to Order*, pp. 13–34. Springer.
[8]Hatvany, N., & Pucik, V. (1981). An integrated management system: Lessons from the Japanese experience. *Academy of Management Review, 6*(3), 469–480.

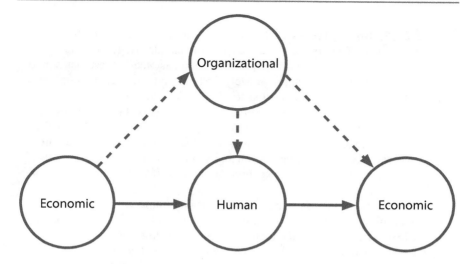

**Fig. 8.4** Toyota's capital creation model

were twice as productive as their US counterparts.[9] Human capital was the new foundation for competition in the vehicle manufacturing business. Sakichi Toyoda, the founder of Toyota, noted, "Workers are [the] treasure of the factory. They are important to me." The Japanese model views human capital as the key success factor in the creation of economic capital. It is complemented by organizational and economic capital (Fig. 8.4).

Henry Ford, Alfred Sloan, and Sakichi Toyoda have distinct signature achievements that resonate with their view of capital creation. The River Rouge Complex asserts that economic capital is the main input capital for creating more capital. The multidivisional corporation, organizational capital, was Sloan's enduring emblem. For Toyota, it was dedicated and well-trained employees who could manage lean production and quality control.

**Bristol Tennessee Essential Services**
The Baldrige Program is a US public-private partnership dedicated to performance excellence. Each year, Malcolm Baldrige National Quality Awards are given for several organizational categories. It is the highest level of national recognition for performance excellence that a US organization can receive.[10]

[9]Holweg, M. (2008). The evolution of competition in the automotive industry. In *Build to Order*, pp. 13–34. Springer.
[10]https://www.nist.gov/baldrige/baldrige-award.

In 2017, Bristol Tennessee Essential Services (BTES) won the small business award. The sixty-eight employees of this electricity and fiber services utility company serve thirty-three thousand customers. It estimates that it has saved its customers approximately USD 70 million over the last forty years. BTES's customer satisfaction levels are close to 100% on many product and performance measures. Some key performance factors are as follows: outages are less than sixty minutes per customer per year, which outperforms the best-in-class averages of around ninety to one hundred minutes; the Average Service Availability Index was 99.99% for 2014 through 2016; the employee retention rate was 100%, while the national industry average is 82%.

Such success is very dependent on high quality human capital, and BTES excels in this area. The percentage of employees with perfect attendance is about 75%. In comparison, the industry average is below 20%. It cares for its employees. There is on-site exercise equipment for employees and retirees, it promotes a healthy lifestyle, and offers educational and advancement opportunities. During extended area power outages and inclement weather, BTES deploys a commercial-grade kitchen to cook meals for its crews in the field restoring power.[11]

BTES demonstrates that human capital is frequently the key ingredient to high performance. This means it needs a system of production for keeping employees healthy and motivated, and ensuring their skills are current. In other words, it needs to have routine procedures for the creation and maintenance of human capital.

*Production (human capital quality)* → *Production (performance excellence)*

## 8.3  Organizational → Economic

Knowledge, patents, routines, and software systems are components of organizational knowledge that individually and collectively can be converted to economic capital. Consulting companies, for example, specialize in converting their knowledge into revenue streams. This knowledge is often intricately tied to their human capital, and consulting companies have well-developed routines for recruiting talent, nurturing it, and finding clients willing to pay for their knowledge. Because organizations usually turn to consultants to solve their most complex problems, projects typically require a team of consultants, and consulting firms need a breadth of human capital with the necessary knowledge to attack a wide range of challenging problems.

---

[11]https://www.nist.gov/baldrige/bristol-tennessee-essential-services.

Patents, the product of an organization's R&D units, can be used internally to produce new products and refine the production of existing products. Such uses create additional economic capital. An enterprise can also elect to license or sell its patents to generate revenue. These seem relatively simple decisions, but many organizations struggle to exploit the full value of their patents.

There is often a disconnect between R&D and business units when knowledge transfer between each is very domain-dependent. The R&D people might have an insufficient comprehension of the marketplace to see a fit for an invention. Similarly, the generic and abstract nature of a patent might obscure opportunities so that business unit personnel overlook them. The ability to transfer across these boundaries is a form of organizational capital, and effective innovators find ways to permeate these barriers in both directions. It means finding ways to create persisting links between units. In addition, each unit must have the capacity to learn from the other.[12] This could mean embedding people in the R&D unit with customer-facing experience, and placing scientists or engineers at field sites to get direct knowledge of operations and customers. In some situations, such as in the following case, it means putting the R&D team in the workplace and continually engaging and refining the intended product.

---

**UPS and the Telematics Project**

Modern vehicles contain technology to sense the state of a vehicle and make associated data available via an automotive bus, which connects components such as an antilock braking system and engine control unit. Sensors for speed, temperature, and so forth can also be connected to this bus. These data enable a system of record to be created for a vehicle. UPS developed proprietary firmware to capture these records to give it access to more than two hundred vehicle-related elements, such as RPMs, oil pressure, when a truck reversed, and time spent idling.[13]

Three senior UPS engineers led the development of the necessary applications to analyze the pool of data (back-end) and the development of the necessary interfaces to share information with drivers and managers (front-end). As veterans each having more than thirty years' experience at UPS, they had deep domain knowledge across many aspects of the firm's operations. To help make sense of the data collected, and to understand how to best communicate them, they spent most of their time in a UPS depot so they could interact frequently with the drivers, supervisors, and mechanics who used the system's reports.

---

[12]Tsai, W. (2001). Knowledge transfer in intraorganizational networks: Effects of network position and absorptive capacity on business unit innovation and performance. *Academy of Management Journal, 44*(5), 996–1004.

[13]Watson, R. T., Boudreau, M.-C., Li, S., & Levis, J. (2010). Telematics at UPS: En route to Energy Informatics. *MIS Quarterly Executive, 9*(1), 1–11.

They innovated, prototyped, investigated, and refined the telematics concept for many years. They did not write information requirements for programmers at some distant corporate campus. Rather, they created a prototype and refined it successfully until it was effective. When the system worked in the field, they handed it over to corporate IS to formalize and manage. Domain knowledge is frequently the key to systems' success, and in this case, UPS started with a very high level of domain knowledge and then grew it rapidly through iterative field development. They went through many (the {*} notation) iterations of inquiry and engagement before a system of production emerged.

*(Inquiry → Engagement {*}) → Production*

Valuing patents is a second problem for a firm seeking to license or sell its knowledge. It might well lack the organizational capital to make an accurate assessment. In this case, it can tap into organizational capital created by another entity, such as reports on how to value patent licenses.[14]

## 8.4  Natural → Economic

There are three approaches to converting natural to economic capital: manage as a renewable resource, deplete as a finite resource, or recycle.

### 8.4.1  Management

The conversion of a renewable natural resource to economic capital is managed when a resource is exploited over a long period. A forestry plantation could last for centuries if harvesting and planting are synchronized to ensure a steady yield of timber. For example, if a tree reaches its optimum yield after twenty years of growth, then it would make sense to harvest about 5% of the forest each year. Changes in forestry science are likely to increase yields, so there can be a steady increase in the $C'$.

Management typically works well when there is a single owner of the resource; however, when it is a common or shared resource, the *Tragedy of the Commons* is often witnessed.[15] The tragedy model predicts that shared resources, such as the

---

[14]Chiu, Y.-J., & Chen, Y.-W. (2007). Using AHP in patent valuation. *Mathematical and Computer Modelling, 46*(7–8), 1054–1062; and Hagelin, T. (2003). Valuation of patent licenses. *Tex. Intell. Prop. LJ, 12,* 423.
[15]Hardin, G. (2009). The tragedy of the commons. *Journal of Natural Resources Policy Research, 1*(3), 243–253.

common land of a village where all can graze animals, will be overexploited and degraded, because those with the right to use the common resource will act in their self-interest and seek to maximize their $C'$. A society's shared resources includes oceans, lakes, rivers, air, and public parks and gardens.

Common property resources have two key features,[16] the first of which is control of access or *excludability*. It can be difficult to limit access to a common resource, such as the ocean or the atmosphere. A fundamental problem for managing carbon emissions is that $CO_2$ cannot be confined within national boundaries, and we are all affected by rising levels. Second, *subtractability* means that each person using a common resource can reduce the value available to other users. Groundwater is particularly susceptible to subtractability because each liter pumped leaves less for others, unless total extraction is below the replenishment rate. Of course, the problem might only become noticeable after millions of liters have been extracted.

The tragedy of the commons can be managed by limiting access to a common resource through enforceable controlled access and setting limits on the harvesting of the resource. The key, obviously, is enforceability of a limit. One approach is to set a quota. Aquifers can be metered, for instance, but it is much harder to monitor quotas for large physical regions, such as a fishing or hunting zone. Additionally, a monitoring agency needs to be established to set limits, enforce them, and sustainably manage the natural capital for a persisting conversion to economic capital.

## 8.4.2   Depletion

The mining industry extracts the earth's nonrenewable resources. Fossils fuels (coal, oil, and natural gas) were created from decayed organic materials, plants and animals, that were subjected to heat and pressure over millions of years. This is a finite resource, and for some years there has been speculation about when "peak oil" will occur. In 1977, Marion King Hubbert speculated that global oil production would peak in 1995. His projection of a peak is valid since oil is finite, but his timing was off because he did not account for technological developments that improved the search for and extraction of oil. Given recent developments, it is likely that peak oil will be caused not by geological factors but rather a shift to electrical vehicles fueled by renewables sources.

Assuming extraction continues to grow at current rates and there are no major discoveries of new ore bodies, several key minerals will be depleted this century (Fig. 8.5).[17] Organizations that have capital conversion processes relying on these minerals will need to find substitutes, such as carbon nanotubes for copper.[18] They might also invest in new capital conversion methods that use more plentiful minerals.

---

[16]Feeny, D., Berkes, F., McCay, B. J., & Acheson, J. M. (1990). The tragedy of the commons: twenty-two years later. *Human ecology, 18*(1), 1–19.
[17]http://www.bbc.com/future/bespoke/BBCF_infoData_stock_check.pdf.
[18]https://www.technologyreview.com/s/425468/nanotube-cables-hit-a-milestone-as-good-as-copper/.

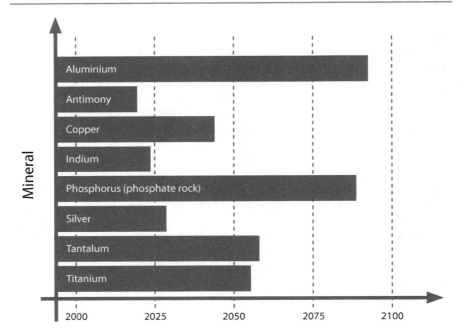

**Fig. 8.5** Year until depletion of some key minerals

The conversion of a finite natural resource to economic capital will ultimately result in its financial depletion because C′ becomes too low. There will always be copper, but the cost of extraction will eventually become too high relative to the technological development of substitutes. Alternatively, we can build better recycling systems.

### 8.4.3  Recycling

For minerals, the resulting processed materials can be recycled. Bauxite, for example, is smelted to create aluminum, which is an energy intensive process. Consequently, re-melting aluminum is financially sensible.[19] Similarly, research indicates that it is possible to recycle the lithium and cobalt in lithium batteries.[20] While no process can recycle 100% of the components of a manufactured product, there is a capacity to capture some of the elements. Designing capital conversion processes that can disassemble products efficiently to enable greater reuse will lower the cost of recycling. Apple has demonstrated a robot, Liam, that can

---

[19]Recycling aluminum requires about 5% of the energy required to create aluminum from bauxite.
[20]Rahman, A., & Afroz, R. Lithium battery recycling management and policy. *Int. J. Energy Technology and Policy*, 2016. 13(3), 278–291.

disassemble an iPhone.[21] Sorting is one of the major costs of recycling, and Liam can reduce an iPhone to eight different pieces in separate containers. BMW, which opened its first Recycle and Dismantling Center in Landshut, Germany, in 1990, designs its cars to be dismantled and the parts recycled.[22] The combination of robotics and machine learning can enable capital conversion processes that capture the value in old products through disassembly and recycling.

**GoldCorp**

In 2000, Rob McEwan, CEO of GoldCorp, a gold miner with headquarters in Vancouver, Canada, assessed that the company's underground mine in Ontario had more potential. It was then producing about 50,000 oz (~ 1,400 kg) annually at the hefty cost of USD 360 per ounce, and company geologists were unsure of the precise location of the best veins. He decided to openly share the mine's 400 Mbytes of geological data and offered a prize of USD 575,000 to the best solution revealing the gold in the ore body.

Launched in March 2000, the competition attracted more than a thousand submissions in a few weeks. The winners were a partnership of two Australian firms who developed a 3D map of the mine revealing more than 110 sites, with 80% of them indicating significant gold reserves. The competition reduced exploration time by two to three years, and the value of gold extracted by late 2009 exceeded USD 6 billion.[23]

Geological surveys, systems of production, created a geological dataset, a system of record, that was shared electronically, a system of engagement, and processed by specialized mining software, a system of inquiry, to create a more precise model of the gold seams in the mine, a system of framing. GoldCorp lacked an adequate system of inquiry, and often a firm discovers that the gold, literally in this case, is in its system of inquiry. Fortunately, in a networked economy, systems of engagement enable the rapid sharing of data sets to take advantage of experts with powerful systems of inquiry. Such access, however, is worthless without a detailed system of record.

*Production → Record → Engagement → Inquiry → Framing*

The GoldCorp case illustrates how the five systems model provides a general method for understanding the conversion of capital, in this case from natural to economic. The CEO was sufficiently astute to recognize that the firm's weakness was its system of inquiry's inability to identify rich ore bodies. Every organization needs to analyze its major capital conversion processes and devise means for remedying any weaknesses.

---

[21]http://www.businessinsider.com/apple-liam-iphone-recycling-robot-photos-video-2017-4.

[22]https://www.bmwusfactory.com/sustainability/corporate-sustainability/recycling-programs/.

[23]https://www.ideaconnection.com/open-innovation-success/Open-Innovation-Goldcorp-Challenge-00031.html.

## 8.5  Social → Economic

Organizations have a lot of experience in converting social to economic capital. Manufacturers and retailers have a variety of sales approaches and distribution channels to reach potential customers to entice them to buy their wares. Many retailers, such as Macy's, have brick-and-mortar stores and an online outlet. A major challenge for most retailers is to retune their capital conversion process to handle the ongoing consumer shift to electronic channels.

Entertainment and information service providers often use an advertising model to gain revenue from their audience. TV, radio, newspapers, magazines, search engines, and social media all use advertising to transform social to economic capital, but the conversion process is under challenge. Newspapers are learning how to shift their readers, their social capital, to a subscription model as advertising no longer provides sufficient revenue to subsidize the news reporting side of the business. Broadcast and cable TV are finding that their viewers, their social capital, are increasingly enticed by ad-fee subscription services from Netflix, Hulu, Amazon Prime, Apple, Acorn, and others.

Social movements, clubs, universities, and charities, who rely on converting their supporters into donors to sustain them, play the same social to economic capital conversion game.

We are typically members of many different social networks (e.g., membership of club) or treated as such (e.g., a customer of a retailer). On any day, you will likely face multiple attempts to engage you in the conversion of social to economic capital. Use of a search engine might result in you generating revenue for a website owner; as a result of clicking on a story on a news aggregator's site, you might be invited to subscribe to a newspaper because you have exceeded your monthly free read quota; and you might receive a message from a retailer announcing its latest products. This is not surprising, because many organizations, and not just for-profits, are based on converting their social to economic capital.

---

**Kakao Bank**

Kakao Bank launched its Internet-only banking service to South Koreans on July 27, 2017. In the first 24 h it opened around 300,000 accounts. After a month, it had 3.9 million customers. In its early days, it opened approximately 6,400 new accounts per hour. In August, it approved about Won1.4 trillion (USD 1.2 billion) in consumer credit loans, about 40% of total loans in South Korean for that month. In contrast, Citigroup announced plans to close 70% of its branches in South Korea, Standard Chartered had already cut its number of branches there by 20%, and the country's largest lender by assets, Kookmin Bank, had shut 55 of its 1,207 branches.[24] Kakao Bank's astounding rate of growth was greatly aided by the social capital created by its parent, Kakao Corporation.

---

[24]https://www.ft.com/content/438e8524-9f6a-11e7-8cd4-932067fbf946.

Kakao Corporation, founded in 2010, developed Kakaotalk, a free mobile message app that is used by 93% of South Korea's population. It has about fifty million active monthly users and also offers a range of services based on Kakaotalk, including games, car-hailing, navigation, mobile payment, and online purchasing.[25] Based on its free app, it has created a vast pool of social capital that it can convert into revenue, economic capital, in a variety of ways, including banking services. The launch of Kakao Bank illustrates the devastating impact on other banks of the combination of social capital and digitization of banking's capital creation processes.

*Engagement (KakaoTalk) → Engagement (KakaoBank) → Production (banking services)*

## 8.6  Symbolic → Economic

Organizations create symbolic capital to grease the creation of economic capital and enhance its return. A well-known brand is more likely to attract a potential customer's interest and a premium price. Organizations have two main competitive levers they can manipulate: price and perception. A person's behavior is the outcome of the blending of their rational and social components. Our rational bent is influenced by price, but our social slant is affected by perceptions, such as a product's brand or popularity, as depicted in Fig. 8.6.

Markets are very efficient for trading commodities, because they can be precisely described. For example, it is impossible to discriminate between a certified kilogram of gold of a specified purity sold by different vendors. The more a product becomes like a commodity, the greater the move toward markets as an exchange mechanism. For companies competing on price, symbolic capital is a costly overhead. Rather, they need to build organizational capital that enables them to have the lowest price in the market. This is the strategy pursued by Walmart, which supports its everyday low price strategy with a highly efficient logistics system and a well-integrated supply chain. Efficiency determines the $C'$ of a price-oriented business.

Alternatively, when perceptions have the upper hand, marketing can be very effective, and firms will attempt to differentiate their products through surrounding them in symbolic capital. This can include establishing the exclusivity and quality of the brand, and building distinctive retail outlets in prestigious shopping centers, stores, or areas such as the Champs Elysées in Paris. When an organization competes on the basis of perception, it needs to invest in symbolic capital to elevate the image and quality of its product to command a premium price and raise its $C'$ by differentiation.

---

[25]https://en.wikipedia.org/wiki/KakaoTalk.

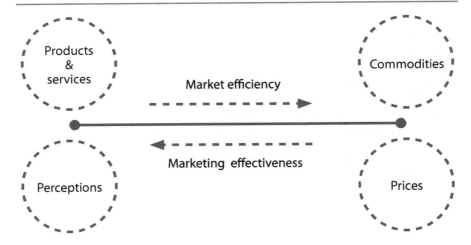

**Fig. 8.6** The major competitive levers: perceptions and prices

**Top Tourism Sites**

In 2016, ninety-one million people chose their vacation destination based on symbolic capital—namely, a country's most famous landmark. This is about a 7.5% of the 1.2 billion tourist arrivals in 2016, according to the UN's World Tourism Organization. In terms of tourism spending, the United States is the leader, with USD 206 billion in 2016, followed by Spain (USD 60 billion) and Thailand (USD 50 billion).[26] The most visited site, according to *Travel + Leisure*, is the Grand Bazaar in Istanbul, with more than ninety-one million visitors per year.[27] Construction of the Grand Bazaar started in 1455 and was not completed until after 1730. It has between three thousand and four thousand shops and covers more than sixty streets.

Six of top-ten most visited sites are in the United States (New York's Times Square, Central Park, and Grand Central Terminal, Union Station in Washington, the Los Vegas Strip, and Niagara Falls). Interestingly, only one of the top-ten sites is natural capital, and the rest are human-made.

A city or nation's landmarks and natural attractions are symbolic capital that draws tourists, whose expenditures create economic capital. The World Travel and Tourism Council estimates that one in ten of the world's jobs are in tourism, and that is 10.4% of global GDP. For five countries in the Caribbean, tourism is between 19% and 35% of GDP.[28] The promotion of

---

[26]http://media.unwto.org/press-release/2017-07-14/strong-tourism-results-first-part-2017.

[27]https://www.travelandleisure.com/travel-guide/istanbul/things-to-do/grand-bazaar.

[28]https://www.wttc.org/research/economic-research/economic-impact-analysis/.

destinations is a system of engagement that attracts tourists, whom the tourism industry serves through a variety of production systems (hotels, tours, restaurants, etc.).

*Engagement (attraction) → Production (visit)*

### 8.6.1  Complementary and Conversion

Presenting capital conversion as a relationship between only two types of capital downplays the complexity of a capital conversion system. Capital creation requires the coordination and integration of multiple capital conversion processes to create the required capital, as we saw with Ford, GM, and Toyota earlier in this chapter.

The comparison of price versus perception directed capital creation extends our understanding of how to create a synergistic capital creation system. In the case of price, the conversion of economic to economic capital is supported by organizational and social capital. A business needs to efficiently (organizational capital) engage customers (social capital) (Fig. 8.7). While customers will be attracted by the lowest price, the firm stills needs to pay some attention to its systems of engagement because customer retention is typically cheaper than customer recruitment.

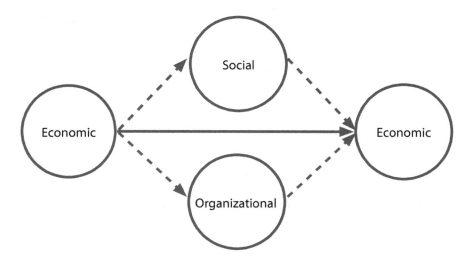

**Fig. 8.7** Price-oriented capital conversion

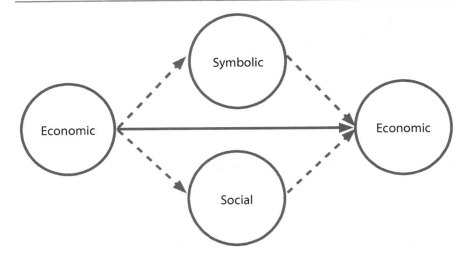

**Fig. 8.8** Perception-oriented capital conversion

For a perception directed business, the conversion of economic to economic capital is primarily supported via symbolic and social capital (Fig. 8.8). The business needs a range or products or services that are perceived to be distinctive (symbolic capital) and interact with customers (social capital) in a manner they also perceive as distinctively engaging. They want to bind their customers to the business through exceptional service.

For both types of organizations, economic capital includes the products being sold and the physical facilities needed to support sales, distribution, and management. However, while one might build a "big box" in a strip mall, the other will likely design a store to fit the ambiance of a prestigious retail zone. Both will likely be surrounded by businesses of their ilk.

## 8.7  Summary

Don't be misled by the simplicity of the diagrams used in this chapter to illustrate key concepts. Modern society is not as simple as the models presented, or indeed those depicted by the five forces model or business model canvas discussed earlier. However, they all follow a common principle: to understand a complex organizational situation, first simplify it to the objects and their interaction that you and your colleagues can comprehend and agree upon, as I elaborated upon in Chap. 7 on objects. This should enable you to develop a frame for discerning what you want to do, how to do it, and what resources are critical to success. You can add complexity once you are sure the core conversions are correct and central to your capital creation goals. Implementation will require dealing with the complexity ignored by a simple vision. For example, "Everyday low prices" or "The customer experience" encapsulate in their simplicity guidance for building successful enterprises. While they can be understood by all, particularly customers and employees, their implementation is a major initial and ongoing challenge.

# Human Capital

9

Human capital is the general health, skills, knowledge, and abilities of the population, a workforce, or an individual. "A country's ability to improve its standard of living over time depends almost entirely on its ability to raise output per worker," according to Nobel Prize–winning economist Paul Krugman.[1] The characteristics of a nation's organizations or a person's human capital determines to a large extent the type of conversions each can undertake and how it can raise C′. Thus we first examine the roles of mass education and public health in the creation and maintenance of human capital.

## 9.1  Mass Education

An OECD Insights' report has a perceptive title, "Human Capital: How What You Know Shapes Your Life."[2] It asserts that education is the key factor in creating human capital, and links higher education levels to economic capital, in the form of higher personal incomes and national economic growth, and increased social capital through greater community involvement. Furthermore, education raises health levels, possibly through greater income and more knowledge of healthy behaviors. Education shapes a person's life and also that of their immediate family members, who will most likely get a better education and health care. The length and depth of a person's education is an investment that can produce long-term returns for the individual, the employer, and the nation.

---

[1]Krugman, P. R. (1997). *The Age of Diminished Expectations: US Economic Policy in the 1990s.* MIT Press.
[2]https://www.oecd.org/insights/humancapitalhowwhatyouknowshapesyourlife.htm.

© The Editor(s) (if applicable) and The Author(s), under exclusive license
to Springer Nature Singapore Pte Ltd. 2021
R. T. Watson, *Capital, Systems, and Objects*, Management for Professionals,
https://doi.org/10.1007/978-981-15-9418-2_9

Knowledge, higher quality human capital, is fundamentally different from other forms of capital. As it becomes widespread, as we saw in the world's first literate society in Greece, knowledge readily expands, becomes more easily acquired, and generates more human capital. It appears to be society's best mechanism for continuous growth in $C'$.

Mass education, particularly at the university level, is critical for building human capital. However, many advanced economies appear to have a major human $C'$ problem in that the spending on education is rising faster than inflation. In the case of the United States, tuition at four-year public colleges had risen more than 100% between 2001 and 2017, after taking inflation into account.[3] Another report notes that public college tuition fees quadrupled in the thirty-five-year period prior to 2014. In addition, government spending on higher education has increased at a faster rate than its spending in general. This is partly due to an increase in the population enrolled in college and the growth in graduate and professional enrollments.[4]

Historically, education has not found a $C'$ escalator to dramatically raise its productivity. The production model has over the centuries been rather consistent. A professor lectures the class. Massive Open Online Courses (MOOCs) promised to ramp up productivity by having the world's best professors lecture to tens of thousands of students at a time, but MOOCs fail to engage students. The current completion rate for an MOOC course is about 13%. Furthermore, those who finish a course tend to be advanced learners, who are capable of self-instruction using whatever method is convenient, such as a MOOC or a book.[5]

Nearly every technology (radio, TV, personal computers, and MOOCs, for example) has had its boosters who promised an education revolution, but they misunderstand two key aspects of education. First, there are features of the traditional class that make it engaging. Students create social capital as they build friendships with others in their classes and learn how to work together on class projects. Some classroom friendships are lifelong. Also, some students want to build a relationship with a professor. Some will maintain lifetime connections with their favorite professors and continue to seek their advice years after completing a class. Humans have a drive to learn and a drive to bond with each other,[6] and the combination of these forces appears very influential in maintaining a strong preference for relatively small face-to-face classes.

Second, education can be focused on building explicit (know-what), or tacit knowledge (know-how and know-why). Explicit knowledge is codified and transferable. This book is an example of explicit knowledge, and most educational technologies are designed to deliver explicit knowledge. In contrast, tacit knowledge is personal expertise, experience, and judgment that are difficult to codify. It is

---

[3]https://www.washingtonpost.com/news/grade-point/wp/2017/10/20/who-is-to-blame-for-rising-tuition-prices-at-public-colleges/?utm_term=.99749788e5e9.

[4]https://www.nytimes.com/2015/04/05/opinion/sunday/the-real-reason-college-tuition-costs-so-much.html?_r=0.

[5]https://wp.nyu.edu/robertubell/2017/01/19/moocs-and-the-failure-of-innovators/.

[6]Lawrence, P. R., & Nohria, N. (2002). *Driven: How Human Nature Shapes Our Choices.* Jossey-Bass.

more difficult to transfer tacit knowledge because it resides in people's minds. For example, a colleague in the paper industry commented that experienced plant operators relied on subtle variations in the sound of equipment to detect problems.

Usually the transfer of tacit knowledge requires the sharing of experiences. For example, tacit knowledge is transferred when an expert helps a novice diagnose a problem, explain its causes, and indicates why the proposed solution will work. The exchange of tacit knowledge requires a problem-oriented classroom where an experienced professor steps into guide students when they get stuck on a problem. The professor should not present a quick solution, but rather point out the clues that reveal the nature of the problem and then give enough hints to set the student on a new course. In today's world, problems are more complex and multilayered, and tacit knowledge is more critical to organizational success. Employers want graduates with critical thinking skills, and these are fostered by building their tacit knowledge. Critical thinking develops through practice, experience, and mentoring.

Technology might give us incremental improvements in advanced education, but it would seem that the creation of tacit knowledge is bounded by the number of students with whom a professor can effectively interact with in a class. Artificial intelligence, especially if it can explain its reasoning, might offer some prospect of a human $C'$ bump, but history would predict this is a false hope.

For individuals, an extra year of schooling increases hourly earnings by 8.8% compared to the US stock market return of 5.6% over the past fifty years. The calculation excludes other benefits, such as the lower mortality rates associated with greater education. The return on additional education is higher for women and for primary education.[7]

Our past capital investments have created today's knowledge society, which requires advanced knowledge, skills, and competencies to maintain capital growth across its various dimensions. If the additional funding for college education results in more capable graduates who are well-equipped to advance $C'$ in the organizations that employ them, then the increasing costs could be a very worthwhile investment because they result in widespread organizational productivity gains. The goal of society is to raise overall $C'$, and thus attention should be focused on the quality of graduates relative to the cost of education. Measuring the quality of human capital is a more difficult assessment that toting up costs.

## 9.2  Health Care

Good health is a key component of human capital. A healthy population results in fewer lost hours due to illness or loss of skills and experience due to disability, early retirement, or death. Notably, the cost of national health care systems as reported in

---

[7]https://www.economist.com/news/finance-and-economics/21741558-returns-education-over-past-half-century-have-beaten-american?frsc = dg%7Ce.

2019 varies considerably across the seven G7 countries from USD 3,649 (Italy) to USD 11,071 (US) per capita.[8] Despite spending more, the United States has, on several measures of population health, worse outcomes than its international peers.[9] The data indicate that the US health care system is a drag on the national C′. It is not my intention to dig further into this issue in this chapter, but rather to point out that when human capital productivity is a key element in overall C′, an effective and efficient health care system is a key national investment. At the societal level, human capital can also have a broad impact on national economic growth. One estimate, for instance, indicates that a national improvement in life expectancy of five years contributes to a 0.5% uptick in economic growth.[10] Given that advanced economics grow in the region of 2 to 3% annually, this is a substantial ramp.

## 9.3  Economic → Human

The conversion of economic to human capital is an individual, organizational, and national investment. Education creates opportunities for well-paid and interesting jobs. Thus it is not unusual for many people to use their economic capital to increase their human capital and those of their immediate relatives, particularly their children.

There is evidence that an investment in human capital is necessary for accelerated economic growth. The birth of mass education around the end of the nineteenth century preceded large-scale economic growth in Germany and the United States. Relatively high literacy levels in Singapore and Korea were present before their economies grew rapidly in the 1980s and early 1990s.[11] Indeed, Singapore has two assets: location and people. Geography was a launching pad, but investment in human capital is the enduring fuel of economic growth.

At the organizational level, we have specialist institutions for converting economic to human capital, In most societies, universities are the main engines for this transformation. While they rely on faculty, human capital, to build and operate the conversion process, they also need economic capital in the form of teaching rooms, laboratories, and field stations. These same types of resources are found in many traditional organizations as many need to continually upgrade the quality of their human capital through education and research.

---

[8]OECD (2020), Health spending (indicator). https://doi.org/10.1787/8643de7e-en (Accessed on 03 August 2020).

[9]http://www.commonwealthfund.org/publications/issue-briefs/2015/oct/us-health-care-from-a-global-perspective.

[10]Keeley, B. (2007). *Human Capital: How What You Know Shapes Your Life*. OECD. https://www.oecd.org/insights/humancapitalhowwhatyouknowshapesyourlife.htm.

[11]Keeley, B. (2007). *Human Capital: How What You Know Shapes Your Life*. OECD. https://www.oecd.org/insights/humancapitalhowwhatyouknowshapesyourlife.htm.

Organizations can use their economic capital to recruit human capital. Some enterprises, particularly those in high-tech, recognize that a bundle of capital, including a financial package, is necessary to recruit and retain talented human capital. Thus Google's office in Zurich includes ski lift gondolas as meeting spots and slides between floors. On the grounds of an old brewery, the building is convenient to Lake Zurich. Larry Page, a Google founder, believes that workplace ambiance impacts human capital productivity.[12]

Nationally, governments invest in systemwide activities to raise the quality of their human capital. They invest in school buildings, establish research labs, and finance education. In some cases, governments elect to make universities tuition free or create schemes to fund attendance. They understand that a key activity of a government is to use its revenue to build human capital for the good of the entire economy.

**KPMG**

Data analysts and scientists are in high demand, and data-oriented businesses, such as accounting and auditing, need a steady flow of recent graduates. Universities are a critical component of their supply chain, and the big four accounting firms have traditionally competed to get top accounting graduates so they have the talent to operate their business. Moreover, auditing is moving from sampling transactions to a complete analysis of all transactions, and this change in its capital creation process creates even more demand for data analytics talent.

KPMG (an audit, tax, and advisory firm) in 2016 took action to increase its supply of incoming data and analytics graduates by working with two US universities to initiate a Masters of Accounting with Data and Analytics. It persuaded the universities to extend their current Masters of Accounting programs to include new courses on data and analytics. In addition, they provided funding to cover tuition and other associated educational expenses for fifty-one selected students. In 2017, it extended the program to another nine US schools, and 135 students entered the program in 2018. While in the program, students work as interns on KPMG audit or tax teams. Successful graduates join KPMG's audit or tax practices through an advanced entry program upon graduation.[13]

When a company's key capital conversion creation process changes, it often needs new human capital skills. KPMG recognized that a major change in auditing, one of its central capital creation processes, required new skills that were in short supply. It took the initiative of convincing universities to also change their capital conversion process, education of accountants in this case, to include more data and analytics education. It invested economic capital in the form of faculty education and student funding to create human capital.

---

[12]http://www.businessinsider.com/google-zurich-headquarters-tour-2018-1/#the-google-campus-in-zurich-is-located-only-a-few-minutes-walk-from-lake-zurich-on-the-grounds-of-an-old-brewery-and-extends-over-four-floors-1.

[13]http://www.kpmgcampus.com/our-opportunities.

As certain forms of human capital become scarcer, we can expect more organizations to pressure the major suppliers, mostly universities, to revise their capital creation systems. KPMG's initiative is likely to be emulated as other organizations recognize that they need to integrate more closely with their human capital supply chain and invest its continuing renewal to meet future needs. Essentially, it engaged with universities to change a system of production (education).

*Engagement → Production*

Today, many of the world's leading enterprises are based on the primacy of human capital in economic capital creation. Indeed, we have a shortage of the highly educated human capital required to manage complex organizations and generate innovations to sustain their competitiveness. As the automotive industry examples illustrate, it took about a century for a shift from economic to human capital dominance, and there is every sign that human capital will remain critical for the creation of economic capital for the foreseeable future. Many organizations might need to follow the KPMG model by investing in new supply chain relationships to ensure they have the needed human capital with the right skills.

## 9.4  Human → Human

In the beginning of this chapter, the roles of mass education and health care were discussed. These are both primarily systems dependent on human capital creating higher quality human capital. They rely on teachers and medical practitioners to educate and cure, respectively. Not surprisingly and appropriately, they are large components of an advanced economy's public and private expenditures.

The cumulative effect of capital creation is very evident with human capital. The well-educated, both countries and individuals, earn more and can thus invest more in their citizens' or children's education. Furthermore, education can open doors for economic migrants because many countries seek their talent. Intellectual migration results in many people with an undergraduate degrees moving to advanced economies for graduate education and staying. For example, in my academic department we have scholars originally from Australia, Cyprus, Canada, China, India, Iran, Sierra Leone, Syria, and the United States. All completed their Ph.D.s in North America.

Universities have long dominated the conversion of human to human capital through their roles of education and research. They recruit students at various levels, such as high school leavers, and require them to complete a set of prescribed educational activities to gain a degree. They also recruit faculty, usually at the assistant professor level, and provide the resources to participate in their fields' system of inquiry to generate knowledge. While the journal and conference systems result in the dissemination of created knowledge, the greatest beneficiary is perhaps the researcher. Decades of immersion in a specific topic or problem creates a deep understanding and level of tacit knowledge. Leading universities seek to nurture faculty that can authoritatively speak on their domain.

Given the high current demand for high quality human capital, many organizations have created internal knowledge creation activities to raise the skill of their human capital. Some operate their equivalent of a university. Steve Jobs established Apple University in 2008.[14] Some enterprises recognize that educating the customers is important. For example, Philips has an online Lighting University, where you can "Learn about lighting from experts."

On the health care side, societies create programs and infrastructures for reducing and curing illness. Thus, mass immunization of children prevents many diseases and has eradicated some. Yearly flu shots can reduce infection rates and lost work hours. The cost of the 2017–2018 flu season is estimated to have been USD 9.42 billion in terms of lost productivity for US industry. In the second week of January 2018, some 6% of all US doctor visits were a result of the flu virus.[15] Immunization and policies that encourage people to stay home when they have the flu are effective in reducing the economic impact. For example, when a flu virus is particularly active, it might make sense for an organization to modify its sick-leave policy so those infected stay home and don't spread the virus to other workers and exacerbate the loss in productivity.

There is also a need for an effective curative system that ensures ill people receive effective treatment that enables them to recover and resume their prior activities. Governments accept this mandate, but to varying degrees. For instance, the US prides itself on its entrepreneurial spirit, but does little to enable start-ups to provide health insurance for their employees. One report indicates that only 28% of US companies with less than 10 employees offer health insurance.[16] This is a drag on mobility for those who need the security of health insurance (e.g., those with young family members). When national $C'$ is dependent on a vibrant startup community, then it is appropriate to have national policies, such as health insurance affordability, that don't limit the movement of talent.

In both the case of adjusting sick leave policy during flu season and establishing health insurance polices for startups, we see a failure of systems thinking. An exploration of the consequences of a lack of action is often missing, and the result is a possible drop in $C'$. A collection of individual independent actions is not always in the interests of an organization or society. On the surface, the policies suggested might be written off by some as nanny-statism or the creation of entitlements, but if you accept that the ultimate goal is to enhance $C'$, then they are eminently sensible.

---

[14]https://www.bloomberg.com/news/articles/2014-02-13/why-apple-university-matters-more-than-ever.
[15]https://www.cbsnews.com/news/flu-season-gets-worse-costs-are-climbing/.
[16]https://www.goco.io/blog/the-secret-weapon-startups-can-use-to-attract-talent/.

**Georgia State University**

Georgia State University's main campus is in downtown Atlanta. Its student body of around fifty thousand is 60% low income and 60% minority. Many are the first in their families to attend a university. Every evening, the university updates grades and reviews eight hundred risk factors for each student. Using this system of record, a predictive analytics package identifies struggling students and alerts their advisers. Based on these alerts, Georgia State advisers held fifty-two thousand meetings with at-risk students during the 2016–2017 academic year. These meetings can direct students to campus tutoring centers, instructors for remedial help, and other academic support services. In 2017 compared to five years earlier, Georgia State graduated two thousand students more per year, and the number of degrees awarded was up 30% during a period when enrollment growth was 5%. Georgia State has demonstrated how a system of inquiry, predictive analytics, can raise significantly the conversion rate of human to human capital.[17]

*Record → Inquiry (analytics) → Engagement (advising) → Production (learning support)*

## 9.5  Organizational → Human

Decision-making, or preparing for the future, is the central activity of modern organizations. Organizations are busy turning out goods, services, and decisions. While increasingly decisions are made by machines, which we will discuss in the section on converting human to organizational capital, there are still a host of problems that require humans to take a decision and follow up with action. Thus enterprises need to consider how they can use their capital to improve decision-making. Organizational capital, because it includes databases, software, and routines, can leverage human $C'$.

Often the terms *data* and *information* are used interchangeably, but they are distinctly different. Data are raw, unsummarized, and unanalyzed facts. Information is data that have been processed into a meaningful form. Many organizations now have a single database, often called a *data warehouse*, that integrates and relates data from separate databases. The value of a database for decision-making is dependent on how well it reflects the fidelity of the environment in which its host organization operates. Missing essential data and missing and incorrect relationships between database tables reduce fidelity and the ability to extract information to support decision-making.

---

[17]https://www.insidehighered.com/digital-learning/article/2017/07/19/georgia-state-improves-student-outcomes-data.

Associated with a database, is query language, usually SQL, that lets analysts customize the processing of data so that they can create information appropriate to their client's current problem.

Knowledge is the capacity to use information. The education and experience that managers accumulate provide them with the expertise to make sense of the information they receive. Knowledge means that managers can interpret information and use it in decision-making. In addition, knowledge is the capacity to recognize what information would be useful for making decisions. For example, a sales manager knows that requesting a report of profitability by product line is useful when she has to decide whether to employ a new product manager.

The relationship between data, information, and knowledge is depicted in Fig. 9.1. A knowledgeable person requests information to support decision-making. To fulfill the request, data are converted into information. Personal knowledge, expertise, and judgment are then applied to interpret the requested information and reach a conclusion. The cycle can be repeated several times if more information is needed before a decision can be made. Notice how knowledge is essential for grasping what information to request and interpreting that information in terms of the required decision. An organization's databases and software are the foundations for creating information to support decision-making. Unfortunately, many organizations are data rich and information poor, because they have not invested in the human capital and routines required to exploit their data.

Decision-making can be improved by applying a systematic set of routines to problem solving. For example, a standard approach to group problem solving might be

- Define the problem.
- Define the characteristics of a good solution to the problem.
- Generate alternative solutions.
- Evaluate the alternatives based on their fit to desirable characteristics.
- Select an alternative.

From my experience, group problem solving is often unstructured. In some cases, each person is solving a different problem or applying different criteria because these topics have not been explicitly surfaced and a consensus has not been reached about them.

A study by Bain & Company[18] reports the executives are attending more meetings because information technology, such as videoconferencing, has lowered the cost of organizing and attending. On average, senior executives are spending more than two days every week in group meetings. Also, 15% of an organization's human capital is tied up in meetings, and this percentage has increased consistently since 2008. Enterprises need to create organizational capital that eliminates meetings, reduces the time of necessary meetings, and applies structure and routine to group decision-making to make it more effective.

---

[18]Mankins, M., Brahm, C., & Caimi, G. (2014). Your scarcest resource. *Harvard Business Review*, 92(5), 74–80, 133.

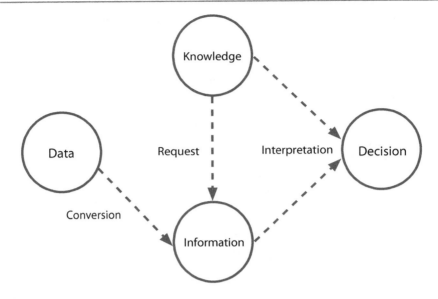

**Fig. 9.1** The relationship between data, information, and knowledge

**Woodside Petroleum**

Woodside, an Australian oil and gas company, had operated as a matrix structure for a number of years. However, decision rights and accountability were poorly defined, and the potential collaborative gains of a matrix format were not fully realized. The time spent meeting to coordinate across functions and business units was an increasing cost, without sufficient discernible benefits.

In 2012, Woodside established operating principles (organizational capital) that explicitly assigned responsibilities, authority, and accountability to business units, functions, and corporate headquarters. An associated training program for senior executives on the new principles ensured these new organizational routines were clearly understood and that Woodside's key decision makers recognized the implications for their business units.

Clearly establishing decision rights and accountability for critical decisions accelerates decision-making and reduces the need for meetings. Human capital gains a productivity jump, because personnel have more time to spend on execution and seeking business opportunities.[19]

*Framing (decision rights) → Engagement*

---

[19]Mankins, M., Brahm, C., & Caimi, G. (2014). Your scarcest resource. *Harvard Business Review, 92*(5), 74–80, 133.

Routines should be designed to improve the productivity of human capital. If they became red tape, then they should be redesigned or eliminated to become green tape that supports human C'. Establishing governance structures and architectures for decision-making are elements of a system of framing because they set forth how human capital is engaged in decision-making. This system of framing needs to be complemented by databases and software that can provide the information required for the decisions that will need to be made. A key purpose of organizational capital investment is to enable individuals to achieve the goals the organization has set them.

## 9.6 Natural → Human

Natural capital, mainly in the form of trees and forests, impacts human health by improving air quality, supporting the growth of medicinal plants, and providing a place for recreation. Beyond trees and forests, natural capital includes mountains, rivers, coastlines, marshes, and grasslands. Natural capital might be thought of as the relatively undisturbed natural environment that has a minimal build environment. Of course, such settings usually include roads, trails, and huts for hikers. However, urban parks and botanical gardens, while more developed, are often more accessible and can also generate health benefits.[20]

The World Health Organization maintains that "health is a state of complete physical, mental and social well-being and not merely the absence of disease or infirmity."[21] Natural capital raises the quality of human capital when it enhances the physical, mental, and social well-being of people. Often, these three goals can be achieved by a single outdoor activity. An energetic mountain hike with a group of friends provides exercise, relieves stress, and reinforces social connections.

The notion that natural settings have restorative effects has been established for some centuries. From the 1600s onward, wealthy Europeans have visited spas to relax and recover from illness. Spas continue to be marketed for their health outcomes, as a web search will reveal. Olmsted, the renowned landscape architect, promoted the healthiness of nature in his books. He was a strong proponent for the creation of national parks.[22]

While in past times people sensed the regenerative effects of nature, in recent times, scientists have reported desirable changes in emotional and physiological states after people have viewed simulated natural and urban environments. After spending forty minutes in a nature reserve compared to a city center or passive relaxation, students exhibited better performance on an attention task (e.g., proofreading). Other studies report a positive association between exposure to nature and health and well-being, including recovery from surgery, treatment for breast cancer, clinical depression, and stress. Furthermore, people have learned that walking in a natural setting is likely to be

---

[20]This section draws heavily on Hartig, T., van den Berg, A. E., Hagerhall, C. M., Tomalak, M., Bauer, N., Hansmann, R.,… van Herzele, A. (2011). Health benefits of nature experience: Psychological, social and cultural processes. In *Forests, Trees and Human Health*, pp. 127–168. Springer.
[21]https://www.who.int/about/mission/en/.
[22]He codesigned New York's Central Park.

revitalizing.[23] Urban dwellers with access to green spaces have less psychological problems than those who don't, and converting vacant lots to green spaces can reduce their depression.[24] Additionally, a city dweller visiting a natural environment is likely to immediately lower his levels of stress hormones.[25]

Walking on a trail compared to a paved footpath is more cognitively engaging. The brain has to look ahead for obstacles, such as tree roots and holes, and continually adjust a person's balance because of surface variations. Hiking on an irregular surface is cognitively intense.[26] Undistracted hiking can also enhance creative problem solving.[27] Walking in a natural setting exercises mind and body.

**Outward Bound**

Outward Bound is based on the principle that learning to live outdoors through an expedition and the development of athletic skills build and develop character, an aspect of human capital. The belief is well-established, and Plato declaimed that outdoor activities developed healthy bodies and souls. Some seventy years after its origins in Scotland in the 1930s, there are now Outward Bound schools in more than thirty countries. It is no longer solely wilderness-focused, and some classes occur in urban settings.[28]

Outward Bound New Zealand, for example, offers a twenty-one-day expedition for sixteen- to eighteen-year-olds. Its description of the course indicates participants will develop a sense of independence and a positive mind-set. Its eight-day course for those forty years old and up is about re-energizing and reassessing priorities. Some aspects of human capital development in a natural setting is the common theme of the description of its approximately twenty courses.

A careful study of the results of multiple investigations of the longer versions of adventure programs (twenty to twenty-six days), such as those offered by Outward Bound, finds consistent evidence of positive effects for self-control, responsibility, and self-assurance. Importantly, these notable effects are found to be persistent. It is important to recognize that there is variability in the outcomes, as not all programs have equal effects.[29]

*Engagement → Framing (character)*

---

[23]Reported in Hartig, T., et al. (2011). Health benefits of nature experience: Psychological, social and cultural processes. In *Forests, Trees and Human Health*. Springer.
[24]https://www.npr.org/sections/health-shots/2018/07/20/630615148/replacing-vacant-lots-with-green-spaces-can-ease-depression-in-urban-communities.
[25]https://well.blogs.nytimes.com/2015/07/22/how-nature-changes-the-brain/?mcubz=0&_r=0.
[26]http://mxplx.com/meme/2622/.
[27]Atchley, R. A., Strayer, D. L., & Atchley, P. (2012). Creativity in the wild: Improving creative reasoning through immersion in natural settings. *PloS one, 7*(12), e51474.
[28]https://www.outwardbound.net.
[29]Hattie, J., Marsh, H. W., Neill, J. T., & Richards, G. E. (1997). Adventure education and Outward Bound: Out-of-class experiences that make a lasting difference. *Review of Educational Research, 67*(1), 43–87.

## 9.7 Social → Human

Poverty not only limits access to education and health care; it also reduces access to social networks that can help grow human capital. The poor, with limited connections to mainstream society, are unable to take partake fully in their local, let alone global, economy. Social connections can expose people to opportunities to enhance their human capital. Some private universities have admission procedures that favor the children of their alumni. While public universities usually operate highly equitable admission procedures, intelligent and suitable applicants might not consider applying if they come from marginalized communities with few university graduates to serve as aspirational role models.

A university's alumni are a key component of its social capital, and many use their alumni relations to help their students find their first job, which is a critical stage to consolidating and extending a university education. Opportunities to apply and acquire skills, knowledge, and expertise build human capital, especially in the knowledge economy, and are essential for personal and societal human capital accumulation. Your network, or someone else's, can often be a more fruitful path to a new job than responding to an advertisement.

Social capital can help a person find their ideal job, one that engages their passion and motivates mastery. For example, a former student in my Energy Informatics course wanted to apply information systems to create sustainable enterprises. Soon after starting her initial job in a top tech company, she connected with its sustainability leadership and made them aware of her goal. Within eighteen months she had been relocated to corporate headquarters to work as an energy analyst. Open organizations that encourage communication across all levels, from new recruits to the C-level, facilitate the creation of social capital that helps effectively match organizational needs to human capital.

> **EY**
>
> In an advanced economy, the major medical threat is no longer contagious diseases. Rather, it is mental health, and social capital has the potential to improve mental and physical health and well-being.[30]
>
> With its headquarters in London, EY, formerly known as Ernst & Young, is a global organization of around 230,000 people delivering professional services to a range of clients. Many of its assignments require teams of professionals, and its success is highly dependent on the effective performance of each team member. In October 2016, it launched "r u ok?" for its 45,000 US employees following a CEO summit on mental health in the

---

[30]Marmot, M. (2010). *Social Capital, Human Capital and Health. What Is the Evidence?* OECD IRDES, Centre for Educational Research and Innovation.

workplace in New York in October 2015.[31] It is part of a broader forty-year-long employee assistance program to support its partners and staff to handle their professional and personal life. The program creates social capital by building a culture of caring.

The r u ok? program relies on training employees to

- Notice signs of change in a co-worker indicating they might need help.
- Ask them "r u ok?" as a one-to-one conversation starter to see if the person wants to discuss an important matter.
- Listen to learn and gain an understanding of the situation.
- Act to remedy the matter by involving appropriate EY personnel or firm leadership.

Note that the program relies on social connections, coworkers, and a key phrase which everyone has been trained to recognize to initiate possible action. Having a cue phrase that everyone understands is part of the firm's social capital because it can help connect people at a critical moment. A coworker's engagement is the first step toward engaging a health professional to help deal with a personal issue.

Engagement (coworker) → Engagement (health professional)

## 9.8  Symbolic → Human

For those seeking to add some glitter to their resumes, some organizations are magnets because of their reputation and name recognition. Think of McKinsey & Co for a management consultant, Rio Tinto for a mining engineer, LMVH for a luxury brand manager, or the Royal Concertgebouw for a musician. Consequently, these organizations can attract top talent who seek the opportunity to work with some of the best human capital in their field.

### Apple's Design Studio

If you an industrial designer, working in the studio headed by Sir Jonathan Ive would be a career highlight. Apple does not need to advertise openings; rather it employs three recruiters whose sole task is to pinpoint designers to join the studio. Perhaps one new recruit is identified each year. In an interview

---

[31]http://workplacementalhealth.org/News-Events/News-Listing/R-U-OK-A-Meaningful-Question and http://players.brightcove.net/1066292269001/V1CXro3Ce_default/index.html?videoId=5430689648001.

in 2015, Ive commented that in fifteen years only two designers had left the studio–one because of illness. At that stage, Apple had a core team of nineteen industrial designers. Design at Apple involves twelve-hour days, and team members can't discuss their work with friends.

Bono, a friend of Ive's, commented, "To watch him with his workmates in the holy of holies, Apple's design lab, or on a night out is to observe a very rare esprit de corps. They love their boss, and he loves them. What the competitors don't seem to understand is you cannot get people this smart to work this hard just for money."[32]

Apple's design studio is a symbolic capital double play—Apple and Ive. It can entice the most accomplished industrial designers in the world because the opportunity to work with Ive in Apple's design studio is rare and unparalleled. They become exceptionally engaged in applying their human capital to operate a system of inquiry for creating iconic hardware and software.

*Engagement → Inquiry*

Not every company or person sits at the top of the pyramid in its domain, but organizations can do much to make themselves a recognized desirable places to work, a form of symbolic capital, to attract the talent they need to raise C'. The symbolism associated with a well-known brand certainly gives it an advantage, but every organization can develop a message for explaining why it is a great place to work and which it complements with a set of attractive benefits. In the battle for the best possible human capital, symbolic capital can play a key role.

## 9.9 Summary

Human capital is a critical resource for many organizations, and many leaders acknowledge that talent can be a winning resource in today's world.[33] For example, Sandy Ogg, while an operating partner at the Blackstone Group, began studying the relationship between human capital and success. He found that 80% of talent-centric portfolio companies hit all their first-year targets and achieved 2.5 times the return on initial investment. The 22 most successful portfolio companies out of the 180 he evaluated managed their human capital assignments by matching critical leadership roles to the value they needed to generate.[34]

---

[32]https://www.newyorker.com/magazine/2015/02/23/shape-things-come.

[33]Charam, R., Barton, D., & Carey, D. (2018). *Talent Wins*. Harvard Business Review Press.

[34]https://www.mckinsey.com/business-functions/organization/our-insights/linking-talent-to-value?
cid=winningtalent-eml-alt-mkq-mck-oth-1804&hlkid=3d7311f398c9479bb4b688f6e3fbfd25&hctky=
1443659&hdpid=b713dac9-a1c5-40c4-b544-2e2b3ffc1f3b.

To ensure success, the allocation of people to projects is just as critical as the allocation of financial resources. Humans manage capital, design, and oversee the execution of capital conversion processes and measure their success. Most importantly, human talent is necessary to critically assess the results of systems of inquiry and determine when a system of framing needs refining or even a massive revision. Maintaining organizational effectiveness in a global and changing world requires human capital that can recognize when a new course is required and chart its implementation.

# Organizational Capital

Organizational capital refers to the wide collection of resources that some label as intellectual capital. It is the knowledge, software, and methods that a firm can deploy to convert capital. It can be organized into databases, applications, procedures, and patents. It is also closely associated with human capital expertise and experience, and it can be embedded in an organization's culture and structure. In the twenty-first century, organizational capital has become increasingly important for raising C′.

The two major categories of knowledge are explicit and tacit. Explicit knowledge can be codified and transferred to many through books, online courses, and videos. Explicit knowledge builds know-what and know-how capabilities. For example, I know that a word processor is suitable for document preparation and know how to use its common commands. I can consult online help to learn how to complete less common tasks, such as indexing a book.

Tacit knowledge tends to reveal itself in a context and through a bilateral or multilateral system of engagement. Tacit knowledge is enduring capital because it can take time to build and requires continuing exposure to a wide variety of problems so you can learn general patterns or recall a past experience and how it was resolved. Companies that rotate their future leaders through multiple positions in different organizational settings build both organizational capital in the form of tacit knowledge and social capital by growing their personal connectivity.

At another level, organizational capital is the structure an enterprise has designed to successfully create capital using the five basic systems. It is the dynamic glue that enables systems to create capital, and the choice of an appropriate structure is an open question in a competitive environment. A fixed organizational chart with well-defined lines of communication once seemed like an effective plan. However, as former champion boxer Mike Tyson said, "Everybody has a plan until they get

R. T. Watson, *Capital, Systems, and Objects*, Management for Professionals, https://doi.org/10.1007/978-981-15-9418-2_10

punched in the mouth."[1] In a competitive environment, an organization is constantly punched all over its corporate body by a variety of assailants. It needs to find the economic structure most able to absorb these competitive jabs and respond.

The economy is a mix of economic structures. In addition to public companies, we see start-ups funded by angel investors, venture capital, crowdsourcing, and private equity firms that have decided that capital creation is more effective when subject to less scrutiny. In some countries, state-run enterprises are major economic actors. For a country, these are all forms of organizational capital. Other include its legal system, which defines permissible structures and how they are regulated. A free market economy fosters organizational structural innovation, and its legal system, part of the national organizational capital, continually adapts to support new forms of organizing.

Some political systems are ideologically constrained and limit organizational forms. For example, the Soviet Union essentially banned any scaling of small private enterprises in favor of massive public enterprises. Today, Russian private enterprises are still heavily state controlled, though it seems more likely by private fiat than the legal system.

The problem of adaption has not disappeared, and in recent years the ecosystem, a collection of firms, has shown to be more adaptive than some traditional structures.

## 10.1  Economic → Organizational

Economic capital, mainly its financial form, frequently provides the wherewithal to create other forms of capital. The conversion of economic capital to the different forms of organizational capital requires a variety of capital conversion capabilities. Digitization is the most recent major innovation, and it has been proceeding for roughly half a century. More recently, though, the intensity of the conversion has accelerated. Software and databases have become the major repositories of institutionalized knowledge and codified experience. Machine learning can capture some forms of organizational knowledge and make it generally available. Routines are embedded in transaction processing systems. Manuals are now PDF or ePub files that can be read on a range of devices. For example, tablet equipped employees can consult product manuals and take orders at a client's location. Videoconferencing and teamwork support software enable distributed and dynamic work structures.

[1]http://articles.sun-sentinel.com/2012-11-09/sports/sfl-mike-tyson-explains-one-of-his-most-famous-quotes-20121109_1_mike-tyson-undisputed-truth-famous-quotes.

With respect to digitization, there are two major conversion challenges. First, organizations need to advance digitization at least to the point of industry competitiveness and ideally move beyond it. Second, they need to ensure that the result of digitization is an integrated and responsive system that results in higher levels of efficiency and effectiveness. Efficiency comes from corporate uniformity in housekeeping routines such as payroll, accounting and email. One system or external service should be able to meet the needs of the enterprise. For example, there are payroll services that can meet the needs of a globally distributed workforce and handle all local requirements. Effectiveness comes from localizing customer facing systems to account for the culture, language, and idiosyncrasies for some customers and markets. Agility and local differentiation is often required for systems of engagement, such as sales, systems of framing, such as marketing, and systems of production.

### Lifebuoy Soap

In many developing economies, regular handwashing, especially after going to the toilet, is not an established practice. Diarrhea is a common problem among poor people in many of these economies, and there is considerable evidence that handwashing with soap reduces its incidence. Unilever recognized that if it could change handwashing behavior in less develop economies, it would improve human capital and increase sales of its soaps.

Unilever set out to change the handwashing behavior of one billion consumers across Asia, Africa, and Latin America. If successful, it could prevent 600,000 child deaths annually and swell sales of Lifebuoy, its popular antibacterial soap that is sold in nearly sixty countries. To increase its reach, in addition to offering a 125 g bar, it also offered more affordable 60 g and 30 g sizes in some markets The manufacturing process was also altered to create a milled bar, which lasts longer.

The project required the creation of several forms of organizational capital. There was an investment in routines and structures for a handwashing education program that could be scaled to reach hundreds of millions. Similarly, Unilever needed to develop routines and structures for marketing and distributing soap in a large number of villages, where some of the poorest live.

The most important change for Unilever was to frame the lack of handwashing by the poor as a problem it could address. Until this frame was surfaced as an opportunity to create social, symbolic, and economic capital, there could be no concerted action. Once the frame was established, Unilever had to create two systems of engagement: one for education and one for sales.

*Framing  (handwashing  reduces  disease) → Engagement  (education) → Engagement (sales)*

## 10.2  Human → Organizational

The introduction of digital data processing has seen a massive conversion of human to organizational capital. Human tasks have been converted to software. Prior to the development of digital computers, NASA employed computers, the term in the 1940–50 s for people, mainly women, who did calculations using manual calculators. In organizations, clerks computed payroll, invoices, and maintained ledgers, among other tasks requiring computations. Increasingly, human capital has been converted to organizational capital, and many now see both opportunities and threats in the use of AI and machine learning as they further this conversion.

Manual tasks have also been converted to organizational capital. Robots have taken over blue collar factory jobs. Medical robots can have a major impact, including a 70% drop in hospital acquired infections with the Xenex Robot.[2] The da Vinci Surgical System enables surgeons to operate with enhanced vision, precision, and control, and the Veebot draws blood in less than a minute.

Autonomous cars are already navigating some streets, and car manufacturers are massively investing in software, organizational capital, to enable safer driving by eliminating the driver. A systems analysis of this transition reveals many consequences. Speeding fines will virtually disappear as a source of revenue, driving schools will no longer be required, organ transplant programs will have a much diminished supply, crash repairers will be looking for jobs, and so forth.

Software captures human capital capabilities and makes them massively reproducible at minimal cost. While we need human capital to create software, the number of required programmers is small relative to those previously employed as clerks, assembly line workers, or taxi drivers, for instance. Converting human to organizational capital has been a $C'$ elevator for half a century.

---

[2]https://api.medicalfuturist.com/9-exciting-medical-robot-facts/.

**Robots Learning by Watching Humans**

While assembling some Lego models with his son, a German robotics professor, David Vogt, gave himself a challenge. Could he teach a robot to put Legos together? Vogt and his colleagues equipped an industrial robot with a Kinect depth camera. Two experienced human Lego builders were fitted with motion tracking tags so the robot could observe their actions as they built a rocket from Legos. After only one observational session, the robot was able to partner with a human and erect a rocket.

Vogt and his colleagues propose that robots that learn from human observation will be more able to assist humans in skilled assembly work and ensure that a worker has the right tool or piece at hand as they assemble a complex product. He observes, "Ideally, humans and robots together should be able to do something that, individually or separately, they wouldn't have been able to do alone."[3]

In early 2018, the Tesla car factory was plagued by slow productivity and quality issues. Its Fremont plant has been described by employees as chaotic. Nimble innovation and extensive robotic automation are not the right mix for mass car production. The major automakers have learned, through experience, that a complementing mix of humans and robots is currently the most efficient car-assembly process.[4]

Trying to convert all human capital into organizational capital is likely to be a time-consuming and expensive process. Rather, teaching robots to do the simple and tedious and letting humans undertake the intricate and irregular is likely to be more successful.

Teaching a robot through observation is a system of engagement that replicates the gesturing of early systems of engagement. Early systems of production, such as flint making, likely used learning by observation with some guidance of movements. Engaging with a robot to teach it a skill can result in a system of production.

*Engagement → Production*

## 10.3   Organizational → Organizational

An organization must continually reinvent itself in order to remain relevant and ensure that its C′ is competitive. Since organizational capital is a dynamic glue, an organization should endeavor to use its organizational capital to create higher

[3]https://www.newscientist.com/article/mg23230973-600-robot-learns-to-play-with-lego-by-watching-human-teachers/.
[4]https://www.economist.com/news/business/21739981-road-ahead-elon-musks-car-company-looking-more-perilous-tesla-heading-cash.

quality organizational capital. Organizational structural reinvention and knowledge generation are likely the two most critical areas for organizational capital creation in most organizations.

The knowledge component of organizational capital can be self-renewing if appropriately funded and managed. Knowledge builds upon knowledge, as illustrated by Bell Labs, which for many years in the' twentieth century was the world's premier research facility. It produced eight Nobel Prize winners and breakthroughs in the areas of radio astronomy, lasers, transistors, and information theory. The Unix operating system and C and C++ programming languages are products of Bell Labs. The fundamental model was to identify an important and challenging problem, explore potential solutions, and develop a massively scalable product.[5] The same approach is taken today by those inspired by Bell Labs, and we see various forms of emulation in Silicon Valley, such as Alphabet Inc., "which is a holding company that gives ambitious projects the resources, freedom, and focus to make their ideas happen."[6] The focus has changed, however, and scientists are now embedded in product teams to emphasize generating profitable products (economic capital) rather than knowledge (organizational capital) that might eventually produce products. Also, the great labs of AT&T, IBM, and Xerox thrived when their parents were monopolies, and they were given some slack because society benefited from their basic scientific research.[7]

The ultimate goal of knowledge creation through systems of inquiry is to raise national and organizational $C'$. A nation has to decide to what extent it leaves knowledge creation to the private sector and the chance that basic science is shortchanged and long-term $C'$ is jeopardized. An organization faces the same balancing act of deciding between basic and applied research.

---

**3M and a Tale of Two Systems**

3M is an American multinational based in St. Paul, Minnesota. In 2016, it had forty- six technology platforms, USD 30 billion in annual sales, employed ninety thousand people worldwide, and made more than fifty-five thousand products.

In 2001, James McNerney was appointed as the first outsider CEO at 3M. He left GE for 3M when Jeff Immelt was appointed to succeed Jack Welch as chairman and CEO. From 2001 to 2005, McNerney was 3M's chairman of the board and CEO. When McNerney left abruptly to become Boeing's CEO, he was replaced by George Buckley, former chairman and CEO of Brunswick Corporation, the owner of several popular boating brands.

---

[5]Gertner, J. (2012). *The Idea Factory: Bell Labs and the Great Age of American Innovation.* Penguin.
[6]https://www.google.se/search?client=safari&rls=en&q=alphabet+inc&ie=UTF-8&oe=UTF-8&gfe_rd=cr&dcr=0&ei=RtuTWrXMI4exX-_apLAP.
[7]http://www.economist.com/node/8769863.

**Table 10.1** Comparison of two 3M CEOs

| McNerney | Buckley |
|---|---|
| Increase profitability | Bring back creativity and maintain operating efficiency |
| Corporate wide adoption of Six Sigma | Reduce Six Sigma use in research labs, but keep it in manufacturing |
| Hold R&D spending constant and allocate funds to promising new markets, such a pharmaceuticals | Boost R&D spending, and refocus on 'core' research and move away from ancillary markets such as pharmaceuticals |
| Instill the GE approach to management | Reignite innovation and encourage risk taking |

The contrasting missions and actions of the two leaders are captured in the following Table 10.1.[8]

3M had traditionally been a science company, a term it uses to describe itself on its website, with consequently a focus on systems of inquiry across a wide range of technologies. McNerney's background in manufacturing at GE and his implementation of the 3M Board's charge to improve profitability resulted in a shift of attention to systems of production, Six Sigma, and efficiency. Buckley swung the pendulum back to systems of inquiry and creativity.

Ultimately, every company must create economic capital, and the traditional path for 3M was

*Organizational* → *Organizational* → *Economic*

3M used knowledge to create more knowledge, which was then converted by engineers into marketable products.

McNerney's actions pushed the template to

*Organizational* → *Economic*

This can be a successful short-term strategy, but as organizational capital ages, engineers have less knowledge to convert into products. At the same time, it is important to recognize that applying the same managerial methodologies, such as Six Sigma, to *Organizational* → *Organizational* and *Organizational* → *Economic* can fail to recognize the fundamental differences between creativity and efficiency. Manufacturing at 3M most probably benefited from Six Sigma and greater attention to costs, but R&D likely suffered.

---

[8]http://integralleadershipreview.com/6176-the-role-of-values-in-leadership-how-leaders-values-shape-value-creation/ and https://www.bloomberg.com/news/articles/2007-06-10/at-3m-a-struggle-between-efficiency-and-creativity

The 3M case illustrates the tension that leaders increasingly face in a knowledge economy. They run a two-sided business, and each side needs to be run differently. One creates knowledge, and the other consumes it to make products. One is about systems of inquiry and the other about systems of production. If the board can't manage a two-sided business, then it should consider creating a partnership or ecosystem for one of the sides. Apple, for example, relies on third parties for many of its system of production.

## 10.4  Natural → Organizational

Organizational capital includes intellectual resources, such as patents and formulas. Medical drugs are among those things that can be patented and thus provide a potential protected source of revenue for some years. Pharmaceutical companies have realized that nature can be a beneficial source of new medical treatments. Millions of years of evolution have resulted in chemical compounds with diverse properties. For example, some animals and plants produce toxins, which enhance their ecological fitness. These toxins might have other applications. For instance, in the 1970s compactin and mevinolin were discovered to inhibit the biosynthesis of cholesterol. They became the foundation of statin therapeutics, a successful medical treatment and pharmaceutical business.

Nature has solved a variety of problems, and biomimicry is aimed at using its solutions to inspire innovation. As Michael Pawlyn observed, "You could look at nature as being like a catalog of products, and all of those have benefited from a 3.8 billion year research and development period. And given that level of investment, it makes sense to use it."[9] Some examples illustrate how natural capital can be turned into useful knowledge.

The flippers of humpback whales have large irregular bumps, tubercles, across their leading edges. Wind tunnel analysis of a model of their fins shows that tubercles improve the flow of air, and can give an 8% improvement in lift and 32% reduction in drag. This discovery has applicability for the design of wind turbines, airplanes, and fans.

Knowledge gained from analyzing natural products and observing animal behavior contributes to an enterprise and society's organizational knowledge. Some might ultimately be converted to economic capital, but there is an interim stage when natural capital is converted to organizational capital by scientists and engineers.

---

[9]https://biomimicry.org/what-is-biomimicry/.

**Shinkansen Bullet Train**

Japan's Shinkansen bullet train can reach speeds of 320 km/hour ( $\sim$ 200 mph), but it has a noise problem. When it emerges from a tunnel, the air pressure change produces a large thunder clap that can be disturbing to residents within several hundred meters.

When diving into water, a kingfisher changes from low drag air to high drag water, and analysis shows that its beak is almost ideal for reducing the impact of the change of medium. The shape of a kingfisher's beak allows water to flow past it rather than being pushed in front of it. Trains face the same challenge when entering a tunnel, as they are moving from low drag open air to high drag confined air.

Eiji Nakatsu, a birdwatching Japanese railway engineer, applied his careful observation of kingfishers to design the front of the Shinkansen Bullet Train so that it now travels more quietly, is 10% faster, and uses 15% less electricity.[10] Nakatsu's inquiring mind led to the understanding that tunnel noise was due to a phase change, and redesigning the front of the train would lessen the noise.

*Inquiry* → *Framing* → *Production*

## 10.5   Social → Organizational

Customers are usually an organization's largest social network, though the strength of their relationship with an organization will vary, but this is no different from any other social network. When consumers feel connected to an organization, they are often willing to share their expertise and contribute knowledge to the organization. We have seen several common forms of this willing sharing fostered as a result of the web.

### 10.5.1   Reviewing Systems

Reviews of products and services prior to the web were typically done by organizations, such as a variety of national consumers' associations funded by subscribers. In addition, word of mouth was an informal and limited source of knowledge among family and friends. When websites started allowing consumers to submit reviews and ask each other questions, they opened up a vast informal knowledge exchange and digitized word of mouth. Customers were able to help customers. The website that can attract the most reviewers or problem solvers has a

---

[10]https://www.greenbiz.com/blog/2012/10/19/how-one-engineers-birdwatching-made-japans-bullet-train-better.

trove of organizational capital and becomes a go-to site for advice. Companies such as TripAdvisor have turned this organizational capital into economic capital by inserting appropriate advertisements among reviews of hotels, restaurants, and so forth.

### 10.5.2  Help Systems

For many coders, Stack Overflow is a valuable forum because coders solve each other's problems. This online community for developers is a knowledge repository. Organizational capital is openly created and shared through Stack Exchange's network of 133 Q&A communities. Stack Overflow, one of its exchanges, serves more than 50 million developers monthly.

### 10.5.3  R&D Systems

Customers use a firm's products every day in a wide variety of circumstances for a range of activities. They discover uses and missing features that even the most creative research lab might never spot. Fortunately, many consumers are willing to freely share this knowledge, and for the organization with an open innovation perspective, their ideas are valued. Traditionally, many new products have been secretively developed in-house, and this might still be appropriate for some items. Many technology companies reveal little about their future products. Open innovation champions such as Henry Chesbrough[11] advocate actively seeking external ideas as a source of inspiration for new products and services. Essentially, they are promoting the development of means for converting social into organizational capital.

Platform businesses, such as Apple, Google, and Microsoft, have found that software developers are a vast R&D lab that can be cultivated to create new products to increase demand for the platform. In addition, the apps created can reveal market needs that the platform architects and developers had not envisaged. This can result in new application programming interfaces (APIs) or new hardware in later releases. A platform's application library should be thought of as organizational capital because it is a resource that reveals the potential of a platform to grow and indicates what features the market values.

---

[11]Chesbrough, H. W. (2006). *Open Innovation: The New Imperative for Creating and Profiting from Technology*. Harvard Business Press.

## 10.5.4 Open Source Software

Programmers have always shared code, but the mass sharing of code did not breakout until the release in 1991 of Linux as an open source operating system. Now open source has a well-established presence in the market place in areas such as data analytics, website management, database management, content management, graphics, cloud computing, and big data management. The Apache Software Foundation lists more than three hundred open source projects.[12] This organizational capital is freely available to all and substantially raises the C' of a start-up because it frees up economic capital to hire human capital to meld a collection of open source software into an innovate product or service.

---

**DeWALT**

DeWALT manufactures high-quality power tools for professionals in the construction, manufacturing, and woodworking industries. A subsidiary of Stanley Black & Decker, DeWALT understands that customers determine the success of a product or service. Consequently, it engages the professionals who use its tools in cocreating new products and services. Before launching a new product, it involves tradespeople in product development from ideation, product testing, and usability, to marketing and packaging. For example, it worked with construction professionals to develop a waterproof and dustproof smartphone that can survive a 2 m (6 ft) drop onto concrete and operate in temperatures ranging from –20 °C to 60 °C (−4°F to 140°F) and be operated while using industrial quality gloves.[13]

The 12,000 member DeWALT Insights Forum enables professional tradesmen and customers to submit ideas for new products. The forum also provides a fast and accurate assessment of how customers will react to a new tool. As a result, DeWALT estimates it has saved over USD 6 million since launching the Insight Forum through reduced research costs.[14]

Cocreation saves costs because consumers are engaged in designing what they want. It is a system of inquiry that provides vital input to the refinement of existing tools and the creation of new products. It helps a company continually adjust its system of framing to match market needs.

*Engagement → Inquiry → Framing*

---

[12]https://projects.apache.org
[13]http://www.bbc.com/news/technology-36082146.
[14]https://www.visioncritical.com/customer-stories/dewalt/.

## 10.6  Symbolic → Organizational

Symbolic capital includes an organization's brand and prestige. For some of those with the highest repute for a specialist expertise, this can be an opportunity to transform symbolic into organizational capital. A field's leaders can often get access to the world's most interesting cases or problems, learn from these, and formally capture the knowledge within their organization.

Harvard Business School is perhaps the most well-known and prestigious of the world's business schools. Harvard's library of case studies on a wide range of organizational problems are familiar to most MBA students. The case method of teaching originated in the 1920s.[15] Today, Harvard sells more than 10 million cases per year, and Harvard faculty write about 350 cases annually. To be featured in a Harvard case is considered by many companies an accolade because cases illustrate important managerial innovations,[16] problems, and issues. Harvard's symbolic position as the leading producer of organizational cases means that companies might seek it out when they have a perplexing managerial situation. Furthermore, the prospect of a Harvard case can get an appointment for a faculty member on many a busy CEO's calendar. The Harvard case library is organizational capital that fuels its MBA and executive education programs and provides source material for managerial and business books written by its faculty.

Founded in 1864, the Mayo Clinic in Rochester, Minnesota, is often ranked as the best hospital in the US. In 2016, 1.3 million people from all 50 US states and 137 countries visited the Mayo.[17] About 80 miles (130 km) from the Minneapolis–St. Paul airport, it is not a convenient location for an ill person, but it has a world-class reputation for the quality of its diagnosis and care. Those with rare diseases or challenging medical situations see Mayo as their best hope, when local or regional hospitals might have fallen short. Thus Mayo has an opportunity to refine its diagnostic and treatment skills by tackling some of the intractable medical problems. Its reputation helps it add to its organizational capital.[18]

---

[15]https://hbx.hbs.edu/blog/post/the-history-of-the-case-study-at-harvard-business-school.
[16]For example, see Applegate, L. M., Griffith, T. L., & Majchrzak, A. (2017). *Hyperloop Transportation Technologies: Building Breakthrough Innovations in Crowd-Powered Ecosystems.* Harvard Business School.
[17]https://www.mayoclinic.org/about-mayo-clinic/facts-statistics.
[18]The Mayo Clinic does many things well that contribute collectively to its success. See Berry, L. L., & Seltman, K. D. (2008). *Management Lessons from the Mayo Clinic*: McGraw-Hill.

**Arup and the Sydney Opera House**

The Sydney Opera House is one of the world's most well-known buildings. It sits in full sail on the expansive Sydney Harbor. In 1957, Danish architect Jørn Utzon won an international competition for his design of Sydney's new opera house, but it was a major challenge to convert Utzon's design into an architectural and engineering masterpiece.

Arup Group International, one of the world's most highly regarded engineering, design, planning, project management and consulting firms, was founded in 1946 by Ove Arup, who was recognized as one the foremost architectural structural engineers of his period. Arup's team had to learn how to design and construct the building's enormous, precast concrete shells—the sails of the Opera House. After four years, including pioneering use of computer technology to calculate the stresses of the design, Ove and his engineers identified a design principle—the shells should fit the chord of a sphere—and a prefabrication approach that would lead to efficient construction.[19]

Arup's reputation as one the world's top engineering firms attracts some of the globe's most challenging engineering problems, and it gets to create solutions and software (organizational capital) that it can apply to solving other complex engineering problems. For example, the software created to design the Opera House shells has general applicability across many architectural settings. Arup creates organizational capital through the strength of its linkage between its system of inquiry to systems of production. It solves engineering problems and builds the solutions.

*Inquiry → Production*

Not every organization has the prestige of Harvard Business School, Mayo Clinic, or Arup. Many will not have the depth of symbolic capital necessary to encounter opportunities, such as being presented with tough problems, that can generate organizational capital. However, I suspect there are organizations that don't fully appreciate that their fine reputation can be a catalyst for organizational capital creation. If your organization fits into this category, conjecture how you might deliberately convert symbolic into organizational capital.

## 10.7  Summary

Since the introduction of computers, human capital has been steadily converted to organizational capital. We have advanced from automating simple low skill routines to applying deep machine learning to high level skills. As a result, software is

---

[19]https://www.arup.com/projects/sydney-opera-house.

now essential to the operation of nearly every organization. Once expertise is codified, it can be scaled at low cost and deployed by many enterprises, as we have seen repeatedly. Digital encoding of data and processes has been the foundation for much of $C'$ over the last half century or so, and there are no signs of its impact lessening. Indeed, digitization, the most recent term for describing this mass conversion, has the attention of many CEOs because it is seen as critical to maintaining a competitive value proposition.

# Natural Capital

Natural capital is the earth's endowment. Some of this bounty is finite, such as the different types of minerals, and some renewable, such as forests. Renewable resources are all powered directly or indirectly by solar energy, and they are a valuable annuity for all life on earth. The term "natural capital" was introduced in 1973 in the book *Small Is Beautiful* by Ernst Schumacher, an economist.[1]

Natural capital includes ecosystem services, the long-term stream of benefits provided by the natural environment. Ecosystem services include wetlands as buffers for flood waters, forests capturing and storing $CO_2$ emissions, dilution of wastes by rivers, trees cleaning the air, and plants detoxifying chemically degraded soil. A 2006 report for New Jersey estimates that value of wetlands at USD 10.6 billion/year and marine ecosystems at USD 5.3 million/year.[2] New Jersey forests provide USD 2.2 billion/year, excluding timber harvesting, because they are part of the water supply, a source of pollen for bees, and provide aesthetic and recreational services. The ecosystem services perspective recognizes that natural capital has value beyond direct exploitation, and the continuing provision of these service and their expansion is capital creation.

The wealth of a nation is often determined by its finite and renewable natural resources and ecosystem services. The early European migrants to the United States were able to exploit natural resources to create wealth based on fishing, trapping, and logging. The plentiful cod of the coast of Massachusetts produced a highly profitable fishing industry that made Boston a major eighteenth century commercial

---

[1]Schumacher, E. F. (1973). Small is beautiful: a study of economics as if people mattered: Random House.
[2]Costanza, R., d'Arge, R., De Groot, R., Farber, S., Grasso, M., Hannon, B.,… Paruelo, J. (1997). The value of the world's ecosystem services and natural capital. *Nature, 387*(6630), 253.

R. T. Watson, *Capital, Systems, and Objects*, Management for Professionals,
https://doi.org/10.1007/978-981-15-9418-2_11

center[3] and initiated a capital creation system that today sees Boston as a global educational and technology hub. The current wealth of many countries in the Middle East is based upon finite fossil fuels, and their challenge is to use this wealth to fashion a capital creation system that survives beyond the time when their oil and gas reserves are depleted or world demand splutters.

Typically, organizations turn natural capital into other forms of capital. Thus, a mining company extracts ore and sells it on a commodities market. Alternatively, the Appalachian Trail Conservancy preserves and manages a hiking path from Maine to Georgia, and creates social capital (working together to maintain the trail) and symbolic capital (hiking the full trail), while maintaining human capital (outdoor exercise). Alternatively, we can create natural capital, which we now consider.

## 11.1   Economic → Natural

Farming and forestry invest economic capital in creating natural capital. They harvest natural capital. These industries fail, however, when they do not sustain the quality of the underlying natural capital, such as the soil, or they are so invasive as to deplete the supply, such as with fishing.

The demise of natural systems through overexploitation has occurred several times in human history. Typically, collapse resulted from the demands that a growing or migrant population placed on natural resources. For example, when the Vikings settled Iceland, they quickly exterminated walrus and sea bird colonies, and within several decades about 80% of the woodland than once covered 25% of the island was cleared.[4] The lack of trees led to severe soil erosion, and vegetation struggled to find a foothold. Loose soil and strong winds combined to create sandstorms that further damaged the land. Today, with little or no vegetation, about 40% of Iceland is a "wet" desert. Rain is plentiful, but vegetation is scarce.[5]

Economic capital is now increasingly becoming a resource for restoring natural capital from a degraded to a bountiful state. Many countries, including Iceland, are investing in afforestation. China, for example, set a target of planting in 2018 enough trees to cover an area the size of Ireland. With forests already covering nearly 22% of China, the goal is to reach 26% by 2035. China had invested over USD 65 billion in new forests in the previous five years.[6] For China, trees are a way

---

[3]Kurlansky, M. (2011). *Cod: A Biography of the Fish that Changed the World*. Vintage Canada.
[4]Diamond, J. M. (2005). *Collapse: How Societies Choose to Fail or Succeed*. Viking.
[5]https://www.nytimes.com/interactive/2017/10/20/climate/iceland-trees-reforestation.html.
[6]https://cleantechnica.com/2018/01/06/huge-china-reforestation-campaign-kicks-high-gear/.

to capture atmospheric carbon and control creeping desertification. Thus the Chinese afforestation project includes creating the "Great Green Wall" by planting billions of trees along a 2,800 mile (4,500 km) strip in northern China to limit the growth of the Gobi desert.[7] China is not alone, and there many national and private afforestation projects. For instance, CarbonFund.org enables individuals and businesses to offset their carbon emissions by contributing to afforestation and other projects investing in natural capital preservation and restoration.

The traditional capital conversion process of investing in economic capital to turn natural capital into economic capital, such as with mining and farming, is increasingly less viable as natural resources are depleted or degraded. We are now in an era where we have to invest in natural capital restoration to sustain or restart the conversion of natural capital to economic capital. This often means rethinking business models or complying with environmental protection regulations. In the case of White Oak Pastures, a fourth-generation US farmer shifted from industrial to organic farming and direct marketing of grass-fed beef and lamb and pastured chicken.[8] Farmers in Western Australia must now obey regulations on the clearing of native vegetation introduced by the state's government in 2014.[9] These new regulations are partly to manage soil degradation prevalent in the state's main agricultural area, where more than 2.5 million acres (1 million hectares) are affected by dryland salinity.[10]

Natural capital investments also extend to areas such as cleaner air, waterways, public parks, and biodiversity so that we reap the health, social, and medical benefits they provide. However, in order to feed the world's increasing population, the bulk of economic capital over the next few generations will likely need to go into creating a sustainable food supply system, protecting natural water resources and forests to control erosion and desertification. We will need to carefully manage natural $C'$ by judicious investments.

---

[7]https://news.nationalgeographic.com/2017/04/china-great-green-wall-gobi-tengger-desertification/.
[8]https://modernfarmer.com/2013/09/white-oaks/.
[9]https://www.der.wa.gov.au/images/documents/your-environment/native-vegetation/Guidelines/Guide_1_-_Exemptions_and_regulations_for_clearing_native_vegetation-1.pdf.
[10]http://www.abc.net.au/news/rural/2017-03-13/wa-salinity-issues-on-the-rise-after-unseasonal-summer-rain/8349042.

## Oconee River Land Trust

The Oconee River runs through my community on its way from the mountains of North Georgia to join the Ocmulgee River, which flows into the Altamaha River on its way to the North Atlantic Ocean. As with many rivers flowing through agricultural areas, it has pollution from fecal coliform bacteria, fertilizer runoff, and sedimentation. Like many rivers, the Oconee is the major source of water for towns along its path, such as Athens, Georgia, who have water treatment plants to filter, disinfect, and chlorinate the water prior to human consumption.

The Oconee River Land Trust,[11] a nonprofit organization, partners with landowners to conserve natural forests and working lands along Georgia's rivers, streams and wetlands. Since 1993, it has encouraged public and private landowners to create conservation easements. In the United States, a conservation easement constrains a landowner's rights in the interests of conservation. It is an agreement between a landowner and land trust or unit of government that preserves ownership subject to the terms of the easement. A conservation easement applies to both present and future owners of the land. An easement reverts all or a portion of economic capital into natural capital. For example, an easement of 127 acres (51 hectares) established in 2017 protects a buffer area around the rivers or streams flowing through the easement, bottom land, and hardwood forests, while the landowners retain rights to continue agricultural activities in certain areas. Since establishment in 1993, the Oconee River Land Trust has preserved 26,000 acres (10,500 hectares) on more than 112 different conservation easements. The US National Conservation Easement Database[12] records 146,236 easements conserving nearly 26 million acres (10.5 million hectares), and it estimates that it covers 60% of all US easements, which in total represent 40 million acres (16 million hectares).

Land trusts partner with land owners to convert land to the production of natural capital.

*Engagement → Production*

---

[11]http://oconeeriverlandtrust.org.
[12]https://www.conservationeasement.us.

## 11.2   Human → Natural

Prior to the industrial revolution, most people lived in rural areas and worked on farms. Human capital was primarily used to support the managed creation of natural capital. Farm workers controlled the growth of domesticated plants and animals, and tried to limit the impact of weeds and wild animals on crops and protect livestock from predators. Routines were very simple and often repeated for long periods or seasonally, such as shepherding or harvesting. Human capital did not need to be literate, and skills were very basic. For centuries, human capital was mainly used to create natural capital that was for self-consumption or converted into economic capital.

**Agroecology in Malawi**

For poor farmers, the use of fertilizers and herbicides imposes costs they cannot afford. As a result, some apply "agroecological" methods, which means adopting practices that mimic nature, such as adding organic material to soil, planting trees on cropped fields, and using natural enemies to attack insect pests. For the last five years, some six thousand Malawi farming families have been learning this new method through the Malawi Farmer to Farmer Agroecology project.

Farmers begin by planting crops that enhance soil fertility, such as peanuts, beans, and pigeon peas. These plants are a source of food, livestock, cash, and fuel. By burying the leaves and branches after harvesting, a crop's residue is turned into a rich source of organic material for the soil.

Agroecology means farmers need additional knowledge on how to grow a wider range of crops. Their farming practices might have to change for some crops. To retain knowledge within a community and to diffuse it across communities, farmers teach farmers. This method of frugal knowledge management ensures that human capital is developed and grown locally and not lost when the agricultural experts leave.[13]

Agroecology can enhance resilience. In 1988, Caribbean hurricane Mitchell caused more than ten thousand deaths and over USD 6.7 billion in damage. Postdisaster research indicates that farmers using agroecological methods before the hurricane had more vegetation, lower soil erosion, and less economic loss.[14]

The transition to agroecology starts with agricultural scientists learning how natural systems operate to sustain soil fertility; they then engage with farmers to transfer knowledge, farmers educate each other (the frugal knowledge management phase of engagement), and finally a new system of production is implemented.

*Inquiry → Engagement      (scientists) → Engagement      (local farmers) → Production*

---

[13]http://soilandfood.org/projects/malawi-farmer-to-farmer-agroecology-project/.
[14]http://theconversation.com/how-low-tech-farming-innovations-can-make-african-farmers-climate-resilient-47684.

## 11.3   Organizational $\rightarrow$ Natural

Environmentalists refer to the three Rs of sustainable society as reduce, reuse, and recycle. The three Rs are about cutting back on the raw materials required for each capital conversion process and thus imposing less demands on the natural environment. They don't create natural capital directly. In the case of renewable natural capital, such as forests and oceans, reducing the impact means that in most cases natural capital will be created because that is how nature works. There are situations, such as desertification, where natural capital will not be restored without human influence. An intact forest continues its cycle of natural capital creation. The indirect effects of the three Rs create more natural capital, and this is what is implied by this section's focus on the conversion of organizational to natural capital. Achievement of the three Rs requires knowledge and procedures, two elements of organizational capital.

**Reduce** is the most effective of the three Rs because it starts at the beginning of product and service creation. An organization needs to apply its current knowledge, or create new knowledge, to design products that require less resources to make, distribute, and retail.

In addition, production methods need to be redesigned to reduce waste. Traditional production methods employ subtractive manufacturing, which starts with more materials than needed and removes them (e.g., grinding or cutting). 3D printing is additive manufacturing, where objects are made layer-by-layer using only the materials needed.

---

**Renault Trucks**

Lighter engines will enable automakers to meet stricter fuel economy and emissions standards, because lighter engines means less weight to be moved and thus lower fuel consumption. For trucking fleets, fuel is usually the highest operational cost.

Renault Trucks' engineers and designers are working on an additive manufacturing process to reduce weight and boost engine performance. They have designed a prototype engine exclusively using 3D printing that reduces the weight of a four-cylinder engine by 120 kg or 25%, and also the number of components by 25%, for a total of two hundred fewer parts.

*Inquiry $\rightarrow$ Production*

---

On the distribution side, products and their packaging can be designed to reduce shipping costs. Changes might be as simple as increasing the number of items that can be placed on a pallet. In the case of a T-shirt manufacturer, using software for optimizing and packaging and pallet layout resulted in 44% less pallets.[15]

---

[15]https://www.esko.com/en/solutions/packaging-management/palletizing.

The goal of **reuse** and **recycling** is to find another purpose for a waste product that might otherwise be discarded or end up in a landfill. At times, the distinction between these terms can be fuzzy. We treat them as very similar ideas because the ultimate goal, to extend the time before a product ends up in the waste stream, is the same. Reuse or recycling of industrial waste is a capital creation opportunity, and the firms involved have created organizational capital, in the form of patents, know-how, and processes, to extend the life of waste materials. In some cases, they manage to reprocess waste into a reusable natural capital, such as water and oil. Indeed, some industrial waste conversion firms become so effective in finding new uses for waste products that they are willing to pay for them.

> **Daiseki**
> Daiseki Co. Ltd. was established in 1958 in Japan to manufacture lubricating oil and recycle waste oil. Today, it is involved in the treatment and recycling of industrial waste, such as waste oil, waste acid, waste alkali, sludge, and other waste. It has processes for converting sludge into a resource for cement manufacturing. Two of its subsidiaries specialize in recycling waste plasterboard, and another recycles used automotive and industrial lead batteries. It also has a business related to research and restoration of polluted soils.[16]
> *Inquiry → Production*

Creating new design knowledge and skills and redesigning capital conversion processes to reduce an organization's environmental footprint has multiple benefits. Using less resources reduces costs, enhances efficiency, and advances sustainability for the benefit of everyone.

## 11.4 Natural → Natural

As discussed earlier, the world has two major systems: natural and human. Natural capital creates more natural capital because its energy conversion systems are fueled by a flow of 120,000 terawatts of solar energy. This is 10,000 times the energy flow generated by all the world's energy consumption systems, such as gas-fired turbines and cars.[17] The world's forests, oceans, and plains are a vast natural capital creation system, which provides inputs to human-designed capital conversion processes. Forests are a potential source of pharmaceuticals, and thus

---

[16]http://www.daiseki.co.jp/english/profile/message.html.
[17]https://www.theatlantic.com/technology/archive/2012/08/visualizing-how-much-energy-the-sun-shines-onto-earth-a-thought-experiment/261436/.

the maintenance of human capital is dependent on the biodiversity found in nature.[18] The challenge for humanity is to determine how much we disturb the natural capital creation process by deforestation, farming fertile plans, and allowing $CO_2$ emissions to increase ocean acidity. We need to recognize that there is a natural capital creation loss when forests are cleared. Of course, computing this loss is not trivial.

**Chernobyl and the Korean DMZ**

There are few places in the world where natural capital is undisturbed by humans for long periods. The Antarctic is an exception, but it is a desert and life is predominantly confined to the ocean edges. Other isolated examples are Chernobyl and the demilitarized zone partitioning the Korean Peninsula.

In 1986, after an accident at the Chernobyl Nuclear Power Plant in Ukraine, a zone of alienation of 30 km (19 miles) radius around the plant was established. The zone was later extended to cover 260,000 hectares (640,000 acres), and within this area public access and habitation are restricted. Despite a high level of radioactivity, by 2005 biodiversity in the zone was higher than before the disaster. Some 100 threatened species, according to the International Union for the Conservation of Nature (IUCN), were found in the evacuated zone, including some species of bear and wolf that were not seen there before the accident. Ecologists posited that if the animals at the top of the food chain, such as bears, were thriving, then the plants and animals they ate were also flourishing.[19] Recent reports continue to confirm that without the presence of humans, and despite radioactivity, wildlife abounds.

The Korean Demilitarized Zone (DMZ), established in 1953, is 250 km (160 miles) long and about 4 km (2.5 miles) wide. It is almost totally free of human habitation and human entry is very limited. The DMZ is a temperate and diverse habitat, with forests, mountains, rivers, prairies, swamps, lakes, bogs, and estuaries. It contains over 1,100 plant species; 50 mammal species, including Asiatic Black Bear, leopard, lynx, sheep, and possibly tiger; hundreds of bird species, many of which, according to IUCN are endangered; and over 80 fish species. The area naturally revived after the devastation of war.[20]

Natural capital creates natural capital even when the conditions are rather harsh. This is not surprising because natural capital creation has operated for millions of years. Humans are also part of this system, but like all dominant species they have strong ecosystem effects. When humans disengage from nature, as the preceding examples illustrate, natural capital production thrives.

*Disengagement → Production*

---

[18]Chivian, E., & Bernstein, A. (2008). *Sustaining Life: How Human Health Depends on Biodiversity*. Oxford University Press.

[19]https://www.nature.com/news/2005/050808/full/news050808-4.html.

[20]http://www.dmzforum.org/about/background-of-the-dmz.

## 11.5   Social → Natural

Some social groups have a strong affinity with the natural environment and are willing to help maintain it. The Adopt-a-Highway and Sponsor-a-Highway programs in the United States and Canada, respectively, enlist the support of local community clubs to keep portions of a highway free of litter. There are similar movements to keep waterways clean, such as in my community where kayakers are encouraged to remove trash from the Oconee River and its banks. Living systems are more able to function when not burdened by human garbage and its sometimes toxic by-products (e.g., heavy metals from electronics).

> **Let's Do It!**
> Let's Do It! began in Estonia in 2008 when 50,000 people united together to clean up the entire country in just 5 h. It is now a civic mass movement, and 20 million people in around 120 countries have teamed up to remove illegal waste from the natural environment.
> In July 2009, a group of friends started "Let's Do It, Portugal!" to galvanize Portuguese residents to clean up litter and trash deposited illegally in dumpsites, including many in forests.[21] Over the next 9 months, they developed a bottom-up social media campaign. This effort was complemented by local media promotion through radio, television, and newspapers. They used crowdsourcing to discover the location of dumpsites throughout Portugal. Citizens were asked to post the coordinates of these illegal trash heaps to a website so that a map of sites to clean up could be created. On March 20, 2010, more than 100,000 volunteers removed trash from about 13,000 illegal dumpsites that had been registered in the previous 9 months. Over 50,000 tons of waste was collected.
> *Engagement → Record (dumpsites) → Production (clean-up)*

On a larger scale, social movements can operate nationally and internationally to protect and extend natural capital. The World Wildlife Fund, Environmental Defense Fund, and Greenpeace are examples of social movements working to promote environmental awareness and action.

---

[21]Cardosa, A., & Boudreau, M.-C. (2012). Think individually, act collectively: Studying the dynamics of a technologically enabled civic movement. Working paper. Department of MIS, University of Georgia, Athens, GA, USA.

## 11.6   Symbolic → Natural

Converting symbolic to natural capital is one of the great problems of time, because as a global society we lack a unified approach to global climate change. This is partly attributed to the decline in the symbolic capital of scientists and experts over recent years, as we see with the strength in several political assemblies of global climate change deniers, the lowering of immunization rates by antivaxxers, and the outcome of the Brexit vote.

The scientific consensus is that the earth's climate is warming, an opinion shared by 97% or more of actively publishing climate scientists.[22] Furthermore, eighteen scientific associations have concluded, "Observations throughout the world make it clear that climate change is occurring, and rigorous scientific research demonstrates that the greenhouse gases emitted by human activities are the primary driver."[23] Despite this high level of concordance, there are political parties that do not support action to reduce greenhouse gas emissions. The loss of scientists' symbolic capital directly results in a lack, in some cases, of national level action to address the impact of global warming on natural capital.

Fortunately, at the organizational level, the symbolic capital of scientists retains its value, and many companies, despite national policies, are taking actions to reduce their environmental footprint. Microsoft, Intel, Apple, and Cisco report that 100% of their energy requirements are met by renewable energy.[24] Combine the symbolic capital of scientists and these major global corporations, and you create an impetus to restore and maintain natural capital by reducing $CO_2$ emissions, along with their other environmentally positive actions. Thus the actions of these corporations have been imitated by many, frequently because sustainability and efficiency often march together.

Why in some countries are the national and organizational level actions at odds? Policies change when systems of inquiry, such as global climate change research, compel systems of framing, such as national and organizational policies, to recognize a new reality and adjust. In free markets, organizations have discovered that paying attention to the nexus between these two systems, inquiry and framing, is critical to long-term survival. They cannot disregard changes in customers' needs, social mores, and technology. They need a close nexus between systems of inquiry and their system of framing to avoid market irrelevance. Indeed data driven organizations, as noted earlier, have a high level of performance, because they pay attention to the results of their systems of inquiry.

Ideologies, such as those of political philosophies and religions, are more rigid than corporate boards. Ideological bounded systems of framing resist systems of inquiry that challenge their credo. Galileo's promotion of a heliocentrism was

---

[22]Cook, J., Oreskes, N., Doran, P. T., Anderegg, W. R., Verheggen, B., Maibach, E. W.,... Green, S. A. (2016). Consensus on consensus: a synthesis of consensus estimates on human-caused global warming. *Environmental Research Letters, 11*(4), 048002.

[23]https://www.aaas.org/sites/default/files/migrate/uploads/1021climate_letter1.pdf.

[24]https://www.epa.gov/greenpower/green-power-partnership-fortune-500r-partners-list.

opposed by some fellow astronomers and the Roman Catholic Church. In 1615, the Roman Inquisition decided that heliocentrism was "foolish and absurd in philosophy, and formally heretical since it explicitly contradicts in many places the sense of Holy Scripture."[25] Similarly, Darwin's theory of evolution was attacked when first published and continues to be savaged by those whose doctrine it confronts. Nevertheless, both theories are now well integrated into science and technology.

Ideologies persist for decades or more because their leadership can lose power when it admits that it was mistaken. In addition, their adherents' faith is highly resilient. Studies of doomsday groups who predict the earth will end on a certain day show that when the appointed day passes peacefully, many followers renew their resolve and commitment to their beliefs.[26]

---

**Pope Francis**

Irrespective of a person's individual beliefs, the pope has tremendous symbolic capital as the head of the Roman Catholic Church,[27] which long ago mastered the art of creating symbolic capital.

In 2016, two Californian venture capitalists asked the Vatican to back a technology competition for start-ups addressing climate change, energy, and managing resources. The Vatican did not offer funding, but it added symbolic capital. It provided a venue, mentoring, and the influence of Cardinal Peter Turkson, Pope Francis's leading adviser on environmental issues. The competition aligns with the Pope's 2015 encyclical[28] urging nations to pull "Mother Earth" out of a "spiral of self-destruction."

In later 2017, nine startups out of about three hundred entrants each received USD 100,000 in equity investment. The pope's support is likely to help the companies secure more financial backing. The unique prestige of the Vatican also attracts tech founders and celebrities.[29]

*Engagement (competition) → Inquiry (startup)*

---

[25]McMullin, E. (1998). Galileo on science and Scripture. *The Cambridge Companion to Galileo*, 271–347.

[26]Festinger, L., Riecken, H., & Schachter, S. (2017). *When Prophecy Fails: A Social and Psychological Study of a Modern Group That Predicted the Destruction of the World*. Lulu Press.

[27]https://www.newyorker.com/news/daily-comment/the-transformative-promise-of-pope-francis-five-years-on.

[28]http://w2.vatican.va/content/francesco/en/encyclicals/documents/papa-francesco_20150524_enciclica-laudato-si.html.

[29]https://www.bloomberg.com/news/articles/2017-12-19/silicon-valley-is-bringing-the-startup-hub-to-the-vatican.

## 11.7   Summary

Natural capital is the foundation of the capital creation system and fundamental to its continued operation. Left to itself, natural capital will multiply, except in the harshest settings. In a resource hungry world with a large and growing population, natural capital is under stress, so it is important to recognize that it has value beyond conversion into economic capital. "Ashes to ashes, dust to dust." Natural capital is at the beginning and end of life.

# Social Capital

**12**

Social capital is the set of relationships, shared values, culture, and context that support group cohesion, trust, and teamwork in a society or organization. At the personal level, it describes a person's ability to benefit from personal connections. It might mean helping a friend in Uruguay connect with a contact in Atlanta to help explore a business opportunity in an emerging field. At the organizational level, social capital is critical as the network of customers or relationship with suppliers and investors are key determinants of success. Nationally, there is a need for mechanisms for building social cohesion, particularly for societies with large numbers of immigrants. The traditional immigrant societies usually have established structures for ensuring most newcomers are assimilated into the social and economic communities. Social capital is the foundation of continuing cooperation because it builds trust within communities. It can also facilitate innovation because in a large social network, such as Silicon Valley, inventors, entrepreneurs, and smart ideas continually collide in daily life and sometimes they mesh to create a new organization.

The first mention of social capital has been attributed to Lyda Hanifan in 1916, who defined it as

> Those tangible assets [that] count for most in the daily lives of people: namely goodwill, fellowship, sympathy, and social intercourse among the individuals and families who make up a social unit.[1]

This is an individual perspective, but the notion is also relevant for organizations and societies. Many people spend much of their daily life as members of organizations, and they are typically attracted by those that provide a setting for goodwill, fellowship, and so forth. Organizations that can fulfill this need build social capital. Similarly, most of us want to live in a society that has the same attributes.

---

[1]*Hanifan, L. J. (1916). The rural school community center.* The Annals of the American Academy of Political and Social Science, *67(1), 130–138.*

In the knowledge economy, social and human capital have a symbiotic relationship that promotes the growth of both. Your social capital is a means of finding people who might help you solve a problem or identify a new job. Alternatively, you might help someone solve a problem or tag them for a new position in your organization. The greater your human capital, what you know, attracts more social connections, and the greater your social capital, who you know, builds human capital through opportunities for exercising your human capital.

## 12.1  Economic → Social

The creation of social capital is facilitated by the availability of venues in which people can meet and gain shared experiences, such as playing sports, tending a community garden, and reliving past experiences. For community decision makers, there is usually not a deliberate connection between building a shared community and creating social capital, perhaps because the drive for social interaction and the creation of bonds with others is an innate human characteristic.

In contrast, organizations are more deliberative and see that creating social capital is often essential for a successful system of engagement. Thus companies will look for opportunities to interact with clients, such as through educational workshops and lunchtime meetings. Organizations also realize that a robust internal network of employee connections can be valuable for executing plans and innovation. Steve Jobs, for example, when he commissioned Pixar's headquarters, set an objective to create a place that "promoted encounters and unplanned collaborations."[2] His specifications included a large atrium space as a central hub for interaction. Pixar's atrium houses reception, employee mailboxes, a cafe, foosball, a fitness center, two forty-seat viewing rooms, and a large theater. As planned by Jobs, it was to house the campus' only restrooms to enable those serendipitous meetings that extend social networks. It is fair to say that you can never have too large a network, and you are likely to be surprised how a connection made years ago suddenly creates an opportunity to create capital.

Compared with many other investments, the conversion of economic to social capital is generally relatively inexpensive. Find a way to mix a few people together for a joint experience, and social capital will be generated. It's in our genes, and organizations need to nourish the means of expressing these genes for internal and external social capital creation.

---

[2]https://officesnapshots.com/2012/07/16/pixar-headquarters-and-the-legacy-of-steve-jobs/.

**Go-Jek**

Two- to three-hour commutes are common in Indonesia's capital, Jakarta, Southeast Asia's largest city with over ten million people. To avoid traffic congestion, some commuters use an ojek (a motorcycle taxi). However, it was not always easy to find an ojek until Go-Jek was established in 2010 and enabled riders to order an ojek by phone. In 2014, it introduced a smartphone app.

Nadiem Makarim, CEO and cofounder of Indonesian Go-Jek, understood that he needed to build a strong social connection with ojek drivers to ensure he could serve the large demand. Thus he set out to augment drivers' incomes by developing services for nonpeak periods. Consequently, Go-Jek also offers Go-Send (a courier service), Go-Food (food delivery), Go-Mart (grocery delivery), Go-Clean (housekeeping and cleaning), and Go-Massage (spa treatments) to help keep drivers busy earning income throughout the day.

The more work he can create for drivers, the stickier their connection to Go-Jek, and thus more motorcyclists are available during peak hour rushes. Makarim correctly recognized that the market was undersupplied and that he had to solve the supply problem to cater for the pent-up demand. To build the Go-Jek fleet, the company held multiple recruitment events in basketball stadiums, signing up tens of thousands of drivers.

Drivers are encouraged to feel a strong sense of attachment to Go-Jek. They can advertise their association by wearing Go-Jek branded attire and accessories, and it is common to see Go-Jek green in Jakarta. Loans are provided to enable drivers needing financial assistance to buy a smartphone, and assistance is provided for completing paperwork to legally register as a driver.

At the same time as Go-Jek was building social capital with its drivers, it was also embedding itself in the fabric of Jakarta. Millions of customers can provide political leverage, as Makarim discovered in December 2015 when the Ministry of Transportation announced a blanket ban on ride-hailing transport apps. Less than 12 h later, however, Indonesian president Joko Widodo rescinded the ban, declaring, "We need to remember that *ojek* exists because the people need it."[3]

In order to build a production system based on a range of ojek-based services, Go-Jek needed to first engage drivers to ensure it achieves network effects, and then engage customers by meeting their demands.

*Engagement (drivers) → Engagement (riders) → Production (services)*

---

[3]https://knowledge.insead.edu/entrepreneurship/digital-lessons-from-go-jek-indonesias-answer-to-uber-and-grab-8871#vCQX7cl7qx3GYEhI.99.

## 12.2   Human → Social

We are a social species and adept at creating social capital. A nudge might be necessary at times and some are more inclined than others, such as those "who have never met a stranger."

Universities are furnaces for social capital creation. Mix large numbers of young people together on a regular basis and give them some joint experiences, and the outcome is social capital. Student clubs, societies, sororities, and fraternities are all common mixing methods. For those seeking a business career, selecting an MBA program based on its social capital creation capabilities is a key factor. If you seek a career in the movie industry, a program in the Los Angeles area would be appropriate.

Many enterprises run off-site leadership and team building programs. Outdoor experiential training is popular, but it is difficult to assess whether it meets leadership and team enhancement goals, because there is little empirical data on enhanced business results.[4] Maybe the real gain is added social capital, but that might be bit hard to sell when social capital creation sounds too much like having some fun and making friends. Having participated in a few of these activities, I enjoyed the white water rafting, rock-climbing, and high ropes courses, but I gained far more from the mealtime conversations and casual chats throughout the day. I don't think my leadership skills changed one bit. The least structured part of the activity was the most beneficial. If you recall, Toyota's approach to human capital is very much linked to social capital creation. It wants employees to be socially connected. If we acknowledge that outdoor experiential training is really about creating social capital, then some redesign will enhance the process.

I have twice taken groups of about fifteen US students to China. In addition to seeing Shanghai and Beijing, we also spent two weeks at the Neusoft Institute of Information, a private university in Dalian specializing in information technology. The American students lived in the dorms, as did the US faculty, and attended class each morning with an equal number of Chinese students with English proficiency. The first hour of each morning was assigned to reporting on key world events, as covered in major national newspapers. Each day fifteen different pairs, one Chinese and one US student, were assigned a different newspaper. They usually spent about ten to fifteen minutes on the task, and then chatted about other matters before commencing to give their news analysis. When we left to return to the United States, there were many tears. The lectures were not the enduring part of the visit, but rather the social connections created. The chats arising from the morning news analysis were probably the most educational experience of the trip.

More educated people are more likely to participate in community groups, such as parent-teacher associations. Community volunteering increments a person's social capital and a community's togetherness. For some pundits, the gain in social

---

[4]Williams, S. D., Graham, T. S., & Baker, B. (2003). Evaluating outdoor experiential training for leadership and team building. *Journal of Management Development, 22*(1), 45–59.

cohesion resulting from mass education is as important as the impact of higher quality human capital on economic growth.[5]

---

**Aussie Rules Footy**

Australian Rules Football, known locally as Aussie Rules footy, is a contact sport played between two teams of eighteen players on a nonstandard oval-shaped field. Originating in Melbourne in 1858, it is now the most popular spectator sport in Australia. Overall participation across all levels, from kids to professional teams, exceeds 1.4 million. Nationally, there are 25,770 teams, including 983 for women.[6] It's a game for all ages, genders, and sizes. Winners of the most prestigious annual award for best male player include a 5'7" (171 cm) rover and a 6'4" (193 cm) ruck man.

Between 1947 and 1969, two million migrants arrived in Australia, which in 1950 had a population of eight million of mainly British Isles origin. Many of the new wave of settlers were from Southern Europe, particularly Greece and Italy. Between 1945 and 1959, there were more than sixty thousand emigrants from Greece to Melbourne. Many settled in the inner-city area, which had a strong football culture and often clubs associated with a suburb, such as Carlton and Collingwood. Many migrants readily adopted the football culture. They could walk to the local footy ground to watch a game, and they could join in the footy conversation at work. Their kids could kick the footy in the local park with other kids and join a local age group team.[7] Integrating new human capital into society is essential if its talents and skills are to be deployed successfully and appropriately. For many Melbourne migrants, football was the pathway to acquiring social capital in a new community and developing a sense of being part of something uniquely Australian.

*Engagement (football) → Engagement (community)*

---

## 12.3  Organizational → Social

Databases and software are major components of organizational capital for many technology firms. For some, their database is the foundation for creating economic capital, such as Google or Facebook. For others, such as Microsoft and SAP, software development is the pathway to economic capital. The conversion of

---

[5]Healy, T., & Côté, S. (2001). *The Well-Being of Nations: The Role of Human and Social Capital. Education and Skills*. OECD. http://www.oecd.org/site/worldforum/33703702.pdf.
[6]http://www.afl.com.au/news/2016-11-22/womens-football-explosion-results-in-record-participation.
[7]Cash, J., & Damousi, J. (2009). *Footy Passions*: UNSW Press.

databases and software to economic capital can be oiled with social capital. Technology products find a wide variety of uses in many different settings, well beyond what a vendor can anticipate. This is knowledge that can be shared with customers if they are networked. A product-oriented conference is a common method for bringing customers together so they can learn from each other and a vendor's technical experts. Most importantly, if a conference is structured to build social connections, then there is the persisting effect of social capital. For example, sessions for people in the same industry and birds of a feather meeting points enable those with a common interest to find each other. Frequently, it is the connections made at a conference that are the persisting value, because they can be incorporated into personal networks and become a source of knowledge and maybe another job.

Some tech companies will host meetings for the C-level executives of their major customers to build linkages with them and also across customers. Such meetings often have a double payoff because the host builds social relationships with the customers and the customers with each other.

In the 1990s, the phrase "communities of practice" entered the business vocabulary. It describes knowledge creation and learning that occurs through participating in an ongoing community that is socially engaged in solving problems of a particular type.[8] Mainly implemented within an organization, the same notion can be extended to learning across organizations. Social capital is the keystone of a community of practice. It creates a mortar that can concentrate attention on a problem. For a software vendor, conferences and workshops are an opportunity to create cross-organizational communities of practice to help customers solve important problems.

**Dreamforce**
San Francisco–based Salesforce.com supplies cloud-based software for customer-relationship management. It helps companies build social capital, a critical step to closing a sale. In 2017, its annual Dreamforce conference had 170,000 attendees and over 2,700 sessions. It is a highly social event, and one delegate reported "4 exciting days, less than 12 h of total sleep, more than 12 miles of walking and 100 s of handshakes." The conference pitch stresses social capital creation: "Dreamforce is all about learning from and connecting with your fellow Trailblazers at all the sessions, keynotes, networking events, parties, and more. You'll make connections that go well beyond Dreamforce and last a lifetime."[9] Dreamforce is an annual system of production to transfer knowledge, educate customers, and connect them with each other.

*Production (conference) → Engagement*

---

[8]Wenger, E. (1998). *Communities of Practice: Learning, Meaning, and Identity.* Cambridge University Press.
[9]https://www.salesforce.com/dreamforce/.

## 12.4  Natural → Social

People need spaces to interact to create new relationships and maintain existing connections. Parks are places for children to play and learn how to share and make friends. They are places for conversations while leisurely strolling. The human drive to bond and to build long-standing relationships[10] emerged in the open space of the African savannah. Thus it is not surprising that we still find natural spaces conducive to creating social capital.

Large natural reserves provide an area for social interactions that can create additional social capital for those involved. They provide a meeting place for growing intact relationships, and there can also be serendipitous meetings that create new friendships. It is quite common when hiking to greet fellow hikers and possibly engage in conversation. Hiking lodges are very convivial, and people readily converse, perhaps because their common shared love of hiking and nature gives a tinge of kindredness to their meeting.[11]

In two Chicago public housing developments, creating nature-like spaces with trees attracted larger groups of people than nature-free settings.[12] Similarly, giving elderly inner-city dwellers access to green common spaces positively correlates with social integration.[13] More trees and plants in an urban setting seem to reduce crime, aggression, and violence, and thus increase the social capital of a neighborhood.[14]

Structured outdoor activities can create social capital and build teams. Some management development programs have activities, as discussed previously in this chapter, that include events in natural settings. These are deliberately designed to build relationships, and typically include meals and entertainment, but the natural setting is often considered key to meeting goals. Indeed, George Hébert, who developed the idea of a ropes course, called it the "Natural Method."

[10]Lawrence, P. R., & Nohria, N. (2002). *Driven: How Human Nature Shapes Our Choices.* Jossey-Bass.

[11]The author, who has hiked in Argentina, Austria, Australia, Norway, and the United States, draws on personal experience.

[12]Coley, R. L., Sullivan, W. C., & Kuo, F. E. (1997). Where does community grow? The social context created by nature in urban public housing. *Environment and Behavior, 29*(4), 468–494.

[13]Kweon, B.-S., Sullivan, W. C., & Wiley, A. R. (1998). Green common spaces and the social integration of inner-city older adults. *Environment and Behavior, 30*(6), 832–858.

[14]Bedimo-Rung, A. L., Mowen, A. J., & Cohen, D. A. (2005). The significance of parks to physical activity and public health: a conceptual model. *American Journal of Preventive Medicine, 28*(2), 159–168.

**Citizen Science**

Citizen science describes scientific research conducted in whole or part by nonprofessional scientists. Thousands of research projects have found ways of engaging citizen scientists in collecting, categorizing, transcribing, or analyzing scientific data. Their efforts span many aspects of the natural environment, including animal observation, asteroid detection, and monitoring water quality. This is not a new phenomenon, as amateur scientists have studied the world for centuries, but today's technology ramps up social C'.

The Internet has fostered rapid growth in citizen science in the last two decades. Projects can now engage people around the globe. For example, eBird collects more than five million bird observations per month. The project records bird distribution, abundance, habitat use, and trends. Data are collected by birdwatchers with a simple, scientific framework. It operates at a scale inconceivable without the voluntary participation of many. At least ninety scientific articles and book chapters on topics in ornithology, ecology, climate change, and statistical modeling are based on eBird data.

Zooninverse offers an opportunity for participants to classify galaxies, transcribe documents written by Shakespeare's contemporaries, and search drone images of the Borneo rainforest for orangutans' nests. Citizen have contributed data for more than fifty articles on topics ranging from galaxies to oceans.[15]

Citizen scientists' interest in the natural world has created extensive and devoted social capital that benefits the world. Zooninverse and eBird have created systems for engagement for various scientific endeavors, which create systems of record that feed data into systems of inquiry.

*Engagement → Record → Inquiry*

## 12.5  Social → Social

A network effect occurs when the value of one person's membership of a group is positively affected when another person joins and enlarges the network. In other words, network effects result in social capital creating more social capital. The goal for many organizations is to create circumstances where customers add value to customers. Customers' review of products and services can create network effects, especially for a site that scales quickly and reaches a critical mass, such as Amazon and TripAdvisor. Those sites that attain a critical mass can reap an almost insurmountable network effect. There are several models of achieving network effects.

---

[15]Bonney, R., Shirk, J. L., Phillips, T. B., Wiggins, A., Ballard, H. L., Miller-Rushing, A. J., & Parrish, J. K. (2014). Next steps for citizen science. *Science, 343*(6178), 1436–1437.

### 12.5.1    A Two-Sided Market

A two-side market has buyers and sellers. More suppliers offer buyers more options, and more buyers entice more sellers. AirBnb and eBay are examples of two-sided markets. When you visit AirBnB, you find many choices for most cities. It is typically not possible, though, for the operator of a two-sided market to limit sellers to their market, and they can lose sellers and buyers to other two-sided markets. Seller and buyers, for example, are not restricted to eBay. Roles need not be fixed, and in cases such as AirBnb and eBay, members can vary between buyers and sellers, though usually one role will be dominant.

### 12.5.2    A Two-Sided Market with Limits

Some two-sided markets have limited network effects because the market gets saturated. For ride-hailing services, there is a limit to how many drivers you can have in a physical area. Once there are sufficient drivers to provide most customers a ride within a few minutes, then more drivers will have little effect on customers' wait times, but they will reduce the revenue of drivers. It is also possible for drivers to have multiple affiliations. In some cities, they operate as taxis, as well as participating as drivers in multiple ride-hailing services.

### 12.5.3    A Platform

Apple's App Store is a two-side market with lock-in effects. A large number of apps attracts buyers, and a large number of buyers attracts app developers. Such two-sided markets can be hard to establish, but once created can be very valuable to the intermediary. In the case of Apple, in addition to getting a cut from the sale of each app, it also benefits from the sale of the hardware required to run the apps. Once customers have invested in Apple's hardware, they have a strong connection to the platform. To move to another platform, they have to buy new hardware and apps, as well as learn a new operating system.

Physical platforms can also exist. John Deere works with manufacturers of add-on equipment for its tractors to ensure buyers have products to meet their needs. Partners manufacture a broad range of Frontier branded products to John Deere's specifications. This ensures Frontier implements meet the company's standards for performance, reliability, and compatibility. The more than six-hundred products marketed under the Frontier name through John Deere's stores and online extend the usefulness of its tractors, making it an attractive platform for tractor buyers and add-on equipment suppliers.

Competitors find it hard to entice customers away from reputable platforms enjoying large network effects, and successful platforms are a barrier to entry.

**ClassPass**

ClassPass markets a monthly subscription service that gives customers access, it claims, to the world's largest network of boutique fitness studios and gyms. As a result, members can participate in a wide variety of workout classes. In early 2018, it offered its more than 250,000 members a global network of 8,500 studios.[16] It covers most major US cities, London, three major Canadian cities, and five Australian cities. While traveling, members can work out at a ClassPass affiliated gym. They can also plan classes with their friends. In 2017, ClassPass was ranked second in Deloitte's Technology Fast 500.

As a two-sided market, ClassPass links gym owners with fitness enthusiasts. Because it can track which workouts members attend, it knows what is popular and can advise gyms on their mix of workouts. Additionally, it could jointly run experiments with gym owners to identify new types of workouts and new products for its network.

ClassPass can continue to grow its social capital by extending its services to fitness enthusiasts. For example, it could add hiking, kayaking, running, and cycling as workout options. It might organize a members-only hiking weekend, for instance, through an experienced provider. This would further build social capital because its members would interact, and as they share a common fitness orientation, some friendships might flourish. In addition, if members advise when they will be visiting a city for a few days or more, it could link those visiting the same city so they can have a gym or outdoor activity buddy. Such extensions increase the value of membership and are attractive to a range of fitness providers. For ClassPass, it can use its social capital to deepen the connection with its existing social capital, gyms and fitness fans, and create more social capital on both sides of the two-sided market.

ClassPass needs to excel at operating two mutually beneficial and interacting systems of engagement: one for gyms and one for fitness enthusiasts. As a by-product, it can maintain a system of records that enables it to help gyms improve their offerings and give members more of what they enjoy.

*(Engagement (gyms)* ↔ *Engagement (fitness enthusiasts))* → *Record*

## 12.6  Symbolic → Social

Some brands and products, such as watches and fountain pens, are collectors' items. When people strongly associate themselves with a particular brand or product, there is an opportunity for the brand owner to build social capital. Collectors of a

---

[16]https://classpass.com.

particular brand already have a social connection with the brand, but this can be potentially multiplied if the collectors are connected with each other. People with the same passion or quirky habits enjoy meeting each other because of the knowledge and experiences they enjoy relating to a willing listener. Organizations can build social capital by supporting their collectors. This is good for the collectors and the organization.

Visit the Coca-Cola Company's website and you can learn about the Coca-Cola Collectors Club. For example, in July 2017, the German Coke Collectors Club's twenty-third convention was attended by 540 people.[17] Similarly, the Mercedes-Benz site details a community of 90,000 members in more than 80 clubs that share a fervor for their cars.[18]

**Porsche Travel Club**

Porsche is best known for its 911, a high performance sports car, but its best sellers are its SUV and crossover SUV. The Porsche 911 is the defining symbol of the company and attracts buyers for its other models. Porsche also works on creating social capital to connect its customers and potential buyers to the firm through its driving club and raceways.

The Porsche travel experience, operating for more than twenty years, extols the opportunity to join a group tour driving one of its iconic cars on the world's most scenic roads, with stays at top hotels and fine dining.[19] For Porsche devotees, this is a chance to share a memorable experience with a small group of like-minded aficionados. Sharing life tales at the end of the day over a glass or two of wine is a proven social capital creator.

The Porsche Experience Center Atlanta[20] is adjacent to the Atlanta International Airport, the busiest airport in the world. It offers a 1.6 mile (2.6 km) track for the customer to spend ninety minutes at the wheel of a Porsche car of her choice with a driving coach. There is also a simulator lab, retail store, meeting space, and a restaurant. Events for six to a thousand people can be handled at the center. Many of those unlikely to buy a Porsche will still be attracted by the opportunity to experience the brand. The center builds social capital for Porsche and can also be used by others to build social capital by using the center for events.

*Production (experience center) → Engagement*

---

[17]http://www.coca-colacompany.com/coca-cola-unbottled/coca-cola-collectors-trade-treasures-in-germany.

[18]https://www.mercedes-benz.com/en/mercedes-benz/classic/community/brand-clubs/.

[19]https://experience.porsche.com/en/travel.

[20]https://www.porschedriving.com/porsche-experience-center-atlanta.

## 12.7   Summary

Because humans are a social species with a strong desire to bond with others, they naturally create social capital if given appropriate settings and opportunities. Organizations can create these circumstances and also shape them using the six forms of capital so they support their social capital creation goals.

# Symbolic Capital

13

Symbolic capital consists of elements, such as brands, prestige, status, and reputation, that distinguish a person, organization, city, region, or country. Generally, entities aspire to have a positive image and a high level of symbolic capital in their peer group. Reputations need not only be positive, as some behaviors might be deliberately molded to create a negative aura. An autocrat might find that maintaining power is advanced by establishing a persona for capricious ruthlessness and seemingly irrational behavior. This chapter is concerned with creating symbolic capital that is widely perceived as positive.

A person's symbolic capital is typically encapsulated in their reputation and status. It can be embellished by where they were born, educated, live, and work; their job title; and a variety of other factors that can stereotype a person and influence opinions about them. For example, completing an MBA at a prestigious business school, even for a mediocre graduate, can generate more symbolic capital than for the top graduate of a less regarded program. Attributes such as reliability and competence can make a career.

Organizations build symbolic capital, often in the guise of a brand, to differentiate themselves. Brands provide benefits for both buyers and sellers. For buyers, brands reduce search costs by helping them reduce the range of products they consider worthy of attention. Brands with an earned reputation for quality can reduce a buyer's concern for performance and reliability. Some brands indicate social standing, and buyers can use them to signal their status. For sellers, an established and well-regarded brand can attract buyers. Brands also lubricate promotion and advertising by giving enterprises names and images on which to focus attention. Brand loyalty can facilitate repeat purchases and the introduction of new

R. T. Watson, *Capital, Systems, and Objects*, Management for Professionals,
https://doi.org/10.1007/978-981-15-9418-2_13

products. In the ideal situation, a brand facilitates premium pricing by creating a level of differentiation that lifts a product out of the commodities' space. Some sellers create a tier of brands so they can serve a broad market with a range of products. This was Sloan's idea behind a car "for every purse and purpose." Hence, there might be a corporate brand, such as GM, and a product brand, Buick.

Cities, regions, and countries often turn economic and natural capital into symbolic capital. Many of the world's major cities are associated with sites that are a must see for many tourists: Red Square in Moscow, the Opera House in Sydney, and Buckingham Palace in London are just a few examples. Some natural settings that have acquired symbolic attributes include El Capitan at Yosemite, Kruger National Park, and Iguzu Falls. Food and culture can also be aspects of symbolic capital, and regions typically build their tourism strategies around their most attractive symbolic capital.

Information is often a key ingredient in creating symbolic capital. Luxury goods embrace words, images, and logos that denote exceptionality. A branding strategy is a system of framing designed to positively differentiate by the careful choice of language, scene, music, and other evocative information. Even the features of a most astounding natural site will be enlarged by information. Thus, when people can be targeted by a range of communication channels and formats, the construction of symbolic capital offers many options and many challenges. We explore some of these by considering how other forms of capital are converted into symbolic capital.

## 13.1  Economic → Symbolic

Building a brand is a key investment for organizations trying to distinguish themselves in a crowded market. Successful differentiation can lead to premium pricing and higher $C'$, as we saw earlier with the prestige car market example. Corporate branding was traditionally envisaged from an organizational standpoint. An enterprise owned and managed its brand exclusively within a closed environment for its benefit and presented the result to consumers. Because of the Internet and social media, these days brands are openly cocreated with customers (Fig. 13.1).[1]

---

[1]This section is based on Pitt, L. F., Watson, R. T., Berthon, P., Wynn, D., & Zinkhan, G. M. (2006). The penguin's window: corporate brands from an open-source perspective. *Journal of the Academy of Marketing Science, 34*(2), 115–127.

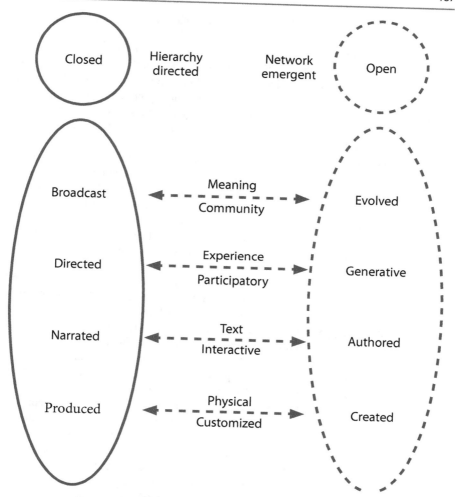

**Fig. 13.1** Dimensions of closed and open brand creation

## 13.1.1 Dimensions of Closed and Open Brand Creation

There has been a shift from the directed hierarchy to an emergent network of participants. Products and services are cocreated, with buyers able to customize purchases to their needs. The Apple Watch customer starts with a choice of material, color, face size, and band, and then with the watch in hand, or more precisely on wrist, can design a face to meet informational and aesthetic preferences and change these as desired.

The text presenting a brand has morphed from corporate narration to dynamic authoring by the public. Twitter hashtags can be devastating for brands. Asking customers to share brand experiences with #CompanyStories can result in over-whelming negative tweets. See what happens when you try #AskCompany to prompt serious questions. Sometimes, #Company becomes a hashtag after a bad customer experience, and can generate a Twitter avalanche of damaging virally shared whinges and whines.

Enterprises once controlled the customer experience, but now, as in the Apple Watch example, customers generate their interface and can change it as desired. For example, before taking a morning run, a jogger can select an app for showing time, distance, and pulse rate; playing inspiring music; and announcing her pace every kilometer. If she preloads a route, she will get an alert before each turn and descriptions of key sights along the route. At the end of the run, she reverts to her usual watch face. Because routes can be shared, customers are freely creating value for other customers.[2]

Finally, the meaning of a brand is coevolved by the community. Broadcast and print media were channels for controlling intended brand meaning, but now citizens can engage through social media in transforming a brand in consequential ways, sometimes positively but often negatively because of the entertaining power of parody and satire. For example, in reaction to a statement by Abercrombie & Fitch's CEO about wanting only "cool, good-looking people" to wear it clothes,[3] a campaign to distribute its branded apparel to homeless people was started, #FitchTheHomeless, supported by a video.[4]

The opening of brand creation means that economic capital is now deployed differently for the creation of symbolic capital. Investing in mass customization permits customers to generate a closer affiliation with a brand because they can transform a product or service to more precisely match their varying needs. Building a listening room to monitor social media is a requirement for many brands so they can respond quickly to customer-created memes that promote or undermine a brand. Different forms of economic capital and capital conversion processes are required to build symbolic capital in the open era.

---

[2]See https://www.rungoapp.com for an implementation of these features.
[3]https://www.theatlantic.com/business/archive/2013/05/abercrombie-fitch-the-homeless/315174/.
[4]https://www.youtube.com/watch?v=O95DBxnXiSo.

**Guggenheim Museums**

Founded in 1937, the Solomon R. Guggenheim Foundation promotes the understanding and appreciation of art. Its three museums mainly feature modern and contemporary periods.[5] Its first, the Solomon R. Guggenheim Museum in New York, was designed by Frank Lloyd Wright and opened in 1959 on Fifth Avenue, one of the most prestigious streets in the world. The museum has a distinctive cylindrical shape, and visitors follow a continuous spiral from the ground to the top level.

The Peggy Guggenheim Collection is housed in an eighteenth-century palace on the Grand Canal in Venice, Italy. A popular attraction for visitors to Venice, it was the home of Peggy Guggenheim for three decades.

In 1997, the Guggenheim Museum Bilbao opened in Bilbao, Spain. Designed by Frank Gehry, it has been lauded by architects and the general public. Sited on the Nervion River, the Guggenheim Museum Bilbao is often ranked as one the finest buildings of the last few decades.

The Guggenheim Museums in New York and Bilbao were designed by arguably the preeminent architects of their time. Their distinctive architecture complements the art collection within. The Guggenheim museums are symbol capital designed by symbolic capital that displays symbolic capital. Wright and Gehry experimented with form and function to create visual masterpieces that became icons of their work and Guggenheim Museums.

Thus, in this book's terms, their approach to design is a system of inquiry because it requires the architect to discover what the client wants, what fits the setting and purpose, what will be visually stimulating, and then create a unique building. Construction is a system of production that converts economic capital to symbolic capital that engages many visitors.

*Inquiry (Design) → Production (Construction) → Engagement (Visitors)*

## 13.2  Human → Symbolic

There are a few people whose names have become symbols. Captain Charles Boycott was ostracized when he evicted tenant farmers in Ireland in 1880. His social exclusion lives on in the verb boycott, refusing to buy or handle certain goods for social, political, or environmental reasons. The infamy of Vidkun Quisling, the Norwegian politician who nominally headed the Norwegian government during the Nazi occupation of World War II, survives because quisling has become synonymous with a traitor who collaborates with occupying enemy forces. An eponym, a noun, or a verb derived from a person's name need not be overly

---

[5]https://www.guggenheim.org.

negative. It might end up as the name of product, such as *biro* as an alternative name for *ballpoint pen* in recognition of its invention by LászlóBíró. A *furphy*, a bit of gossip or a tall story, derives from the Furphy family's eponymously named mobile water tanks around which soldiers gathered and shared yarns during World War I.

A common theme of advertising is to build an association between a well-known person, typically a sports star or celebrity, and a brand. Some become corporate icons and others festooned with logos for several brands. The advertiser's intention is to convert human into symbolic capital.

In 2017, ESPN ranked Portuguese soccer player Cristiano Ronaldo as the world's most famous athlete.[6] According to *Forbes Magazine*, in 2016 he received USD 35 million from endorsements for companies such as Tag Heuer, Abbott Laboratories, Herbalife, and Nike.

However, celebrities seem to be losing their ad appeal. In 2004, they appeared in nearly 20% of all US ads. By 2012, the number had decreased to 9%. Authenticity is proposed as one answer to this decline, because it is doubtful that many customers believe that celebrities actually use the products they endorse. A former Buick marketing executive wryly observed regarding a golfing celebrity: "I'm not sure anyone really believed that Tiger Woods drove a Buick."[7]

As was mentioned earlier, social media results in the cocreation of brands by their corporate owners and consumer pundits. Peer-to-peer marketing through online reviews, electronic word of mouth, YouTube, and blogs, to name a few channels, is considered more authentic. She Media reports that women find online experts more influential than big brands.[8] An overwhelming 52% of them say these social media influencers have more impact on their opinions, compared with 12% for brands and 11% for celebrities. Celebrity-driven symbolic capital creation has lost its oomph, and new means of creating symbolic capital need to be unearthed.

---

[6]https://www.espn.com/espn/feature/story/_/page/worldfame100/espn-world-fame-100-top-ranking-athletes.

[7]https://www.adweek.com/digital/why-peer-to-peer-marketing-does-more-than-celebrity-endorsements/.

[8]https://www.fastcompany.com/3051491/female-shoppers-no-longer-trust-ads-or-celebrity-endorsements.

**Dos Equis and "The Most Interesting Man in the World"**
With the waning of the symbolic capital creation capacity of authentic celebrities, maybe the answer is to create a fake celebrity embellished by entertaining feats of audacity. In 2006, Dos Equis, a Mexican beer brand, introduced "The Most Interesting Man in the World," a gray-bearded, stylish, and charming gentleman. His fictitious life was relayed through a series of humorous ads of adventurous or dangerous exploits, such as freeing a bear from a trap. Improbable claims were made. *At museums, he's allowed to touch the art. ... His blood smells like cologne. ... Sharks have a week dedicated to him. ...He once had an awkward moment, just to see how it feels. ... The police often question him, just because they find him interesting ... His personality is so magnetic, he is unable to carry credit cards.* The ads concluded with the most interesting man stating, "I don't always drink beer. But when I do, I prefer Dos Equis." His signature sign-of was: "Stay thirsty, my friends."[9]

In 2009, US case sales of imported beer were down more than 4% compared to 2008. Dos Equis was up almost 22%. In Canada, in the same period, its sales more than tripled.[10]

There is more to the story beyond the ads. Jonathan Goldsmith, the actor portraying the most interesting man in the world became an authentic celebrity and a friend of President Obama.[11]

"The Most Interesting Man in the World" advertisements successfully distinguished Dos Equis from other brands. The framing in terms of the persona, the one-liners, the stories, and the settings engaged viewers, and it is an exemplar of how to create symbolic capital from human capital.
*Framing (Ads) → Engagement (Sales)*

## 13.3 Organizational → Symbolic

An enterprise's history is an element of its organizational capital, and those with an interesting or inspiring tale, preferably some time ago, can convert it into symbolic capital. The history of the company becomes part of its allure and resonates with the brand. A founder's beliefs, triumphs, and perseverance are a capital inheritance that can add color to a company's reputation and prestige.

---

[9]https://www.newyorker.com/magazine/2011/02/07/interesting.
[10]https://www.macleans.ca/economy/business/king-of-beer-sales-amigo/.
[11]https://www.politico.com/magazine/story/2017/06/02/most-interesting-man-world-friends-barack-obama-215215.

**Johnnie Walker Whisky**

Johnnie Walker was in 2017 the world's top-selling Scotch whiskey brand.[12] A visit to its website extols its founding in 1820 by John Walker when he sold the family farm to set up a grocery store in Kilmarnock in western Scotland. Learning that the single malt whiskeys most grocers sold were of inconsistent quality, Walker starting blending whiskeys so the taste did not vary. This proved a canny move, and the business prospered. In 1867, his son Alexander launched the first commercial blend, "Old Highland Whisky." He continued to innovate by appointing Scottish ships' captains as his agents to acquaint the world with his whiskey, introduced a square bottle to reduce breakages, and designed an easily discerned label slanted at twenty-four degrees. In 1909, the range of whiskies were branded as Johnnie Walker Red Label or Johnnie Walker Black Label, after the color of their labels. About the same time, the "Striding Man" was adopted as the logo, and is reflected in its "Keep Walking" motto and ads. By 1920, Johnnie Walker Whisky was sold in 120 countries, perhaps the first global brand. In 1934, King George V awarded John Walker & Sons a Royal Warrant, which it still holds, to supply the royal household with whiskey.[13]

John Walker & Sons' history provides a rich set of themes for conveying its origins and prestige. It can stress that it sold the first blended whisky of consistent quality, the square bottle, a slanted label, walking man, global brand leadership, and Royal Warrant. It has taken advantage of its many opportunities to convert organizational to symbolic capital.

*Framing (Ads) → Engagement (Sales)*

Of course, not every organization has John Walker & Sons' symbol-laden history, but it is worth reviewing your enterprise's organizational capital to see what can be extracted and transformed into symbolic capital. For Silicon Valley, the founders garage is an exploited symbol. For Dell and Facebook, it is the university dorm room.

---

[12]https://foodanddrink.scotsman.com/drink/the-10-best-selling-scotch-whisky-brands/.
[13]For a blend of the main episodes in Johnnie Walker's history, see https://www.youtube.com/watch?v=LQ16EHwnQjk&list=PLEGJxlcPVUgC7-mgURG2OAi1PGqScbGuZ.

**The Sino-Danish Center in Beijing**

Occasionally, there is a conversion of capital from an organizational to a national setting. The Danish House of Finn Juhl is highly regarded for its distinctively designed furniture.[14] Finn Juhl was an interior and industrial designer who was a leading contributor to "Danish design." The various designs for his furniture are part of the organizational capital of the House of Finn Juhl and other firms associated with Danish design. The Sino-Danish Center in Beijing,[15] a research and education partnership between Denmark and China, is recognizably Danish and includes Danish furniture on every floor, much of it designed by Finn Juhl. The Danish government has wrought the organization capital created over many years by its architects and designers into a center symbolic of Denmark.

*Framing (Design) → Engagement*

## 13.4  Natural → Symbolic

The image of a nation, region, or city is mainly inspired by its natural and economic capital. When you think of Japan, Mount Fuji and high-speed trains might come to mind. The southern region of Argentina evokes the Andes and pampas. The portrait of Sydney in Australia is a bricolage of its harbor, bridge, and opera house. The ability to turn natural capital into an evocative image creates an identity for both locals and tourists.

---

[14]https://finnjuhl.com.

[15]https://www.onecollection.com/portfolio-item/sino-danish-center/

**Yellowstone National Park**
Yellowstone National Park, the world's first large-scale preservation of a wilderness area for the public, was established on March 1, 1872, with an area of over 2 million acres (over 800,000 hectares). Its designation as a national park is partly attributed to American's interaction with the natural environment. The wilderness was a central image of the American identity, and creating a wilderness park differentiated it from the Old World, where parks were prim gardens. Nature was conceived as at its best when it remained untamed and lightly touched by humans. Thomas Cole, the landscape artist, noted, " … the most distinctive, and perhaps the most impressive, characteristic of American scenery is its wildness."[16] Yellowstone became a symbol of the extensive natural endowment of the United States.
   *Framing (Wilderness) → Engagement.*

## 13.5  Social → Symbolic

Groucho Marx, a twentieth century American comedian, said "I sent the club a wire stating, PLEASE ACCEPT MY RESIGNATION. I DON'T WANT TO BELONG TO ANY CLUB THAT WILL ACCEPT ME AS A MEMBER." For many people, belonging to a club that included Groucho Marx would have been a name-dropping point of pride. Membership of certain social networks is much sought after when belonging to a distinguished group transfers symbolic capital to its members.

   The challenge for an organization is to find ways to convert its social capital, such as its relationship with its customers, into symbolic capital. The relationship needs to be deeper, however, than a simple transactional sale, but rather include customers having linkages with each other. Furthermore, it helps for the social capital to have some exclusivity. Hosting a major sporting event has enabled some organizations to convert their social into symbolic capital.

---

[16]Cole, T. "Essay on American Scenery," *American Monthly Magazine*, 1(1836), 4–5.

**All England Lawn Tennis and Croquet Club**
Started in 1868 as the *All England Croquet Club* with six male members, it held its first croquet competition in 1870 at the new club's grounds in Wimbledon. Croquet was at that time more popular than lawn tennis. In 1875, the club converted one lawn into a tennis court, and in 1877 held the first Gentlemen's Championship in Singles. In the same year, the club changed its name to the *All England Croquet and Lawn Tennis Club*, and in 1899 adopted its present name. Currently, the club has 375 full members and a number of honorary members.[17]

The decision to hold an annual tennis championship has proved to me one of the most astute conversions of social to symbolic capital. Wimbledon is *The Championship*, and the most prestigious of the four major tennis titles. The annual tournament reinforces the symbolic significance of Wimbledon. The tournament is still played on grass, the players must wear white, and there is a break on the middle Sunday of the event. Plus, members of the Royal Family attend games and award prizes.
*Framing (Event) → Engagement (Attendance).*

## 13.6  Symbolic → Symbolic

Symbolic capital extension or elevation has become a common strategy for many companies with a well-established brand to gain further value from their symbolic capital. Under brand extension, an existing brand name is used for a new product in a new category. The aim is to benefit from the existing symbolic capital and perceived attributes to gain consumer attention and retail space for the new category. Thus it might start with a fountain pen, as did Mont Blanc, and then add its brand to other categories, including watches, leather goods, smart devices, and belts. These categories are reasonably close in the broad gift category, around the same price, and seem appropriately displayed together in a retail setting. At another level, the automaker Porsche extended its brand into categories such as pens and eyeglasses, which would seem to have little affinity with the parent category of prestige cars. Brand extension should be carefully considered, as the majority of attempts fail. The attributes that apply to one category might not transfer to another.[18] The accolade of the "finest writing instrument" might not easily work for a leather belt, and a car labeled "spark of the future" might not fit well with eyeglasses.

With symbolic capital elevation, an organization builds a new brand on the basis of an existing reputation. Several of the Japanese auto companies have taken this route: Toyota with Lexus, Nissan with Infiniti, Honda with Acura. Their goal was to

---

[17]https://en.wikipedia.org/wiki/All_England_Lawn_Tennis_and_Croquet_Club.
[18]Batra, R., Lenk, P., & Wedel, M. (2010). Brand extension strategy planning: Empirical estimation of brand–category personality fit and atypicality. *Journal of Marketing Research, 47*(2), 335–347.

transfer their reputation for reliability and quality to create a prestige car brand. The new brand is elevated beyond the status of the parent and marketed separately, though most customers are aware of the relationship. The goal is to transfer symbolic capital to create a premium product that will gain consumer attention because of its heritage.

Individuals can also extend and elevate their symbolic capital. As people rise through a particular skill domain, such as finance, they can extend their reputation for handling financial matters. If they were to move laterally, say to marketing, they would be attempting to elevate their reputation by showing they had general rather than specific skills. Similarly, a move to a managerial position in another company, especially in a quite different industry, could elevate a reputation, as might a move to another country.

### Athensmade[19]

Athens, Georgia, is home to the University of Georgia (UGA), the first chartered public university in the United States. The city of around 115,000 is widely known because of the university, the local music scene, and the charm of its downtown. Famous bands associated with Athens include REM, the B52s, and Widespread Panic. Many UGA graduates delight in returning to the city for football games and catching up with the local scene.

In 2015, a group of Athens entrepreneurs realized that Athens was a well-known city and its symbolic capital could be extended to promote Athens-based enterprises. There were stories to be told that could leverage the existing symbolic capital to create more. As a first step, the Athensmade logo was established with the objective of making Athens nationally known as a community for entrepreneurs and creative professionals. Athensmade intends to introduce at least one hundred Athens brands to local, regional, and national audiences.

In order to use the Athensmade logo, a company must be headquartered in Athens. Some of the companies eligible to use the logo include Sons of Sawdust, which specializes in using reclaimed wood to custom-build dining tables, furniture, and transform spaces; Creature Comforts Brewing Company, which repurposed an old tire store in the downtown area as a craft brewery; and Lil' Ice Cream Dude, which in 2019 was operated by a thirteen-year-old who started selling ice cream from a cart when he was seven. All have interesting stories that add to the symbolic capital of Athens and at the same time benefit from it. Indeed, the creation of Athensmade says a great deal about the spirit of the community. This book is Athensmade.

In this case, the local business community is engaged through the creation of Athensmade, and then under its logo and members' stories engages many other communities.

*Engagement (Local Community)* → *Engagement (Multiple Communities)*

---

[19]https://athensmade.com.

## 13.7 Summary

Most of us would like to be remembered for our character strengths. For an organization, positive thoughts about its products and services can be a distinguishing factor that contributes to a pricing and sales volume advantage. It can spend economic capital fashioning a brand, and by complementing these efforts by building on other forms of capital, it can further differentiate its standing.

# Part III
# Capital and Systems Measurement

You can't manage capital unless you can measure its stock (what you have) and flow (conversion from one form to another).

The effectiveness of a capital creation system can be assessed by the quality of capital it produces, the demand for this capital, and its impact on other facets of a capital creation system. For example, a high-quality human capital creation system might have a multiplicative effect on mainstream natural to economic capital creation system because it trains human capital to identify high-yielding natural capital sources.

While much attention has been paid to measuring economic capital, the other forms have been relatively neglected until recently. However, given their growing importance in the current knowledge economy, and future economies that are likely to emerge, their measurement is a key issue for organizational leadership.

The efficiency of a capital creation system is founded in the systems deployed to create or enhance capital. The performance of these capital conversion engines should be continually monitored and improved. Attention should be paid to detecting new technologies or managerial techniques that can raise systems efficiency. Techniques, such as Six Sigma, and new technologies, such as AI, can improve system throughput and quality.

# Capital and Systems Measurement

14

The measurement of performance is an essential feature of capital creation because management of a capital creation process requires knowing what was produced, the quality and value of the product, and what resources were consumed in the process. Of course, this is the ideal situation that enables one to compute $C'$. Unfortunately, the science of capital measurement is rather lacking for most forms of capital. Most of the attention has been given to developing and reporting metrics for economic capital. In this chapter, I mainly consider current practices for measuring the stock of each type of capital at the organizational level. Individual and societal measures are important, and they are set aside at present because of the primarily organizational focus of this book.

All measurements have some uncertainty, especially when trying to assess a broad concept such as capital. There can be uncertainty related to data sources, data collection, measurement techniques used and their accuracy, and measurement choices made. Nevertheless, a flawed measurement is generally better than no measurement. Additionally, the measurement process is informative because it forces a deeper understanding of the components that create value and how they affect the organization.

Measurement can be of two forms:

- Scoring and rating systems, where values are given to some aspect of capital. For example, an organization's efforts to develop its human capital might be rated as 4 on a 5 point scale
- Monetization, placing a monetary value on a form of capital. For instance, valuing eco-services in dollars
- Monetizing all measures makes comparisons across capitals possible and supports the computation of $C'$. It will, however, typically create controversy because significant assumptions need to be made in valuing capital, including economic capital. Nevertheless, I am in favor of such approaches because they force organizations to determine what their stock of capital is worth. A flawed measurement system is better than ignorance.

© The Editor(s) (if applicable) and The Author(s), under exclusive license to Springer Nature Singapore Pte Ltd. 2021
R. T. Watson, *Capital, Systems, and Objects*, Management for Professionals, https://doi.org/10.1007/978-981-15-9418-2_14

The capital creation system has stocks and flows of capital. Examples of stocks include buildings, employees, customers, brands, and forests. These inputs to capital creation all have a value, but a value that is often hard to determine objectively and precisely. The problem is compounded when you convert capital from one form to another, when they are of different forms and both measurably troublesome. What value is created when symbolic capital attracts human capital to join a long-lived project team? Is any symbolic capital consumed? Maybe it is enhanced if a well-known person joins the team. Furthermore, an effective leader might improve a team's human capital while adding her human capital to the group.

When capital is converted to another form of the same type, such as social to social, then the units of measurement should be the same. However, when capital is converted to another form, such as social to organizational, then there needs to be a common unit of measurement. Almost universally, both forms of capital can be expressed in the local currency. Thus we often face a double measurement problem of first trying to assess the value of a type of capital by some reasonable metric and then deciding on the currency equivalent of that metric. For example, if a firm decides that one measure of social capital is to count of currently active customers, it then has to impute the value of each of them in monetary terms. Don't expect measurement of capital to be an exact science, but rather a process of learning more about an organization's value beyond standard accounting procedures.

## 14.1  A Historical Perspective

Humans have been measuring the state of their affairs for several thousand years. In 3000 BCE, Mesopotamians recorded measurements of their inventory in cuneiform, an early script. Today, we capture exabytes of data every day to feed a multitude of measurements systems. The billions of devices of the emerging IoT will be a vast measurement system to support a myriad of decisions both small and large, from whether I need an umbrella in the next 15 min to what the price of electricity should be for the next hour across western Sweden.

The dominant issue facing each type of economy has changed over time, and capital measurement issues reflect the stage of the economy, as shown in Table 14.1.[1] One dominant issue does not replace another, but rather issues remain in place but typically with reduced importance. Thus some societies still occasionally struggle to produce, import, or distribute enough food during a drought to feed their population. Even in advanced economies, governments devote resources to ensuring food and nutritional security. In some advanced economies, sustainability is now the dominant issue or close to the top, though production and customer service still exist as key elements of the capital creation system.

---

[1]This section is based on Watson, R. T. Lind, M. & Haraldson, S. (2012). *The emergence of sustainability as the new dominant logic: Implications for information systems.* Paper presented at the International Conference on Information Systems, Orlando, Florida. http://aisel.aisnet.org/icis2012/proceedings/GreenIS/4/.

**Table 14.1** Societal focus and capital

| Economy | Subsistence | Agricultural | Industrial | Service | Sustainable |
|---|---|---|---|---|---|
| Question | How to survive? | How to farm? | How to manage resources? | How to create customers? | How to reduce environmental impact? |
| Dominant issue | Survival | | | | |
| | | Production | | | |
| | | | | Customer service | |
| | | | | | Sustainability |
| Key capital | Natural | Economic (land and animals) | Economic (factories), organizational, human | Economic, human, organizational, social, symbolic | Economic, human, natural, organizational, social, symbolic |
| Key systems | Engagement | Production, record | Inquiry, production, record | Engagement, framing, inquiry production, record | Engagement, framing, inquiry production, record |

Survival in a subsistence economy is highly dependent on natural capital and a few tools for killing, slaughtering, cooking, and carrying food. Measurement is based on observation and memory, such as "Near the big bend on the river was a good place for berries last summer." As explained earlier, a system of engagement enabled cooperation to enhance survival. There are still some indigenous people living in a subsistence economies, and refugee camps have many features of a subsistence society.

Agrarian society was concerned with farming, a system of production based on natural capital. Farmers also needed a system of record to keep stock of how many animals they had, their gender, age, condition, and so forth. In terms of flow, they needed to measure the yield of each field by type of crop. For early farmers, many of these measures were likely kept in mind rather than recorded. For today's farmer, such measurements are part of their system of record, and some are generated automatically. For example, modern harvesters can measure and record crop yield and other factors such as moisture content by location as they reap. While measurement is now more granular and precise, a farmer's fundamental emphasis on a system of production for converting natural capital to economic capital has not altered.

Society's focus shifted during theindustrial era to the management of resources (e.g., raw materials, labor, logistics) and creating procedures for efficient large scale systems of production. Josiah Wedgwood developed cost accounting (organizational capital) in the late eighteenth century to manage his pottery factory. Using this system of record as input to a system of inquiry, he learned that his costs were either economic (modeling, molds, rent, and fuel) or human (bookkeepers and wages) capital. Measurement of human capital was relatively simple because the skills required to manage a factory were limited. By the mid-twentieth century,

Japanese manufacturers, as discussed earlier, had learned that skilled and dedicated human capital were a competitive advantage. Assessing the true value of human capital was no longer a simple counting of heads exercise.

The industrial era created a great deal of organizational capital, such as procedures for running an assembly line or chemical process, and techniques such as Six Sigma, lean manufacturing, just-in-time, and project management. Perhaps the most important development was the invention of enterprise resource planning (ERP) systems, which give a detailed and integrated view of a company's operations. Measuring the value of such software (organizational capital), though, seems not to have advanced beyond the financial cost to buy, install, and operate.

In the mid-1980s, the advent of a service economy was recognizable. There was a shift in attention from production of goods and services to systems of engagement for customer creation and retention. There was an oversupply of many consumer products (e.g., cars and household white goods), and companies had to adjust to learn how to identify services and product features that would attract customers. They became concerned with determining what types of customers to recruit, finding out what they wanted, and building a relationship with them. As a result, we saw the rise of systems of inquiry, such as business analytics and customer relationship management (CRM). There was widespread acknowledgement that social and symbolic capital needed to be created, managed, and of course measured.

We are in transition to a new era, sustainability, where attention shifts to assessing environmental impact because, after several centuries of industrialization, atmospheric $CO_2$ levels are alarmingly high. We are also reaching the limits of the planet's resources as its population now exceeds seven billion people. When the earth had a small and less affluent population, natural capital processes operated to meet most needs, though in urban areas, there could be water and air pollution. Now, we put such pressure on natural resources that their management, and thus the precursor of measurement, is essential. We have reached the point where many firms and societies realize that we should assess the stock of the full panoply of capitals. We are all invested in the earth as our only home, and reporting on the state of the six forms of capital gives all stakeholders a clearer picture of an organization's integrity and capabilities.

Dominant economic logics don't disappear but rather aggregate in layers, so today's business needs to be concerned with survival, production, customer service, and sustainability. As a result, a firm's need for data never diminishes, and each new dominant logic creates another set of capital measurement and parallel systems' needs. It requires new forms of accounting that can assess the value of noneconomic capital[2] and provide data necessary to managing the future. Because of the almost exclusive focus on economic capital, current corporate reporting might account for only 20% to 30% of a firm's value, compared with 90% some

---

[2]Elliott, R. K. (1992). The third wave breaks on the shores of accounting. *Accounting Horizons, 6*(2), 61.

decades ago when factories and the production of physical goods dominated the economy.[3] Before considering other forms of capital, let's first consider traditional economic capital.

## 14.2   Economic Capital

Measuring the stock of economic capital has been a concern for accountants for some years, as preparing a balance sheet requires measurement of tangibles such as financial and visible assets. Similarly, accountants have experience and techniques for creating an income statement, which measures the flow of economic capital. Accountants apply generally accepted accounting principles (GAAP) in preparing a firm's financial statements, and these provide some latitude for interpretation and even deception. Auditors can vary in the aggressiveness of their GAAP interpretation when assessing the quality of a firm's financial reports.[4] The system for measuring economic capital is arguably the strongest of the six capitals, with its strong focus on monetary value, but it occasionally fails to alert investors, creditors, and suppliers to fraud or failure. As nearly every organization is required to account for its financial assets, I will not dwell on the measurement of economic capital, but rather leave it to the accountants.

## 14.3   Human Capital

As economies develop, high-quality human capital becomes essential to success. As routine tasks requiring low skill requirements are converted to organizational capital in the form of software, organizations become increasingly human capital intensive. Indeed, the world has a shortage of high-level skills, and the battle for talent is driving intellectual migration from developing to developed economies. This is not a new phenomenon, because creative thinkers and artists have gravitated to intellectual hubs for more than two thousand years.[5] Human intellect is uniformly distributed, but for centuries few had the chance to be educated, but this has changed in the last few decades as many countries have invested in university-level education. Now it is possible for those living in some of the world's poorest countries to get an education that develops their intellectual talent to a high level. Some countries, such as Australia, have migration policies that are slanted toward attracting this talent.

---

[3]Gleeson-White, J. (2014). *Six Capitals: The Revolution Capitalism Has to Have—Or Can Accountants Save the Planet?* Allen & Unwin.

[4]Bradshaw, M. T. & Sloan, R. G. (2002). GAAP versus the street: An empirical assessment of two alternative definitions of earnings. *Journal of Accounting Research, 40*(1), 41–66.

[5]Schich, M., Song, C., Ahn, Y.-Y., Mirsky, A., Martino, M., Barabási, A.-L., & Helbing, D. (2014). A network framework of cultural history. Science, 345(6196), 558–562.

Given the growing importance of human capital to national and organizational success, it is imperative that the value of human capital is assessed. There are two metrics that are commonly used for measuring human capital: educational attainment and job-related training. Human capital can be further divided into general purpose and domain-specific knowledge, skills, competencies, and attributes.[6]

### 14.3.1  Educational Attainment

A starting point is to establish a record of educational attainments, such as documenting for each employee their degrees, the field of specialization, and whether this is general or domain specific. For example, an MBA is general and a Masters in Business Analytics is domain specific. Additionally, skills might be graded on a level of low to high. Given this book's emphasis on capital creation, I advocate adding further dimensions by identifying capital conversion competencies, such as social to economic, and systems expertise, such as systems of record. This can be a useful database discovering what knowledge exists within an enterprise. For example, you might want to assess how many employees have experience in converting economic to human capital for operating a system of engagement.

Monetizing this record of human capital is problematic because human capital generates value only when it is matched with organizational needs. A data scientist running simple queries is unlikely to generate the same value as if she were building a machine-learning model to reduce customer returns. Moreover, human capital can have a multiplying effect. A successful leader can enhance the contributions of each member of his group by facilitating teamwork, inspiring creative thinking, and creating a healthy culture. Of course, the reverse can happen when a leader and a team don't gel and performance declines.

If you wish to monetize human capital, then consider its replacement cost, which is essentially the current total payroll plus a multiplier to account for recruiting costs. This simple measure will get you started and then develop a method to assess the value of deployment actions that carefully match human capital to specific tasks or teams.

### 14.3.2  Job-Related Training

Most human capital, particularly those employed in rapidly changing and advancing areas, needs continual education. Training can also be part of a retention strategy as it sends a signal that the organization considers a person as someone worth investing in for the long term. There are four types of training (Fig. 14.1), and they vary in their potential value to an organization.

---

[6]United Nations Economic Commission for Europe. (2016). Guide on Measuring Human Capital. United Nations. https://unstats.un.org/unsd/nationalaccount/consultationDocs/HumanCapitalGuide. web.pdf

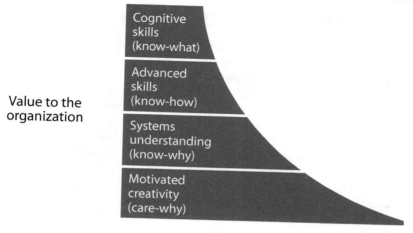

**Fig. 14.1**  Skills values[7]

Cognitive skills cover *know-what*, such as knowing what products or services to offer customers based on their inquiries. Advanced skills, *know-how*, mean that a person knows how to use a machine or software to execute a procedure. It includes knowing how to make a coffee latte to building a machine-learning algorithm. Systems understanding, *know-why*, includes understanding why an organization follows certain procedures. This book is about building understanding of the capital creation system so you can comprehend the essence of all organizations and can contribute to improving C′ in your organization. Finally, motivated creativity is about developing *care-why*. This typically requires the top management team to develop and continually communicate a framing that makes employees feel proud of their employer and its contribution to society. When advertising to consumers, it is also important to think of the impact on employees, because when ads generate pride in a person's organizational affiliation, they motivate them to be more responsive to customers.[8]

Organizations tend to spend more on developing cognitive skills than they do on fostering creativity.[9] This is, unfortunately, the wrong priority. Returns are likely to be much greater when higher-level knowledge skills are developed and employees are committed to an organization's goals. Placing more attention on creating know-why and care-why skills recognizes that knowledge is a key competitive weapon and can have a significant impact on C′. Consequently, I recommend that you report regularly on organizational training via the four skill levels.

[7]Quinn, J. B., Anderson, P., & Finkelstein S. (1996). Leveraging intellect. *Academy of Management Executive, 10*(3), 7–27

[8]Celsi, M. W., & Gilly, M. C. (2010). Employees as internal audience: how advertising affects employees' customer focus. *Journal of the Academy of Marketing Science, 38*(4), 520–529.

[9]Quinn, J. B., Anderson, P., & Finkelstein S. (1996). Leveraging intellect. *Academy of Management Executive, 10*(3), 7–27.

## 14.4  Natural Capital

The measurement of natural capital is complex because it can be freely available to everyone, such as the air, shared with private enterprise, such as the ocean and commercial fishing, or exclusively owned by an enterprise, such as a mining lease. Furthermore, while a company might have the right to a coal mine, side effects such as polluted rivers can be borne by local residents, and the $CO_2$ emissions from burning coal affect all of us. Economists call such societal costs *externalities*. These are costs created by private actions that are borne by nature and society. For example, the US EPA's Superfund program is responsible for cleaning up some of the nation's most contaminated land. The EPA can force those who created an environmental hazard to pay for its remediation, but too frequently the responsible party is no longer an operating entity, in which case the Superfund, funded by US taxpayers, gives the EPA the money and authority to clean up contaminated sites.

Externalities, when they are allowed to persist, weaken the capital creation system because they inflate $C'$ and lead to a misallocation of resources. Externalities are a form of corporate subsidy that can distort international trade because of varying national environmental regulations. The fairest approach is to establish fees, taxes, or regulations that internalize externalities so they become a cost of production and are ultimately borne by those who consume the resulting products.

For extractive natural capital industries, such as oil and gas, mining, forestry and fishing, accountants and industry specialists, such as geologists, have developed methods for assessing the value of their resources. In its 2017 Annual Report of Rio Tinto,[10] one of the world's largest mining companies, the chief executive's statement has a section on mine-to-market productivity (natural capital $\rightarrow$ economic capital) and the many initiatives to raise $C'$. The report also includes details of its proven and probable mineral reserves in millions of tons and the percentage of the mineral in the deposit. The assessment of what is proven and probable is very dependent on projected long-term commodity prices. For an extractive business, there will always be some uncertainty as to the value of its natural capital, but there is typically a level of detail, such as the breakdown of ore reserves for each mine in the Rio Tinto annual report, to get some grasp of the level of uncertainty.

When we turn to shared natural capital, valuation becomes more uncertain, and metrics of each component become difficult to identify in terms of the measurement unit and its value. The first major attempt to measure the world's natural capital in 1997 conservatively estimated its value as in the range of USD 15–54 trillion.[11] At the same time, global GNP was about USD 18 trillion.

---

[7] Quinn, J. B., Anderson, P., & Finkelstein S. (1996). Leveraging intellect. Academy of Management Executive, 10(3), 7–27

[10]http://www.riotinto.com/documents/RT_2017_Annual_Report.pdf.

[11]Costanza, R., d'Arge, R., De Groot, R., Farber, S., Grasso, M., Hannon, B.,... Paruelo, J. (1997). The value of the world's ecosystem services and natural capital. Nature, 387(6630), 253.

When natural capital is converted to economic capital, it is counted as part of GNP but not deducted from a measure of gross natural capital store. For a country with extensive mining or oil operations, every ton of ore or barrel of oil extracted is a decrease in its natural inheritance and that national balance sheet should be so amended. We can no longer treat natural capital as if it were free and unlimited. Developing methods for putting a value on natural capital is an important step toward double entry book keeping for all capital. With such thinking in mind, in 2012 the United Nations formally introduced natural capital accounting as a parallel to GDP.

## 14.5   Organizational Capital

Organizational capital, according to the earlier definition, includes institutionalized knowledge and codified experience (software and databases), routines, patents, manuals, and structures. Essentially, it is the knowledge, skills, and information that stays behind when employees go home. From a measurement perspective, we can break this into three categories: operational, analytical, and strategic.

### 14.5.1   Operational Systems

Operational organizational capital includes an enterprise's databases, software, and operating procedures. These prior investments determine how well an organization performs real-time because they enable it to transact with stakeholders, such as placing an order, recording receipt of goods, and answering a query about a reservation. These are systems of engagement, production, and record.

At the extreme, if all operational systems were not available, most organizations would quickly cease being an operating entity. Thus their value could be assessed as the discounted value of all future cash flows generated less the fire sale value of the organization's economic capital and patents. Even the loss of one component, such as the database of outstanding loans or credit, might doom a business. Therefore, for some operational systems, the true value is not the original cost to buy or create it, but rather what would be the loss if it were not available for certain specified times and how long the organization could go without it.

The criticality of operational systems is exacerbated by the singular and integrated nature of many such systems. For efficiency, it makes sense for an organization to have a single version of many systems, such as payroll, rather than one for each division or country. Similarly, a single integrated enterprise database facilitates operational consistency. A company can disperse its economic capital, such as factories, across multiple countries. Thus the loss of one factory might be disruptive but not disastrous. While digital forms of organizational capital can also be distributed, they typically need to be networked to enable business integration. This connectivity is the weak link because a cyber attack on one part of the system could spread across the corporate network very quickly.[12]

Every so often, the fragility of organizational capital is exposed, such as the eleven-hour power outage at the Atlanta airport in December 2017. In this case, the organizational capital was intact, and once power was restored operational systems reactivated. In a world of cyber ransoms, complete loss of a database for long periods is conceivable.

The quest for business continuity, in the face of accidental and deliberate disruption, requires massive investment in redundancy, replication, cybersecurity, and recovery testing to protect operational systems. Paradoxically, an organization wants to reduce the value of its organizational capital by reducing its absolute dependency on it. It needs to find ways to partition essential operational systems into divisible but connectable components. A useful analogy is to consider how a ship is composed of watertight compartments that are normally connected but can be quickly sealed during an emergency. Thus, when a cyber attack occurs, ideally many digital circuit breakers would be activated to isolate the effect. For instance, if an organization could isolate 90% of its revenue generation within milliseconds of an attack, then it has effectively reduced the intrinsic value of its operational systems by a factor of ten. While this might seem counterintuitive, the goal is to avoid an operational shutdown by isolating vulnerability.

Connectivity and integration have ramped up C' and also created the conditions for total destruction of an organization's capital creation capability. In the worse case, the value of operational organizational capital is the value of the organization, and organizations need to develop methods for reducing dependency on this capital and improving resiliency.

### 14.5.2  Analytical Systems

Systems of inquiry, an organization's analytical systems, create an organizations future. R&D can generate patents and product and process refinements. Systems of engagement and production produce systems of record, which are ideally integrated into a single system of record for data analysis. These systems create value by providing information to identify possible framing changes—such as refining existing products, services, or processes; introducing new product or services; entering new markets; varying methods of engagement; and so forth—that are intended to maintain market relevance. One way to value these systems is to assess how much each system of inquiry generates in terms of innovations or how change impacts C' over an appropriate period.[13]

---

[12]See   https://www.wired.com/story/notpetya-cyberattack-ukraine-russia-code-crashed-the-world/ for the spread of an attack on Maersk and the resulting disruption.
[13]See   https://www.mckinsey.com/business-functions/strategy-and-corporate-finance/our-insights/ taking-the-measure-of-innovation?cid=other-eml-alt-mkq-mck-oth-1804&hlkid= c6016c9ccbf346cea94b75a2147c5164&hctky=1443659&hdpid=ee57b820-7d9b-4138-9166- 80432e03a152 for particular metrics for R&D.

### 14.5.3 Strategic Systems

The ability of an organization's leadership to continually modify its system of framing for incremental and radical changes in C′ determines the longevity of an enterprise. Systems of inquiry can indicate what might be done differently, but reality is determined by the top management team successfully implementing relevant frame changes. Measuring the rate of change of C′ is an indicator of the value of senior leadership. For a publicly-listed firm, its market value can be used for assessing the change in C′. For organizations targeting noneconomic capital, they need to develop similar holistic measures based on the type of capital they primarily create.

## 14.6  Social Capital

For an organization, social capital includes all those people, communities, and organizations who have some relationship with it. It includes a wide range of stakeholders, such as employees, customers, suppliers, and investors. Unfortunately, measuring social capital is a challenge, and there is no simple instrument. Measurement relies upon inferences based on the potential impact of social interactions and the results generated by social capital. There are multiple constituencies to consider when assessing social capital, and I review a few of the more salient.

### 14.6.1  Management Relationships

Established and respectful relationships can be key to resolving the issues that inevitably arise in any partnership. Linkages between top management teams can be important for strategic issues, and well-connected middle managers can often help untangle operational misunderstandings or disruptions. Thus an organization needs to assess the breadth and quality of top and middle management's relationship with key suppliers and customers. Similarly, relationships with appropriate national, regional, and local politicians, administrators, and regulators in those geographic areas or industries where an organization has a significant presence can be crucial to long-term success. For an energy company, effective relationships with national ministers for energy and local environmental regulators will likely be essential. As a start, I recommend that an organization develops a list its key stakeholders, and then for both senior and middle management assesses the quality of the relationship on a five or seven-point scale anchored on "very weak" to "very strong." This will identify areas for adding social capital and should help identify pathways for deploying social capital when required. Knowing who you know is an asset that needs to be formally defined, deliberately extended, and measured regularly.

### 14.6.2  **Customers**

For most companies, customers are their critical social capital. All things being equal, more customers is more income. Thus the number of customers is a very direct measure of social capital. Recruiting and retaining customers is an ongoing task, and it typically costs more to recruit than retain a customer. It is important for a business to know the costs of these two actions, and these are two metrics it should continually review, as they can be important components of C'.

Moving customers from a sales to a subscription model can be an effective strategy for reducing customer defection. However, it can be expensive, as customers can be wary of long-term commitments to a vendor, and the cost of acquiring subscribers needs to be kept in mind. Also, when the initial term of a fixed commitment expires, a company might have to offer incentives to induce customers to maintain their subscriptions. In the United States, when you try canceling your cable subscription, you will generally get a discount or additional premium channels, which for the provider is the cost of retention For a subscription model, it is important to assess the cost of acquiring and retaining subscribers and understand the C' consequences of each of these.

Under either a sales or subscription model, it is important to estimate the annual net value of each customer by various major factors that discriminate among them, such as location, gender, and age. This is a measure of the annual value of your customer-base's social value and also a guide as to which demographics to target.

A nonprofit can have several types of social capital, including donors (e.g., a charity), alumni (e.g., a university), and subscribers (e.g., a city's orchestra). Similar metrics as discussed previously apply, such as how much it costs to recruit and retain a donor and the value of their contribution. Nonprofits might also measure how many people benefit from their services and, if possible, the value of that benefit, as beneficiaries are another form of social capital.

Customers and donors are an asset, just like a factory, that can generate revenue. The cost of replacing your customer or donor base is thus a way of valuing it, just like valuing the replacement of any potentially destroyed asset.

- Value = total customers * cost of recruitment per customer

A less extreme perspective is to treat the annual cost of maintaining a customer base as an investment, in which case

- Value = retained customers * cost of retention per customer + recruited customers * cost of recruitment per customer

Alternatively, as customers generate revenue, then compute the net present value of the estimated net cash flow over, for instance, the next five years.

- $CF_t$ = number of customers$_t$ * net cash per customer$_t$ is the cash flow for year t.
- Value $= CF_1^*(1+r)^{-1} + CF_2^*(1+r)^{-2} + \cdots + CF_5^*(1+r)^{-n}$, where r is the discount rate

Those who contribute revenue determine the future of an organization. Some customers, however, go further in that they provide ideas and product reviews, for example, that can spawn innovations and retain and attract customers. Their contributions increase the value of the customer component of social capital.

My recommendation is to make a first approximation of the value of your customer base, using one of the approaches described previously, and when you are convinced you have good estimates for the various parameters, then consider the incremental value customers add through contributions beyond buying your wares.

## 14.7  Symbolic Capital

Symbolic capital, mainly in the form of brands, is sometimes an organization's most valuable asset, because strong brands can contribute significantly to C'. As a result, brand value is the most developed element of symbolic capital measurement. In marketing, brand equity describes the value of having a well-known and well-regarded brand compared to a nonbranded equivalent. However, there are two fundamental issues with this approach. First, there are few nonbranded products as a basis for comparison. One workaround is to compare brands that are of equivalent quality and use the price differential as a relative measure of brand equity.[14] Second, how do you measure the brand equity of organizations such as Médecins Sans Frontières, the international humanitarian body that provides medical services in conflict and endemic disease zones? Médecins Sans Frontières clearly has considerable symbolic capital, and this is necessary for the success of its fund-raising activities. At this point, let's get some insights regarding the measurement of symbolic capital by examining the more tractable problem of assessing brand equity for public companies.

Yearly, several organizations report a list of the world's most valuable brands. For example, in February 2018, Brand Finance published its report on this matter.[15] It reports on brand value and a brand strength index score (BSI) in the range 0–100, based on marketing investment, stakeholder equity, and business performance.

---

[14]Blair, A. J., Atanasova, C., Pitt, L., Chan, A., & Wallstrom, Å. (2017). Assessing brand equity in the luxury wine market by exploiting tastemaker scores. Journal of Product & Brand Management, 26(5), 447–452.

[15]http://brandirectory.com/Brand-Finance-Global-500-Report.pdf.

### 14.7.1   Brand Value

ISO 10668,[16] to which Brand Finance contributed, specifies procedures for measuring the monetary value of a brand. The purpose of the standard is to make brand valuation transparent, reconcilable, and repeatable. It breaks up the valuation process into legal analysis (such as trademarks and logos), behavioral analysis (such as the opinion of stakeholders across a range of regions and segments), and financial analysis (applying one of three methods to calculate a brand's value).

Brand Finance bases brand evaluation on four elements that incorporate ISO 10668 and extend it as follows:

- Enterprise value, the value of the entire enterprise for a firm with multiple brands, such as a car company or hotel chain
- Branded business value, the value of a particular brand within a firm, such as Lexus within Toyota
- Brand contribution, the brand's contribution to shareholder value
- Brand value, the value of the trademarks and associated marketing intellectual property with a particular branded business.

Amazon, founded in 1994, has built enormous brand value very quickly. It has spread its brand from selling physical books online to a full range of merchandise and areas such as web services, video and music streaming, and branded electronics. It has demonstrated an outstanding capacity to create capital in a relatively short period (Table 14.2).

### 14.7.2   Brand Strength

A brand's strength is a measure of its performance relative to competitors'. It has three components:

- Marketing investment, based on the factors that create brand loyalty and market share
- Stakeholder equity, concerned with how various key stakeholder groups, particularly customers, perceive a brand
- Business performance, derived from quantitative market and financial measures of a brand's price and volume premium, which reflect that the purpose of creating symbolic capital is to raise $C'$.

In comparison to Amazon, Disney is approaching a century of operations since its founding in 1923. Disney becomes known to many consumers early in life through children's cartoons and movies and sustained by its focus on family entertainment. Its brand efficacy is partly a result of being able to spread its

---

[16]https://www.iso.org/standard/46032.html.

**Table 14.2** The ten most valuable brands

| Rank | Company | Brand value (in billions) | Brand rating |
|---|---|---|---|
| 1 | Amazon | 151 | AAA- |
| 2 | Apple | 146 | AAA+ |
| 3 | Google | 121 | AAA+ |
| 4 | Samsung | 92 | AAA+ |
| 5 | Facebook | 90 | AAA+ |
| 6 | AT&T | 82 | AAA- |
| 7 | Microsoft | 81 | AAA+ |
| 8 | Verizon | 63 | AAA- |
| 9 | Walmart | 61 | AA+ |
| 10 | Industrial and Commercial Bank of China | 59 | AAA+ |

http://brandirectory.com/Brand-Finance-Global-500-Report.pdf

**Table 14.3** The ten strongest brands

| Rank | Company | BSI score |
|---|---|---|
| 1 | Disney | 92.3 |
| 2 | Visa | 91.6 |
| 3 | Ferrai | 91.5 |
| 4 | Neutrogena | 90.9 |
| 5 | Facebook | 90.8 |
| 6 | Lego | 90.6 |
| 7 | Google | 90.6 |
| 8 | PWC | 90.6 |
| 9 | Johnson's | 90.4 |
| 10 | Microsoft | 90.4 |

http://brandirectory.com/Brand-Finance-Global-500-Report.pdf

influence from the young child watching a cartoon to grandparents taking their grandchildren to a Disney theme park, where they stay in a Disney hotel and eat at Disney restaurants (Table 14.3).

### 14.7.3 Measuring Your Organization's Symbolic Capital

I suggest you can adopt ISO 10668 and follow its procedures. Don't expect an exact answer, as the process requires some subjective judgments, but trying to apply the standard will give you insights into the value of your symbolic capital and a level of understanding of how it contributes to performance. If you are a nonprofit organization, the process will likely be more difficult and the answer more fuzzy, but this should not discourage you from making an annual effort to assess your symbolic capital and learn how you can increase it.

## 14.8  Integrative Reporting

The capital mix for many organizations has changed over recent decades, and it is not surprising that intangibles now represent about 80% of the S&P 500's market value.[17] There are several events in the capital space driving this shift to intangibles:

- Tech companies are highly reliant on human capital to design new products and services.
- Manufacturers create symbolic capital as they try to differentiate their products in a crowded market.
- Recent developments in machine learningand AI accelerate the conversion of human into organizational capital.
- Social media have provided new channels for creating social capital.
- Organizations are responding to the environmental movement and global warming by recognizing the need to move to renewable energy and conserve natural resources.

Financial reporting that lumps all capital, except economic, under the nebulous heading of intangibles provides insufficient information to key stakeholders to make informed decisions about the long-term prospects of an organization. As a result, several organizations are now taking steps to ensure internal stakeholders, such as corporate boards, and external stakeholders, such as investors, and other key stakeholders are better informed.

Headquartered in Amsterdam, the **Global Reporting Initiative** (GRI)[18] was established in 1997 as an independent international organization to pioneer sustainability reporting. It has developed standards to facilitate reporting details of issues such as climate change, human rights, governance, and social well-being to influence business and government decision makers to adopt a broader perspective of those who might benefit, or suffer, from their decisions. It is particularly aimed at those public corporations who might consider only maximizing shareholder value in the bulk of their decision processes. According to GRI, some 93% of the world's largest 250 corporations report on their sustainability practices.

The mission of the **Carbon Disclosure Project** (CDP),[19] founded in 2002 in the UK, is to establish environmental reporting and risk management as a standard business practice. It reckons that measuring environmental impact, particularly carbon emissions, will create the understanding and motivation to transition to a sustainable economy. On its website, it quotes Ban Ki-moon, a former UN Secretary-General, as stating, "No other organization is gathering this type of corporate climate change data and providing it to the marketplace."

---

[17]Gleeson-White. (2014). *Six Capitals: The Revolution Capitalism Has to Have—Or Can Accountants Save the Planet?* Allen & Unwin.
[18]https://www.globalreporting.org.
[19]https://www.cdp.net/en.

In 2009, the UK's Prince Charles formed **Accounting for Sustainability** (A4S).[20] The future monarch wants to know more about the environmental impact of the Royal Household's investments in public companies. A4S developed a reporting framework identifying five essential environmental indicators: polluting emissions, energy, waste, water, and other significant finite resource usage. A4S aims to influence financial decision makers to design resilient businesses and a sustainable economy.

Established in the United States in 2011, the independent, private sector **Sustainability Accounting Standards Board** (SASB)[21] aims to enhance the efficiency of capital markets by fostering the disclosure of high-quality information to investors. It develops and maintains sustainability accounting standards for public corporations in 79 industries in 11 sectors. When SASB mentions *capital markets*, it means *financial capital markets*. Also, the focus is on environmental, social, and governance, which it calls ESG factors. Attention is mainly paid to natural capital and the community element of social capital.

Concerned by the global financial crash in 2008 and continuing his drive for greater environmental consciousness, in 2009 Prince Charles hosted a meeting that included the heads of major accounting standards boards and accounting firms, the World Bank, the United Nations Environment Programme, the World Wildlife Fund, the World Business Council for Sustainable Development, GRI, and A4S. As a result, the **International Integrated Reporting Council** (IIRC)[22] was formed. It is a global coalition of regulators, investors, companies, standard setters, the accounting profession and NGOs. Its purpose is to improve corporations' communication of how they create value. In other words, it wants to redesign and broaden traditional financial accounting to include integrated reporting on all forms of capital creation.

In 2013, the IIRC released the International Integrated Reporting (IR) Framework Version 1.0 with the motivation of providing an organization's appropriate data for making decisions that enhance financial stability and sustainability. Integrated reporting is intended to give a broad capital creation perspective to top management teams and governance boards so that holistic systems thinking is embraced. While it synchronizes well with the thinking of this book, I believe key decision makers, such as corporate boards, would also benefit from detailed reporting on the state and effectiveness of each of their key systems. An organization is a capital creation system, and it needs to pay equal attention to all its capital stocks and the systems that created them, which is addressed in the next chapter.

---

[20]https://www.accountingforsustainability.org/.
[21]https://www.sasb.org.
[22]https://integratedreporting.org.

## 14.9  Summary

Nearly every organization has to create several forms of capital in order to have an effective capital creation system, and to make it more efficient and effective, you need useful metrics for each type of capital so that investments are made wisely and contribute to $C'$ improvement. In one of his plays, Oscar Wilde observed that a cynic is "a man who knows the price of everything and the value of nothing." I would rephrase this as "a well-run organization knows the value of every form of capital."

# The Measurement of Systems

# 15

Systems are the engines of capital creation, and every organization should be very aware of the state of its critical systems. The emphasis in the prior chapter was on measuring outcomes, the capital created, and in this chapter attention is paid to assessing the processes that generate capital.

Because systems have some common features, I first discuss these and then particular measurement issues for specific types of systems.

As a starting point, first create an inventory of the most important systems by type. This system of record does not need to be exhaustive because most of the gain will likely come from focusing on the 10% of systems that matter in each category. I urge you to design a database for recording these data rather than setting up a spreadsheet, because this should be a long-term investment in systems management that shows the key relationships between systems and capital.

For each system, capture in a database the characteristics listed in the following Table 15.1.

## 15.1  Systems of Engagement

The purpose of a specific system of engagement is to build relationships with a particular segment of a target stakeholder group. For example, a pharmaceutical company might have different systems of engagement for hospitals compared to general practices. Within the hospital category, the engagement process might be different based upon hospital size or specialty. A large urban hospital might have a team led by an account executive, and a small rural hospital might be handled by a single account representative. Other systems of engagement might target community leaders. Systems of engagement can also be inward facing toward employees.

The target audience of each system of engagement should be identified and associated KPIs clearly defined so that performance can be regularly assessed. For customer engagement systems, suitable measures might be how many contacts were

**Table 15.1**  System characteristics

| Characteristic | Comment |
| --- | --- |
| Type | One of the five fundamental types |
| Capital maintained or created | Capital(s) directly and significantly affected by the system |
| Importance to capital maintenance or creation | High, medium, low or a 1–10 scale |
| Operational cost | Annual cost of running the system |
| Investment | Annual investment in enhancing the system |
| KPIs | Metrics for measuring the performance of the system |
| Improvement | Continuous improvement method(s) for the system |
| Technology | Critical technologies for operating the system |
| Human skills requirement | Human skills required to maintain the system's effectiveness assessed as high, medium, low or a 1–10 scale |
| Competitive quality | How well this system compares with market leaders as high, medium, low or a 1–10 scale |

made through each channel each year, the response rate of each channel, and the cost per contact and response for each channel.

## 15.2  System of Framing

An effective system of framing is central to guiding an organization in adapting to its environment through its governance structures. In particular, the top management team and board of directors need a robust system of framing. Enterprise systems of inquiry should provide the input to drive systems of framing, so it is essential to assess the dynamics of the relationship between the two systems. Does the system of inquiry produce useful information? Does the system of framing make full use of internal and external systems of inquiry to inform its environmental scanning?

The research on board effectiveness, which is surprisingly limited, indicates that a process-oriented boardroom culture contributes to a board's effectiveness.[1] However, it is an open question on what processes a board should use. I recommend several key actions for ensuring that the findings of internal systems of inquiry are appropriately considered by the board:

- There is a robust procedure for evaluating frame changed related information.
- Procedures and roles for avoiding group-think are established.
- Decisions regarding incremental and radical reframing are clearly communicated to key stakeholders.

---

[1]Minichilli, A. Zattoni, A. & Zona, F.. (2009). Making boards effective: An empirical examination of board task performance. *British Journal of Management, 20*(1), 55–74.

Many corporate boards have a separate Audit Committee to oversee organizational responsibilities for financial reporting and disclosure. The past is beyond change, but the future is malleable. It would thus seem very appropriate to have a separate Framing Committee that has oversight of the board's system of framing to ensure that the board is receiving the information it needs to continually invent the organization's future. Additionally, it should establish processes for the execution of its system of framing, as suggested in the prior paragraph. The Framing Committee should assess regularly the effectiveness of the board's systems of framing. It is well-positioned for such an assessment because its members are drawn from the board, and as the saying goes, "They eat their own dog food."

## 15.3  Systems of Inquiry

Systems of inquiry vary in their nature, and they include R&D, data analytics, digital twinning, and white papers. Because of their different features, the processes behind each should be measured separately.

### 15.3.1  R&D

To produce applicable knowledge, an R&D process must be open to inspiration. There are three open innovation processes: outside-in, inside-out, and coupled.[2] First, decide which model applies in your organization and then establish appropriate metrics.

### 15.3.2  The Outside-In Process

An outside-in process means an organization builds knowledge through the engagement of suppliers, customers, and external knowledge sources to stimulate creativity. Innovation occurs within the company based on gleaned external knowledge. Process measurement is thus based on evaluating the system of engagement for each input channel and its productivity in terms of ideas that pass an initial screening.

### 15.3.3  The Inside-Out Process

An inside-out process is driven primarily by internal innovation to produce marketable products and services and salable IP. The goal is to learn what processes

---

[2]Gassmann, O. & Enkel, E. (2004). *Towards a theory of open innovation: three core process archetypes*. Paper presented at the R&D Management Conference (RADMA). https://www.alexandria.unisg.ch/274/.

work. First, there is a need to map the processes for some key winners and losers to see if there are general process features that determine success. Second, R&D projects should be evaluated on the extent to which they incorporate high-success phases. The balance between measurement and creativity should be carefully managed, and erring on the side of innovation is preferable to stifling creativity through bean-counting. The goal is to continually assess projects to find features that would benefit most projects. Such evaluation is a soft form of measurement that fits the fuzziness of innovation, where a breakthrough idea can come from the observation of a kingfisher diving into water, as you read earlier.

### 15.3.4  The Coupled Process

The coupled approach to R&D links the outside-in and inside-out so that an organization harvests ideas from one group of stakeholders, innovates, and then markets to another group of stakeholders. Some stakeholders might be on both sides of the chain. For example, customers can suggest product improvements and then consume them. Many software companies use a coupled process by working with key customers to produce a development road map and then delivering on this plan. A coupled R&D process requires multiple systems of engagement for effective idea gathering and commercialization. Thus the sorts of metrics and evaluations suggested for outside-in and inside-out are also relevant. In addition, it is also appropriate to evaluate the effectiveness of coupled process for stakeholders on both sides of the exchange, as these might well be the most valuable customers. They most likely have advanced product knowledge and will be early adopters of new products.

### 15.3.5  Data Analytics

Data analytics has become a high demand skill in recent years because many organizations now realize that their immense and growing data sources are the foundation for data-driven decision making. There are four major types of data analytics: descriptive, explanatory, predictive, and prescriptive.

**Descriptive analytics** produces tables and charts with the objective of helping decision makers see patterns. The main measurement issue is whether the current tools are adequate for decision-making. While you can produce tables and graphs with a spreadsheet, there are better tools and delivery mechanisms. For example, one of my former students who is a data analyst converted the day-long grind of spreadsheet-driven monthly reporting to an R script that he could execute in minutes at the end of each month. Furthermore, his script could directly create a slide deck for the managerial team.

**Explanatory analytics** is concerned with identifying the critical factors for determining a key outcome, such as sales, conversion of leads to sales, or product failure rates. An explanatory model can help managers understand what matters and where they might direct resources. Statisticians have developed rigorous procedures for ensuring that an explanatory model is valid, and organizations need to assess whether these processes are followed. Indeed, it might make sense that for each major explanatory model there is a third-party internal audit process to check its validity. Yearly, the same internal audit process might verify that the model is still valid. In a competitive environment, actions taken by others might nullify a model.

**Predictive analytics** produces forecasts at various levels of granularity for future outcomes, such as the expected value of a new customer or corporate revenue. A prediction model might be based on explanatory analytics work or use techniques, such as neural networks,[3] that can produce forecasts without a corresponding explanatory model. One data scientist advises that he builds both an explanatory and neural net, and only applies the later if its predictive accuracy is 5% better.

**Prescriptive analytics** refers to a class of algorithms that solve complex problems, such as the route for each vehicle to minimize the cost for operating a fleet each day or how to pack the most packages of a given size on a standard pallet. Such algorithms are embedded in many systems of production and are solved as needed to optimize costs or maximize profit. Key evaluation questions include continually reviewing the production landscape to ensure that prescriptive analytics are fully exploited and also to determine the right frequency of solution. For example, the vehicle routing problem could be solved daily, but because of computing costs, it might be solved weekly. At some point, changes in computing costs and algorithm efficiency might make a daily solution profitable.

With the growth in data analytics, governance has become progressively necessary because data analytics is often distributed across the enterprise. A generation ago, because data were widely fragmented, organizations started the move toward integrated single instance databases to avoid the problems of data inconsistency and an inability to relate data across functional silos. Similarly, organizations now need to guard against siloed data analytics. Having separate data models, for instance, for predicting sales in both the marketing and production function is inefficient and potentially causes inconsistent decisions. Thus measurement of data analytics performance needs to include assessing the effectiveness of model governance.

## 15.3.6  Digital Twinning

A digital twin is a high-fidelity digital representation of a physical product or process. For instance, Maserati has partnered with Siemens to create digital twins of its cars and the assembly line for their production.[4] These new forms of systems

---

[3]A neural network is an algorithm based on the operation of neurons in the human brain. Like humans, it uses examples to infer rules for recognizing patterns.
[4]https://www.siemens.com/stories/cc/en/driven-by-data/.

inquiry enable an organization to have a generic digital twin of each of its products from which a precise clone can be generated for each product it makes. In the case of a car, a clone would include details of added accessories and so forth. As the car is driven, the digital data streams it creates can be used to calibrate the matching clone, and features of the physical car customized based on the driver's behavior and typically trips. If the owner, for example, scrapes the bottom of her car as she drives up a steep driveway from her garage to the local street, this could be detected by the car and streamed to the manufacturer's clone. The clone's system of inquiry would identify the regular scrapping events and send a software change to the physical vehicle that raises the car's suspension for the period when the car is moving from the driver's garage to the local street.

Digital twins are systems of inquiry for understanding how individual products are used and how to modify their behavior based on a customer's usage patterns. Furthermore, with situations such as autonomous driving, the system of inquiry must create a dynamic digital twin of its surrounding environment so that the vehicle can navigate it safely. Thus organizations need to continually measure the fidelity of their digital twins, both static and dynamic. They must ensure that the digital data streams they harvest to calibrate the digital twin of each product have sufficient resolution to meet the tolerance needs for safe and effective operation.

### 15.3.7  White Papers

The term *white paper* describes an authoritative report providing background on a problem and possibly proposing solutions. White papers can be a key component of an organization's system of inquiry and are frequently used by governments to promote a public discourse on a proposed policy or aid in the development of policy.[5] Appropriate metrics for organizational white papers might include:

- What is the process for determining topics?
- How many papers were published?
- What is the audience and distribution of each white paper?
- What feedback process exists for evaluating a white paper's relevance and organizational impact?
- Who are the authors, and what are their competencies?
- What processes are in place to ensure white papers canvas a range of perspectives and challenge established practices and beliefs?

---

[5]For an example, see "The United Kingdom's exit from and new partnership with the European Union White Paper" at https://www.gov.uk/government/publications/the-united-kingdoms-exit-from-and-new-partnership-with-the-european-union-white-paper.

## 15.4  Systems of Production

Systems of production are the core activity of most organizations. When we think of an auto manufacturer, we might envision an assembly line, a classroom for a university, or planes in flight for an airline. With the rise of ecosystems, an organization might use multiple partners' systems of production for making its products. For a complex electronic product, different systems of production will create the many components. For a smartphone, for instance, there will be a chip maker, battery maker, camera maker, and so forth. Finally, an assembler might put the pieces together to deliver the product to the company who will market it. FoxConn, for example, assembles some of the products Apple designs and markets. In many industries, the creation of a good is the result of many layers of systems of production making inputs to higher layers to eventually create a consumer good, such as a laptop computer.

Ecosystems create problems of control and transitivity. Members of an ecosystem do not have the same level of control over activities performed by partners as they do those undertaken internally. They might rely on contracts, site inspections, and quality control measures to gain some oversight of another's system of production. For each external system of production, data about its performance need to be collected and analyzed for managerial reporting.

The transitivity problem is perhaps the less apparent measurement problem, but potentially the most risky because an organization might not realize the different levels of risk it faces in a supply network. Consider the example of a smartphone; part of the supply network might be something like that illustrated in Fig. 15.1.

If a lithium miner has a national sovereignty issue, such as a change in government, it might disrupt lithium production. Because of transitivity effects in the supply chain, there might be insufficient batteries to produce working phones. To

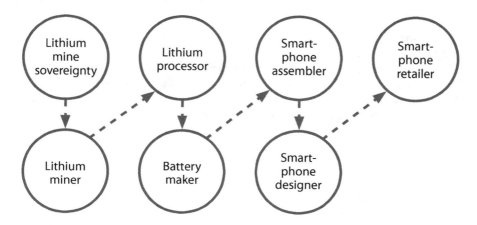

**Fig. 15.1**  A linear portion of a supply network for a smartphone

avoid dependency on a single source or supplier, many companies diversify their supplier network throughout the entire set of systems of production. To clearly understand the level of exposure and the required risk reduction actions, the transitivity risk of each system of production needs to be documented and regularly reviewed. This is a key measurement problem for systems of production and fits well the capabilities of graph database technology.

Coincidentally, within a few hours of writing the previous paragraph, I saw a news report of Ford stopping production of its F-150 truck in all its plants because of a major fire at a parts supplier. Production at Fiat Chrysler, GM, BMW, and Mercedes-Benz was also impacted. The shutdown was expected to last several days.[6]

Transitivity exposure is not limited to manufacturing. A bank can have a risk chain because of the failure of the customer of one of its customers. The rise of ecosystems means we live in a highly transitive world where a failure in one part of a network has multiple effects, and enterprises should analyze potential system of production disruptions in order to develop mitigation plans.

My advice is to create a database that records all major relationship networks and to regularly review the risk of a system of production failure in each of these relationships. When a disruption risk is medium to high, then create alternative systems of production.

The transitivity problem is likely to grow in importance for two reasons. First, digital connectivity has enabled complex webs of relationships to be established among organizations, and this trend appears to be increasing. Second, global climate change will result in more frequent and more intense disruptive weather events. A US Department of Homeland Security official reported to the US Senate in 2014:

> The projected impact of climate change, including sea level rise and increasing severity and frequency of extreme weather events, can cause damage or disruptions that result in cascading effects across our communities, with immeasurable costs in lives lost and billions of dollars in property damage...[7]

Note the reference to cascading effects—another way of expressing the transitivity problem.

Building a resilient system of production means thoroughly exploring transitivity issues across the entire set of contributing production systems, understanding the disruption risk of each ecosystem change, and factoring in exposure to severe weather events for connected systems of production.

---

[6]https://www.detroitnews.com/story/business/autos/ford/2018/05/09/ford-trucks-production-halted/34718903/.
[7]https://climateandsecurity.org/2014/02/13/homeland-security-and-climate-change-excerpts-from-senate-hearing/.

## 15.5  Systems of Record

Depending on the type of data and its intended use, there are a number of data management technologies. Thus a first step is to assess regularly whether the match between intended use and current technology is still a sound choice. For example, in the last few years many organizations have invested in data storage technologies, such as Hadoop, designed to support analytics better than traditional relational databases, which are more suited to transaction processing. Blockchain is now being assiduously promoted by some as data management technology for when distributed and immutable ledgers are advantageous.

Ensuring systems of record are compliant with national or regional data privacy laws has gained more attention following multiple data breaches and misuse of social media data. In April 2016, the EU adopted the General Data Protection Regulation (GDPR), which governs the ways an individual's private data can be collected and exploited. It went into effect in Europe in May 2018, and many companies outside the EU were affected because they had customers in the EU. As it is administratively complex to manage each customer's data according to the jurisdiction in which they live or where the data are stored, many organizations find it pragmatic to comply with the most demanding standards, so they comply with all regulations.

Major security breaches of systems of record have become so common that it would appear very few are invulnerable. Of course, this does not mean organizations should slacken their efforts to secure their data, In addition to employing an in-house security team, a regular review by security consultants is advisable because of the dynamic nature of cyber protagonists and their often extensive, sometimes state-funded, resources. Despite continuing internal vigilance and external assurances, organizations should be prepared to handle the aftermath of a breach. Notably, in 2016 IBM opened a center in Boston where executives can practice responding to cyber breaches and responses.[8]

In brief, the measurement of systems of record should answer the following:

- Is the current match of needs and data management technology appropriate and cost-efficient?
- Are all systems of record compliant with GDPR or similar regulations?
- When was the most recent external review of the security of all systems of record and what was its report?
- When did the senior leadership most recently rehearse its reaction of a security breach?

---

[8]https://www.bostonglobe.com/business/2016/11/16/ibm-unveils-new-kendall-cybersecurity/N9ox2YbhYQHU0q70tqaYGK/story.html.

## 15.6   Business Process Modeling and Mining

There are well-developed methodologies[9] and tools for recording details of a process.[10] These can be used to document each system as to how it ought to work. Furthermore, these models can be stored in an organizational repository for reference and analysis. Because procedures are not always followed as defined, process mining[11] can be used to analyze actual practice. While process mining is feasible for manual systems, the usual practice is to mine computer system logs to reveal common patterns of behavior and anomalies in transaction processing systems.

## 15.7   Summary

Systems are the means for generating outcomes, and most public reporting systems focus on outcomes. This one-sided view of the dual nature of a capital creation system can miss opportunities to rigorously and regularly examine the engines of capital creation. Stakeholders would have a greater understanding of the value of an organization if they knew more about how outcomes were produced. Since reporting on systems is not mandated by accounting standards bodies, this is an underdeveloped field. This chapter has presented some advice on how to go about systems reporting, but you should recognize it is an immature field. As such, it is an opportunity to gain a competitive advantage and improve performance by analyzing an essential underexamined organizational component.

---

[9]vom Brocke, J. & Rosemann, M. (Eds.). (2010). *Handbook on Business Process Management 1: Introduction, Methods, and Information Systems.* Springer; and vom Brocke, J. & Rosemann, M. (Eds.). (2010). *Handbook on Business Process Management 2: Strategic Alignment, Governance, People and Culture* Springer.
[10]https://www.signavio.com.
[11]https://fluxicon.com/technology/.

# Index

CPSIA information can be obtained
at www.ICGtesting.com
Printed in the USA
LVHW080903300621
691553LV00001B/1